The Many Deaths of Tsar Nicholas II

How did Nicholas II, Russia's last Tsar, meet his death? Shot point blank in a bungled execution by radical Bolsheviks in the Urals, Nicholas and his family disappeared from history in the Soviet era. But in the 1970s, a local geologist and a crime fiction writer discovered the location of their clandestine mass grave, and secretly removed three skulls, before reburying them, afraid of the consequences of their find. In 1991, as the Soviet Union collapsed, the bones of Nicholas and his family were again disinterred, this time with official sanction, and positively identified through DNA testing. They were re-interred with great ceremony by the Russian state beside the tombs of their Romanov ancestors, despite vociferous scepticism from the Russian Orthodox Church about the authenticity of the bones.

Yet the history of Nicholas's execution and the discovery of his remains are not the only stories connected with the death of the last Tsar. This book recounts the horrific details of their deaths and the thrilling discovery of the bones, and also investigates the alternative narratives that have grown up around these events. Stories include the contention that the Tsar's killing was a Jewish plot, in which Nicholas's severed head was taken to Moscow as proof of his death; tales of would-be survivors of the execution, self-confessed children of the Tsar claiming their true identity; and accounts of miracles performed by Nicholas, who was made a saint by the Russian Church in 2000. Not least among these alternative narratives is the romanticization of the Romanovs, epitomized by the numerous photographs of the family released from the Russian archives.

Wendy Slater taught Russian history at the University of Cambridge and the School of Slavonic and East European Studies, University College London, until 2003. She is deputy editor of *The Annual Register* and writes regularly on Russian affairs for *Keesing's Record of World Events*.

Routledge Studies in the history of Russia and Eastern Europe

Modernizing Muscovy
Reform and social change in seventeenth-century Russia
Edited by Jarmo Kotilaine and Marshall Poe

The USA in the Making of the USSR
The Washington Conference, 1921–1922, and 'uninvited Russia'
Paul Dukes

Tiny Revolutions in Russia
Twentieth century Soviet and Russian history in anecdotes
Bruce Adams

The Russian General Staff and Asia, 1800–1917
Alex Marshall

Soviet Eastern Policy and Turkey, 1920–1991
Soviet foreign policy, Turkey and Communism
Bülent Gökay

The History of Siberia
Igor V. Naumov (Edited by David N. Collins)

Russian Military Intelligence in the War with Japan, 1940–05
Secret operations on land and at sea
Evgeny Sergeev

Cossacks and the Russian Empire, 1598–1725
Manipulation, rebellion and expansion into Siberia
Christoph Witzenrath

The Many Deaths of Tsar Nicholas II
Relics, remains and the Romanovs
Wendy Slater

The Many Deaths of Tsar Nicholas II

Relics, remains and the Romanovs

Wendy Slater

Routledge
Taylor & Francis Group

LONDON AND NEW YORK

First published 2007
by Routledge
2 Park Square, Milton Park, Abingdon, Oxon OX14 4RN

Simultaneously published in the USA and Canada
by Routledge
270 Madison Ave, New York, NY 10016

Transferred to Digital Printing 2007

*Routledge is an imprint of the Taylor & Francis Group,
an informa business*

© 2007 Wendy Slater

Typeset in Times New Roman by
Florence Production Ltd, Stoodleigh, Devon
Printed and bound in Great Britain by
Antony Rowe Ltd, Chippenham, Wiltshire

All rights reserved. No part of this book may be reprinted or
reproduced or utilized in any form or by any electronic,
mechanical, or other means, now known or hereafter
invented, including photocopying and recording, or in any
information storage or retrieval system, without permission in
writing from the publishers.

British Library Cataloguing in Publication Data
A catalogue record for this book is available from the British
Library

Library of Congress Cataloging in Publication Data
Slater, Wendy, 1967-
  The many deaths of tsar Nicholas II: relics, remains and the
  Romanovs/Wendy Slater.
    p. cm. – (Routledge studies in the history of Russia and
    Eastern Europe series)
  Includes bibliographical references and index.
  1. Nicholas II, Emperor of Russia, 1868–1918 – Death and
  burial. 2. Nicholas II, Emperor of Russia, 1868–1918 –
  Family – Death and burial. I. Title.
  DK258.6S63 2007
  947.08'3092 dc22   2006039267

ISBN10: 0–415–34516–2 (hbk)   ISBN13: 978–0–415–34516–3 (hbk)
ISBN10: 0–415–42797–5 (pbk)   ISBN13: 978–0–415–42797–5 (pbk)
ISBN10: 0–203–53698–3 (ebk)   ISBN13: 978–0–203–53698–8 (ebk)

Contents

	List of illustrations	vi
	Note on transliteration	vii
	Acknowledgements	viii
1	Cruel necessity	1
2	True crime	16
3	The many deaths of Nicholas II	44
4	Gothic horror	60
5	False Alexeis	81
6	Tsar Martyr	106
7	Family portraits	128
	Conclusion: Miscalculating history	152
	Notes	157
	Bibliography	173
	Index	188

Illustrations

2.1	Diagram by archaeologist Ludmila Koryakova of the bones found in the mass grave outside Sverdlovsk (Ekaterinburg)	26
6.1	'Heavenly Glory': Icon of Nicholas, Alexandra and their children	120
6.2	'The Tsarist Martyr Nicholas II': Nicholas in seventeenth-century court dress for a costume ball in 1903	121
6.3	Myrrh-streaming icon of Nicholas II	122
7.1	Romanov family portrait, from the series of pictures taken to celebrate the Romanov tercentenary in 1913	133
7.2	Formal photograph of Nicholas II	136
7.3	Wartime photograph of Tsarevich Alexei	139
7.4	Nicholas II, with guards, under arrest (March to December 1917)	140
7.5	'The Russian Royal Household': Cartoon of Nicholas and Alexandra, with Rasputin, 1916	142

Note on transliteration

In the sources and notes, Russian names are transliterated using the Library of Congress system.

In the text, I have used a modified version of this system to make names easier on the eye. I have also used the English version of some names (e.g. Nicholas II, not Nikolai II).

Acknowledgements

This book grew from the very small beginnings of a paper to a seminar series on death and immortality in Russian culture, at the School of Slavonic and East European Studies (SSEES), University College London, in the winter and spring of 2000 to 2001. While groping around for something to write for my own contribution to the series, I stumbled upon the story of the Tsar's severed head. The rest was history, as they say, but not just history: it was also stories and myths about Nicholas II and his death, and about what they mean in Russia and beyond.

Susan Morrissey organized the seminar series, and was an inspiring colleague and a good friend during my years at SSEES. Her company made our commute to work much more bearable.

Bettina Weichert, during her own field research in Moscow, generously scooped up Romanov material that I needed and brought it back to London. I thank her for using her excess baggage allowance on my project, and for her insights on Russian Orthodoxy today.

Other colleagues at SSEES passed on items that they thought might interest me: they include Lindsey Hughes and Geoffrey Hosking. Beyond SSEES, Janet Ashton, John M.L. Kendrick, Peter Kurth and Bryan Sykes all answered specific queries by email and in some cases provided source material. Marc Ferro wrote with suggestions for further reading about Romanov claimants and kindly gave me a copy of his book on taboos in history.

At Cambridge, the participants in the Department of Slavonic Studies research seminar in 2003 were, as I had anticipated, constructively incisive. I want to thank in particular Simon Franklin, Chris Ward and Emma Widdis.

Alun Munslow at *Rethinking History* cheerfully encouraged me to write a piece on the narratives about Nicholas II; Peter Sowden has been a most patient commissioning editor at Routledge.

Nicholas II and his many deaths have accompanied me and my family through two house moves, a burglary – in which the first three chapters I had written disappeared – and, more happily, emigration to France.

Stephen Lewis encouraged me to start this book, and then he made me finish it. His expertise as an editor improved it immeasurably, but I owe him most for his enthusiasm for the way I wanted to write the stories and his forbearance over the demands that this made. For our daughter Heléna, 'mummy's book' will never match *The Little Wooden Horse* as a bedtime story, but I hope, nevertheless, that she will read and enjoy it one day.

This book is for them, with all my love.

1 Cruel necessity

> During my walk in the hills with Natasha today (the weather was almost like summer), I mulled over the conversation with Lenin about putting the tsar on trial. ... Punishing the tsar's family would, of course, have been impossible in the legal sense. The tsar's family was a victim of the principle that forms the very axis of monarchy: dynastic inheritance.
> (Lev Trotsky, diary entry of 10 April 1935)

> Many people
>   are charmed
>   by a sun crown.
> Excuse me,
>   nobles and gentlemen,
> A crown
>   may be bestowed
>   by us,
> But only
>   with a mineshaft.
> (Vladimir Mayakovsky, 'The Emperor', Sverdlovsk, 1928)

It took so long to finish them. Especially the girls. Later we found out why. When we came to strip them we saw how their corsets were packed with jewels. Rubies, diamonds, emeralds – we'd never seen anything like it. So like the Commandant said, they had only themselves to blame. It was greed that made their deaths so cruel.

At the time, mind you, I wondered if András and Captain Lepa hadn't been right to duck out. They told the Commandant that they'd execute the Tsar, but they wouldn't shoot the women. He was furious. Just as well he never knew about András and one of the girls. The one with grey eyes, the nice one. András was keen on her. He'd even shown her the picture of his mother back in Hungary that he used to carry in his wallet. I don't know how far it had gone. She was probably just bored, or scared, or maybe sex-crazed, like they said her mother was with Rasputin. Who knows? But András was a good-looking lad, young, too, like her. We were all young back then ... before that night. All except the Commandant. When András and Captain Lepa refused to do it he gave them such a roasting. 'Shameful failure to do their revolutionary duty at the crucial moment', I remember him saying, and something about 'the necessity of wiping out the dynasty'.

He was right. Of course he was. In the Party School I'd read what Lenin had said about the Romanovs, that we should execute a hundred of them to teach them not to organize pogroms. Not that Nicholas could have organized anything. As an Emperor he was laughable.... Pleasant enough, I suppose, in his way, as a man. He even tried to get talking to one of our Special Detachment, one of the Kabanov brothers it was, though I don't recall which one. Turned out he'd been in Nicholas's Grenadier Guards for a short spell. The wife though, Alexandra Feodorovna, now she was a different matter. What a woman she was, an Empress to her fingernails. She had the whip hand alright. Nicholas couldn't even blow his nose without her say so. As for the girls, they were just trying it on all the time, especially the younger two. I wouldn't want to see my sister behaving that way, so familiar with strangers. But we'd already been warned about them by the Commandant and most of us kept our distance. Except András of course.

And then there was the boy ... such a weakling. Strange to think that a cripple like him would have been the next Emperor of Russia. If he'd lived. That's the dynastic principle. And that's why they all had to die. It was what they taught us in the Party School. The rule of the tsars had given way to bourgeois democracy, and then to the real Revolution, the socialist one. In that sense the Romanovs were already irrelevant. But they were still important for the Whites. The counter-revolutionaries needed them as figureheads for their reactionary government. It had to be done.

Mind you, I would have organized the whole thing differently. He was a fool to have chosen that room. He should have done it outside. Two rounds each with Winchesters in the courtyard would have finished the job cleanly, especially if the prisoners had been properly searched beforehand and those jewels discovered. But he wanted to use the cellar. I mean, what the hell did he think would happen if he put eleven people in a room less than 50 meters square and then crammed a ten-man firing squad in the doorway? There was almost no light in there either. There was only one bare bulb overhead, and it was so dim that after the first volley we could see nothing through the smoke. And why in the dead of night? I suppose he wanted to keep it secret. But not even the old Cheka trick of revving a truck outside could mask the gunfire and the sound of all the screaming.

The Party called it the House of Special Purpose, but we knew it as the Merchant's House. The seven of us from the factory had been sent there as guards in early July when we were picked to replace a unit of Russian workers. We were a mixed lot, but good lads. We'd all worked for the local Cheka, too. A few of us were prisoners from the Habsburg army who'd been through the Party School in Omsk, and then got drafted to the Upper Isetsk factory as Red Guards. There were a couple of Latvians as well, from the Rifles Battalion. That was a crack unit. Only one of us seven was Russian, an ex-Red Army man called Netrebin. We were all good Communists. We lived downstairs on the ground floor of the Merchant's House, and the prisoners had the top floor.

The Commandant – his name was Comrade Yurovsky – was a Russian and an important man in the Cheka. He'd been given command of the House when we were drafted there. He took over from another comrade who'd been stealing from the prisoners, or so it was said, and had been too slack about security. The Commandant soon put a stop to all that. He reorganized the guard rota and put us in the key posts. He dismissed the guards who'd become too friendly with the prisoners. He even had the family seal up their valuables in a box which he inspected every day. Still, like I said, he wasn't as thorough as he should have been with those jewels.

He was a tall man, dark, around forty years old, with a small moustache and a beard a bit like Lev Trotsky's. He'd been a medical orderly in the War, and a photographer before that, and he'd been in the Party since 1905. He could speak a bit of German, too. Picked it up in Berlin before the Revolution, I think. Now he was Deputy Commissar of Justice for the whole Urals Region. His second-in-command in the House was another Russian, called Nikulin. The Commandant used to rely on him a lot. I think Nikulin was the only one he trusted completely.

It wasn't a bad posting. I mean, there was no real work. It was boring, but then guard duty is always boring. It was hot, too. The city got more tense as the summer wore on. The Whites were closing in on Ekaterinburg. It was those bastards in the Czech Legion who'd rebelled and gone over to the reactionaries. The fools couldn't see that their best hope of national liberation lay with us. But that's another story. In the Merchant's House things got worse by the day. Everyone was talking about the possibility of a rescue. There were all kinds of monarchist sympathizers hanging around in the city. We'd see them outside the high fence that surrounded the house. The perimeter guards were constantly having to warn them off. We even arrested some of them. The prisoners definitely expected to be rescued. They never said so, but you could tell. You could see it in their eyes, hear it in the way they were always whispering to one another. The Cheka comrades had even proved it. Before we were posted to the House, they'd written a letter which they pretended was from a group of monarchist officers. Petr Voikov, the Urals Commissar of Supplies, drafted it in French, and Rodzinsky, who had the neatest handwriting, copied it out. Then they gave it to one of the inner guards who'd got friendly with the prisoners, and he passed it on to that stuck-up-bitch Alexandra Feodorovna. The prisoners thought it was real. I saw some of their replies. They gave plans of the House, details of the guard rotas, everything.

So of course it was the right thing to do. They could have been rescued at any moment, especially given the way the last lot of guards had been fraternizing with them. Even if only one had escaped, it would have been a disaster. We had to keep them secure. The Whites would have made any of them into a figurehead. Even one of their corpses would have been a holy relic. Even part of a corpse. But it was more than that. We weren't just there to stop them escaping. We had to protect them, too. The workers of Ekaterinburg wanted to lynch them. Especially after the city garrison went over to the Whites just a few days after we arrived in the House. And if that had happened, there would have been no trial. Until a few days before the execution, you see, we thought we'd be taking them to Moscow. Lev Trotsky was to be Chief Prosecutor. What an event that would have been! He would have run rings around Nicholas and he'd have shown the bloodthirsty tsarist system for what it was. I'm still sorry that it didn't happen. In the end though, the calculation was simple. We were fighting for the survival of the Revolution. While the prisoners remained alive, three hundred men were deployed to guard them when they should have been serving in Red units at the Front. With the Romanovs dead, those men were free to fight.

You ask about the servants? Yes, they had to die too. They'd been given the chance of freedom and they'd chosen to stay with their masters. I had no sympathy for them. They made their choice. The Commandant knew they were all beyond redemption. All except young Leonid, the kitchen lad. The Commandant thought he might be re-educated. Leonid used to play with the boy, the heir, and kept him amused even on days when the boy couldn't leave his wheelchair. But he played like children do, like equals. The other servants were cringing lackeys but Leonid was alright. So the Commandant sent him away on the evening of the execution, saying that he should be kept in the guard house across the road until it was all over. At heart, the Commandant was an idealist.

The night it happened was hot, oppressively hot. Hardly a breath of air. All day it had been close and humid. It was high summer, and the house was unbearably stuffy because the windows had been sealed to stop the prisoners from attempting an escape. I heard that the family made such a fuss about this that eventually one of the upstairs windows was opened to let in some air. Of course, they'd used it straight away to signal to their supporters outside and one of the guards had fired a warning shot. When he took over, the Commandant had a heavy grate fitted to that window. Naturally the prisoners complained about it. They were always complaining about something.

All through that last afternoon the lads from the outer guard shifted furniture from the basement room. It was hot work and they grumbled about it, but we needed the space. They could have saved themselves some trouble actually. No sooner had the prisoners entered the chamber than her High-And-Mightiness demanded to sit down, so the Commandant sent his deputy out for chairs, one for her and one for the boy whose legs had been bad for days. Nikulin was laughing as he came through the antechamber where we were waiting. He was carrying two cane chairs, and I remember him joking as he passed us. 'The heir, it seems, wants to die in a chair.'

Once they were in the room and were seated to their liking, we were ordered in. We had our backs to the doorway and we were facing the prisoners. They seemed curious, not nervous. The Empress looked at us with contempt, as usual, and the others were whispering to one another. It was a relief to be doing something at last. We'd been waiting for hours in the antechamber, waiting for them to wash and dress. The Commandant had asked the Doctor to wake them up, around midnight, but it must have been two in the morning before they finally came downstairs. They were used to making people wait. It came naturally to them. I could see the Commandant was getting edgy. Summer nights in the Urals are short, and he still had the bodies to deal with. It was only later on that we realized why they'd taken so long to dress. The Commandant had spun the Doctor a story about there being shooting in the town and about needing to move the family downstairs where it would be safer. He'd said they shouldn't bring anything with them. But they were still hoping for a rescue and had put on their special clothes. They were carrying bags and cushions, too, as though they were going on holiday somewhere. Such greed, even in their final moments.

Like I say, the Commandant had wanted it to happen earlier in the evening, and it would all have been so much easier if he'd had a few more hours of darkness. But before beginning the operation he had to wait for the truck that was going to transport the bodies, and predictably enough that puffed-up nonentity Ermakov was two hours late with it. Not only was he late, he was also drunk, although we didn't realize that until afterwards.

It started badly, and it didn't get any better.

I had seen how it would go from the minute the Commandant called us to his room that afternoon. That was when I learned what the execution squad was going to do. What we were going to do. That was when András and Captain Lepa refused to take part. Each of us was allocated a prisoner to shoot, because the Commandant thought it would be more efficient that way. He distributed the Nagant revolvers that Nikulin had collected from the outer guard that afternoon. There was more than one each, I remember. The Commandant and Nikulin had their own weapons, and so did Kudrin from the Cheka, so in the end Ermakov took three, stuffing them in his waistband like a comic book bandit. Then there was a big argument between the Russians about which of them would shoot the Emperor. Eventually, the Commandant pulled rank and claimed Nicholas for himself, although Ermakov grumbled that he had done hard labour and so he was entitled to shoot 'bloody Nick'. I was given the valet, a scrawny old man, always grovelling before his master. I didn't really care who I got. Although a part of me was glad that it wasn't one of the girls.

The trouble was, once we crowded into the doorway of that little room, I saw right away that it wasn't going to work. None of us was facing the right target because the Commandant had let the prisoners stand wherever they liked. They weren't lined up properly. The Tsar was to one side, standing in front of the boy who was on one of Nikulin's chairs. The Empress was on the other chair next to the boy, with three of the girls around her. The fourth girl was somewhere towards the back, standing with the maid near a closed door that led to a lumber room. It was so dim back there that they were just pale shapes. My target, the valet, was standing in the other corner with the Doctor and the chef, behind the Emperor. It meant that I was facing one of the girls, the pretty one who liked András.

It was so crowded and hot that it was difficult to breathe. I knew the moment had come and I felt calm. But it seemed to take so long. As we looked at one another, that family in the semi-darkness and us in the lighted doorway, it seemed as though time had stopped for a moment. They were the past and we were the future. Something new was being born. ... The Commandant stepped forward and pulled a scrap of paper from his pocket. I'd seen him earlier in his room, scribbling on it, muttering phrases that would bid a grand farewell to three hundred years of Romanov history. In the end, it was very ordinary. He was brief and to the point. 'The Executive Committee of the Urals Soviet of Workers', Peasants' and Soldiers' Deputies has resolved that you are to be executed.'

Until then I don't think they had any idea that they were about to die. That all their magnificence was to end there, in that tiny underground room. Nicholas couldn't believe it. He turned to his wife, and then back to look at the Commandant. 'What?' he said, 'What?' He said it twice. And those were the last words of the last Tsar of All the Russias. As he spoke he fell backwards. Actually, he was lifted off his feet by the hail of bullets fired at him by all the Russians in the room. It didn't matter what they'd agreed in the Commandant's office. Nothing was going to stop every single one of them from taking a shot at their Emperor. I decided to follow orders and aim at the valet, even though I wasn't directly facing him. I couldn't shoot András's girl who was my nearest target. I think I hit the valet. I suppose that he and the chef and the Doctor all got some of the bullets meant for the Emperor because they went down quite fast. I can't be sure, though, because after that first volley, with all the smoke and dust, it was hard to see anything. No one had given the order to fire and the shooting was completely random. I did see the Empress slump from her chair. She'd been shot in the side of the head.

It got worse. Once it began, the girls started to run away, hammering on the door to the lumber room and screaming to be let out. And those of us who were standing in the second row, crammed in the doorway, barely had room to aim. Then a couple more lads from the outer guard joined in. It was madness. One of the squad got badly powder burned from the man shooting next to him. The noise was incredible. Women screaming and bullets flying around the room. We couldn't understand why there were so many ricochets in a room that had been chosen specifically because of its soft plaster walls.

It seemed to go on for ever. Eventually the Commandant gave the order to cease firing, and then the choking smoke lifted a little. Now we saw the result. Two girls crouching by the side wall, their arms wrapped around their heads. The boy still sitting in his chair, shaking and crying. He'd pissed himself. I remember the pool on the floor, spreading into the slick of blood from his mother. The Doctor was alive, too. He was on the ground next to the shredded body of the Emperor, but he was still moving. The Commandant walked up to him and shot him in the head. Then Nikulin moved towards the boy with his weapon raised. Even in the smoke and the darkness I could see that his hand was trembling and he'd gone completely white. My ears were ringing from the gunfire but I could hear him shouting something about how he'd used up a whole clip of bullets and the boy was still alive. The Commandant just growled 'nerves, Grigory', walked up to the boy as cool as you like, and shot him in the head with his Mauser. The shot blew open the child's skull and threw him from the chair. Then the girls started screaming again. The two crouching by the side wall tried to stand up, but were too badly wounded and their legs buckled under them. The Commandant finished them both with shots to the head. Then he and Kudrin went from one corpse to the next, trying not to slip, rolling them face up with their boots, checking for signs of life. Someone from the outer guard ran in yelling that the shots had been heard on the street.

And then we heard a woman shriek. 'Thank you, Lord! I'm saved!' It was the maid at the back of the room struggling to her feet. The other two daughters were behind her, and they were alive too, moaning on the floor. Ermakov grabbed a bayonet from his belt and marched up to them. He started to stab one of the girls, but the blade would not penetrate her bodice. She was the youngest of the four, I remember. She was screaming like she used to do when I'd hear them play in the garden. The bayonet wouldn't silence her. I thought it was because Ermakov was drunk. Evidently so did the Commandant, because he pushed him aside and shot the girl, then turned to her sister and did the same. By this time, Ermakov had started on the maid, and she was trying to parry his bayonet with the little cushions she was holding. Eventually, Ermakov wrenched them away from her and stabbed her in the chest. We didn't know it then, but the cushions were like the girls' bodices, stuffed with jewels.

At last it was still, apart from the engine of the truck rumbling outside. Pavel Medvedev, in charge of the outer guard, told a dozen of his lads to take the bodies to the truck. They had to carry them through the basement of the house and out to the yard in front, blood dripping on the floor all the way. I went to help him get something to make stretchers with, and found him in the lumber room, vomiting. I can't say I was surprised. The stench of blood and cordite in that airless chamber was overpowering. As the eleven bodies were taken away on improvised stretchers, some more lads from the outer guard came with buckets of sand and rags to start cleaning up the slime of royal blood and brains on the wooden floor. We had another shock when we were rolling the youngest girl on to a stretcher. She stirred and moaned, still not dead. Ermakov spun round and went for her again, trying to finish her in the same way, but he couldn't push the bayonet through her breast-bone, so in the end he pulled his third revolver from his belt and shot her in the head.

While this was going on, some of Medvedev's stretcher party had started pilfering the trinkets that the prisoners had brought with them to the cellar – cushions, handbags, stuff like that. They were searching the pockets for anything worth taking and ripping jewellery off the bodies. When he realized what was going on, the Commandant demanded it all back or else he would have them shot. The lads surrendered their loot. They knew that we from the Special Detachment wouldn't have hesitated. One of them gave up the Emperor's cigarette case. That thing was worth a fortune, solid gold inlaid with diamonds, just to carry tobacco in. Another lad reluctantly pulled the Doctor's gold watch from his jacket pocket. It was this business, I think, that convinced the Commandant he had to supervise the burial. To see that it was done properly. Ermakov was supposed to dispose of the bodies, but he'd already proven himself unreliable by turning up drunk and two hours late. He still had a half-empty bottle of vodka tucked in his trousers. I know, because he offered it round after the shooting. I never liked the man, but I was grateful for that swig of vodka.

The next part of the night was worse in a way. I didn't want to go along, but the Commandant needed reliable people, with Ermakov as incapable as he was. I was one of the three from the Special Detachment that he ordered to ride in the back of the truck with the bodies. One of the others, would you believe it, was András. Maybe it was the Commandant's way of teaching him a lesson. And he left Nikulin in charge at the House. I remember that we were pulling a tarpaulin over the corpses and the driver was revving the engine when one of the lads ran out of the House with something impaled on the end of his bayonet. He tossed it into the truck muttering 'dogs die a dog's death'. It was the little white and tan spaniel that one of the children kept for a pet. A harmless enough creature, I suppose, although I never could see the point of having a dog as small as that.

It must have been about three in the morning when the truck pulled out of the yard. It was a heavy Fiat, with a 60-hp engine and a closed cab. The Commandant and Ermakov sat up front with the driver, Lyukhanov, who was the official chauffeur assigned to the Merchant's House. We three climbed into the open back with the bodies. We lit up. I needed that smoke. But as we set off down Voznesensky Prospekt, I realized that there were no spades, no picks or tools of any kind. I knew then that it was going to be a long night.

We went slowly west out of town along the Upper Isetsk road towards the Zlokazov factory. Ermakov had worked there once. Now he was Military Commissar for the whole area, and full of self-importance. We swung north, turning off the main road along what was really just a track that led through the forest. It was slow. The vehicle was overloaded with the weight of all those bodies in the back. I had no idea where we were going, but after about two hours of crawling along, the truck stopped. It was where the railway line from the local factories cut across the path. A group of about two dozen men was waiting for us, some on horseback and some in light carts. It turned out that Ermakov had organized a welcome party from Upper Isetsk for the prisoners. The men had been drinking. It got ugly when they realized that all we'd brought them were corpses. Ermakov's lads had expected to get them alive so they could have some fun before they killed them. They'd been looking forward to having some Romanov women. They were going to show Nicky what his German bitch got up to with Rasputin behind his back.

The Commandant tried to take control. He ordered Ermakov's men to lift the bodies on to the carts, so that we could take them deeper into the forest. Ermakov had said there were some disused mineshafts there where we could dump them. At this point, the looting began again. These corpses were expensively dressed with trinkets in every pocket and around every wrist and Ermakov's men couldn't resist. Then, when they were swinging the bodies off the Fiat and on to the carts, someone saw a diamond flash in the bodice of one of the girls where her clothes had been ripped. We all crowded round to look, and then I saw what was hidden in the undergarments of the female prisoners. The men began pawing at the dead women's clothes. One of them raised the Empress's lilac skirts and sniggered that he could die happy now that he'd touched the 'royal cunt'. Then another did the same. It was beginning to fall apart. The Commandant ordered them to back off, and when they hesitated he used us – the members of the Special Detachment – to make them. We levelled our revolvers, forcing the men back. The Commandant dismissed the two who had groped the Empress and any others he'd seen looting. They grumbled, but they obeyed, and things calmed down a little. He told the rest of the men to fan out along the road and stop anyone approaching from either direction. And after they'd gone he tore into Ermakov for having 'jeopardized the operation'.

The Fiat set off back to town. It was too heavy to make it down the path ahead. Actually, it was a relief to be rid of the truck. It had already got stuck a couple of times, and we'd had to struggle to free it. We went deeper into the forest with three carts containing the corpses, leading the horses on foot. It was already getting light. Ermakov eventually brought us to the disused mine, which was in a large glade at a place called the Four Brothers. He didn't seem too sure of the way, but he pointed out where the 'brothers' had once stood – four pine trees that grew out of a single trunk, he said, although now there were only a couple of stumps left. The mine shaft didn't live up to its name either. It turned out to be just a shallow pit from a prospecting mine. There were lots of pits like that nearby, the region was rich in copper. It was obvious that the bodies wouldn't stay hidden for long if we dumped them there. But we were exhausted and it was already dawn so the Commandant had no alternative. He ordered us to strip the corpses and burn the clothes. He told Ermakov to smash in the faces. This was harder than anyone imagined, and the drunkard only managed to disfigure a couple, before giving up, complaining that he was exhausted.

We stripped the bodies in the dawn light to a chorus of birdsong. We tried to do it fast, desperate for that night's work to be over. I remember thinking: how can a woman wear so many clothes? Under the dark blue suits those girls had blouses, petticoats, frills, ruffles, and then, on top of yet more chemises, those bloody doubled corsets. As I wrenched apart the metal fastenings at the front, jewels came tumbling out from between two layers of stiffened fabric. Diamonds, sapphires, rubies, each one wrapped in wadding. Whole necklaces and bracelets. Rings, brooches, medals, earrings, all packed closely together to form a kind of body-armour made of the most priceless things. It was then we finally understood why the girls had taken so long to die in the cellar. With Ermakov's thugs dismissed, the Commandant had reliable people with him, and we worked properly, ripping the doubled corsets to get at the valuables which we placed in a sack that the Commandant himself carried from one body to the next. I was shocked at the quantity of jewels they'd hidden. Next to her skin the Empress was wearing several ropes of large pearls that she, or someone else, had sewn inside a cloth belt. She also had a spiral of thick gold wire wrapped around her upper arm underneath her chemise. I couldn't begin to guess its value. Even the buttons of their clothes turned out to be enormous precious stones covered with fabric. The boy wore a kind of undergarment lined with valuables, and he had jewels sewn inside the band of his cap. When the Commandant's sack was full, it weighed about eight kilos.

I can say this with pride: all the valuables were collected. Not one of us took anything for himself. At least, we took none of the precious items. In the chamber, the Commandant had tossed Nicholas's cap to Kudrin, 'as a souvenir', he'd said. It was a regular army cap so Kudrin just ripped off the cockade and pocketed that. I admit, we did want to share out the footwear. Boots were almost impossible to come by at that time, you see, and it seemed criminal to burn such good ones. But they were soaked in blood and would have incriminated us, so they had to go on the fire along with the rest of the clothes. The Commandant promised us the pick of the boots left in the House. I'd heard say that the Emperor had forty pairs with him in his luggage, although I only ever saw him in the same old ones he was wearing that night. The Commandant kept his promise, but it turned out that my feet were too big for the Emperor's boots, so I took a pair of the Doctor's brown brogues. They were well made. They lasted me for years.

We lit two large fires to burn the clothes. The blood on them was beginning to harden and it made the flames hiss and smoke. The naked bodies lay sprawled on the ground. White corpses, which looked no different from any other dead body. I'd seen plenty of corpses before, at the Front, men sometimes so disfigured that they were barely human. But these looked out of place in the forest at daybreak, and I was glad to dump them. Working in pairs, we took them by the arms and legs and swung them into the pit. There was no particular order. They were equals in death. However, the hole was not so deep, and at the bottom there was less than a metre of water. The last corpses to be thrown in were quite close to the surface, and clearly visible. Someone had the idea of tossing in grenades to make the pit collapse over the bodies, but we decided against it because the noise would have drawn too much attention. Instead, we cut branches to cover the hole. It was about six in the morning by now, and the Commandant left for town on horseback. He took Ermakov and the sack of jewels with him. He left orders for us to keep the fires stoked until all the clothes were destroyed, and to allow nobody to approach the pit. He'd be back that night, he said, with the right tools to finish the task properly.

So we three from the Special Detachment spent that day by the mine, building up the fires and taking it in turns to get some rest. I couldn't sleep much. We found fresh water, but there wasn't a lot to eat, except for a few biscuits that András had in his pocket and whatever berries we could forage. We had to scare off some peasants from the village nearby who'd wandered in our direction, attracted by the fires and the noise of the previous night. The Commandant had told Ermakov's men to say that the Czech Legion was in the area and the villagers shouldn't stray into the forest. But it seems that word had got out about the Romanovs being executed. We spent most of the day smoking or playing cards to pass the time. As we waited for the Commandant to return, I even began to wonder whether the town had fallen and he'd been taken prisoner by the Whites. The idea made me nervous. I knew those bastards were only days away, and I could imagine what they'd do to us if they caught us.

For a second night, we didn't sleep. In the early hours of the morning another group of men – about a dozen of them – arrived at the Four Brothers clearing. These lads made quite a contrast with Ermakov's lot. They were reliable Chekists from the Kusvinsky Works in Ekaterinburg, with orders to assist in burying the bodies. We told them what had happened, and they began poking around in the ashes of the bonfires where we'd burned the clothes. It wasn't long before someone found a diamond ring and then several other jewels. Not long after the Kusvinsky contingent arrived, the Commandant himself turned up in a cart loaded with spades and ropes – the equipment that Ermakov should have arranged to bring in the first place. The Kusvinsky men said that the whole town was talking about where the Romanovs were buried. The word was that Ermakov had got a dressing down from his boss, Military Commissar Goloshchekin, for botching the burial and for bringing his gang of workers to see the corpses. I noticed that the Commandant was looking uncomfortable, and wondered if he'd been reprimanded too. He was limping. Said he'd fallen off his horse.

Then we had to get the bodies out of the mineshaft. Two of the Kusvinsky men lowered themselves into the pit, up to their waists in freezing water, and tied ropes around the ankles of the corpses. We hauled out the naked bodies. They emerged feet first in the moonlight over the lip of the mineshaft. The bloody corpses that we'd tossed in the night before had been washed clean in the cold water, and their limbs looked smooth and white, like holy relics. The little dog? We left it down there, I think. We laid the bodies beside the pit, and covered them with a tarpaulin. By the time we'd finished, it was dawn on the morning of July 18, and we still didn't know how to dispose of the bodies. We had to hide them – or destroy them – and we had to do it fast. Too many people already knew, and we couldn't be sure they wouldn't tell the Whites.

The Commandant was describing some deep mines that he'd been told about, mines with proper shafts, not like Ermakov's shallow pit. They were out on the Moscow Highway, he said, back to the west of town. The three of us from the Special Detachment wanted to bury them right there and then. We'd been dragging those bodies around for two nights and a day. And taking the carcasses of Their Imperial Majesties back through Ekaterinburg when it was about to fall to the Whites seemed like madness. So the Commandant ordered the Kusvinsky men to start digging a pit that could hold at least some of the corpses. It would be better to split them up, he said. They began digging with a will, but they soon struck rocky ground and had to give up.

We three who had been in the Merchant's House that night and had brought the corpses this far were completely exhausted by now. The Commandant told us to rest, set some of the new contingent to keep watch, and said that we'd have to wait for it to get dark before we took the bodies to the deep mines on the Moscow Highway. He set off back to town to requisition a truck. He was thinking about burying some of them along the way, too. He was still keen to break up the group. Perhaps some could even be burned, although no one seemed to know how. Frankly, I no longer gave a damn what we did with them, and I lay down on the ground and slept like the dead.

All that day we waited, with sentries posted to guard access to the clearing. Anyone not on sentry duty dozed in the shade. Someone went to the village for supplies and came back with milk and hard-boiled eggs. The Commandant showed up again about 9.30 in the evening, by car this time, bringing some more provisions with him. We drew back the tarpaulin, took the corpses by the arms and legs, and loaded the carts to take them to the truck which was waiting on the forest road nearby. But now, last night's relics didn't look so holy. They were bloated and stinking, with flies buzzing around the eyes and the open wounds. Imperial bodies rot the same as proletarian ones. We had to tie rags over our mouths and noses. We led the carts along the path, and found the truck, with Lyukhanov at the wheel again. There was a second vehicle too, loaded with barrels and boxes. We swung the putrefying corpses on to the back of the truck and set off.

This time we headed south, back towards Ekaterinburg on the forest road, but intending to turn right on to the Moscow highway, rather than left into town. It all went fine at first. We negotiated the difficult intersection with the factory railway line quite easily. Then, about half-way back to town, the truck got bogged down in wet ground. It was where the road went down into a slight depression. Probably it was always damp there. We gathered brushwood to wedge beneath the wheels and attempted to push the truck out. But all the traffic of the last two days, the overloaded truck driving back and forth to Ekaterinburg, had made deep ruts, and Lyukhanov had driven right into them.

Once again we found ourselves grappling with the bodies. Pulling them off the truck, I felt they were still alive and resisting me. Their weight would suddenly collapse on top of you as you moved them, making you lose balance and footing. I thought we were cursed. Even when it was unloaded we struggled with the truck for nearly two hours, trying to free it from the ruts, in the darkness, with those stinking corpses piled nearby. Eventually, some of the men brought some old railway sleepers that they'd found stacked outside the watchman's hut by the railway crossing. When these were wedged under the wheels the vehicle broke free from the mud and made it to firmer ground. But by now it was after midnight. We'd been stuck with those bloody corpses for three days. We were hungry and exhausted and wanted it to be over. The Commandant said to press on, but there was nearly a mutiny when he ordered us to reload the truck. We'd had enough.

Then someone – I forget who now – had the idea of burying the corpses right there. Right there, in the shallow dip in the road where the vehicle had been stuck. The ground was soft, so digging would be easy. We could get rid of the bodies at last, and we could even cover the grave with the railway sleepers that we'd just used to free the truck.

No one wanted to start digging again. Yet we could see that the plan made sense, so some of us grabbed spades and set to, and the others soon joined in. The Commandant, though, still insisted that the bodies shouldn't all be buried together in the same grave. So, when we refused to dig two pits, he decided to burn some of them. We split into two groups. The grave diggers began to dig, and the cremation party gathered dry brushwood and logs and made a funeral pyre. They doused it in kerosene that the Commandant had brought. It would have been best to burn Nicholas, I thought, if he wanted to be sure the Whites would never find him. But the Commandant didn't seem convinced that the bodies would burn at all, and he chose the smallest corpses to experiment with – the boy and one of the daughters. They built the fire downwind of the grave we were digging – about fifty metres away – but we could still feel the intense heat and taste the stench of burning rotten flesh. The Commandant kept shouting at them to build up the fire. It's hard to burn a body.

After a couple of hours, we'd dug a squarish pit right in the middle of the track where the ground was softest. It wasn't all that big, about two metres by one-and-a-half, and not much more than a metre deep. The Commandant had wanted it deeper, but once again we struck rock not far below the surface, towards the northern edge. We dragged the nine remaining bodies into this hole. The first to go in was the valet who had been my target. Nicholas went in on top of him, quite by chance – the valet's final service to his master. I remember thinking how old the Doctor looked without his false teeth. And how the young girls were no longer pretty.

The Commandant had brought several boxes containing large jars of acid. When all the bodies had been dragged into the hole, we poured the acid on top, mostly over the faces. The flesh and hair melted immediately. We poured the rest of it over the torsos, hoping to minimize the stench that would come from the grave. The pit was not that deep after all. Some of the acid splashed on to my grey uniform, burning a hole in one trouser leg and stinging me, which made me even less well disposed towards the whole affair. We backfilled the pit, put the railway sleepers on top, and scattered some brushwood around the site. Then Lyukhanov reversed the truck over the sleepers, going back and forth, back and forth, until he'd packed them down tight and made it look as though that little bridge had always been a part of the road. And at last, around dawn, the two bodies on the bonfire seemed to have disappeared, more or less, and the fire was allowed to die down. We used our spades to smash up the lumps of burned wood and the larger charred bones, and then we dug the bits into the earth. Finally, we lit a new fire on the same spot, and when this died down we stamped out its embers, to disguise the makeshift cremation.

At last it was over. The Commandant gathered us all together and solemnly told us that the remains must never be discovered, that for the sake of the Revolution we must never speak of what we had done, that we should forget what we had seen.

'We hid them so well that the world will never find them,' was what Commissar Voikov boasted afterwards. Well, he didn't do the hiding, but

I believe that we did it well. The Commandant's fires at Four Brothers, where we burned the clothes, were a perfect decoy. The world certainly thought that all the bodies had been burned, completely destroyed, because when the Whites took Ekaterinburg – which they did only a few days later – they sent their gendarmes to poke around in the forest and look for the Romanovs' remains. We were all long gone by then, but they searched hard, for us and for their precious Emperor's body. I know that they found the little bridge of railway sleepers, and the remains of the bonfires at Four Brothers, and some debris that hadn't quite burned in them – boot buttons, small trinkets, stuff like that. I believe they even got part of the Doctor's dentures.

It was about ten years later, when I'd left Russia for good, that I came across one of the books they'd written about it. It had a photograph of Ermakov, standing by the bridge, all puffed up with pride. But only we knew what was beneath the bridge. People in Ekaterinburg, though, still remembered. I heard that the Commandant used to go to Party meetings to talk about the Emperor's execution. And Mayakovsky wrote a poem about it. But for the rest of the world, Nicholas and his family had been burned to ashes. There were no remains. There was nothing left to find.[1]

2   True crime

> That bodies die is one of the most fascinating things about them.
> (Jean Bethke Elshtain, *Politics and the Human Body: Assault on Dignity* (1995))

> 'Oh them,' she said, 'they're just a pile of bones.'
> [Russian student on the Romanovs].
> (Orlando Figes, 'Burying the Bones', *Granta*, 64, winter 1998)

The first finders[1]

When the soil they extracted with their makeshift drill showed traces of oily black matter, they knew that they had found the grave. Back at the Avdonins's apartment in Sverdlovsk that evening, they tested the soil samples and found that they were highly acidic. This was proof. From the testimony of Yakov Yurovsky – the man who had organized the shooting and the burial in 1918 – they knew that the bodies had been disfigured with acid before being interred. The acid, Yurovsky had written, would also serve to disguise the smell of decay, for 'the pit was not deep'.

The following day – a hot Friday, 1 June 1979 – all six of them rendezvous at the site, a largish glade deep in the forests outside Sverdlovsk. The two women, Galya Avdonina and Margarita Ryabova, have gone to buy some bottles of mineral water, and arrive to find that the men have already lifted off a layer of grass and topsoil to reveal, about sixteen inches down, the railway sleepers mentioned by Yurovsky. Galya bustles about setting up camp. Among the scrubby trees she manages to find a wooden crate for a table and an old lorry tyre that will make a comfortable seat on the wet grass. All around is the silent forest of pine and birch. The men have brought the equipment one might need for a geological survey: spades, bags for samples, notebooks. Geological research will be their cover story if they are discovered. Avdonin's friend Gennady Vasilev, a geophysical engineer, has even gone to the local authorities to obtain the requisite authorization, the all-powerful *spravka*, for permission to dig.

They have been waiting for a whole year to excavate. The summer before Avdonin and a colleague, geologist Mikhail Kochurov, surveyed the old forest road that leads north west from Sverdlovsk to Koptiaki village, looking for the place near railway crossing No. 184 where the forest road had been bridged by wooden sleepers, as Yurovsky had described. The site was mentioned in other sources, too. The White Russian investigator, Nikolai Sokolov, had come across it in 1919 and had photographed the spot where he believed that sleepers had been laid down because the Bolsheviks' lorry had become mired in the track. Sokolov thought that the lorry had been on its way back to Ekaterinburg from the 'Four Brothers' clearing, where he was convinced that the Bolsheviks had incinerated the bodies of their victims. What Sokolov had failed to realize, and what Avdonin had suspected from reading his account, was that it was precisely here – where Yurovsky and his gang had halted for five hours, far longer than it should have taken them to free their lorry – that the Tsar was buried. Since then, of course, the sleepers had become buried under the mulch of sixty winters. Kochurov, however, with a scout's expert eye, had seen a small declivity in the road near the old railway crossing and he suspected that this might be the spot. When he and Avdonin carried out test boring with a home-made probing rod something like a giant corkscrew, they found what they were looking for. About sixteen inches below the surface they hit a layer of rotting wood that extended over an area of some six-and-a-half by ten feet.

Geli Ryabov, back in Moscow, could barely contain his excitement when Avdonin wrote to him of their discovery. 'What shook me most was that your colleague has found the layer of sleepers,' he wrote back on 5 October. 'I'm not exaggerating when I say that a shiver ran up my spine.' When he arrived in Sverdlovsk in late May 1979, this time with his wife Margarita, Ryabov was certain that they were about to open the grave of the last Tsar. He hoped to have a more significant role in the excavation once the remains were discovered. Lacking the scientific expertise of the others, and without their local knowledge, he had been of little help in finding a small patch of ground in the trackless undergrowth. But his years in the police service had taught him to recognize human remains and, as a film-writer, he was acutely aware of the dramatic potential of the moment.

Two layers of decaying sleepers are lifted off, followed by rubble. Further down is yet another layer of sleepers, and a trickle of water begins to run into the hollow that forms. The men dig down into the flooded clay beneath the rotten sleepers. Mosquitoes gather, attracted by the pooling water, and Ryabov tells his wife to build a bonfire to drive them off. It is hot and humid in the forest and the men begin to sweat. Finally, about two-and-a-half feet down, they lift the first bone fragments from the liquid clay that bubbles gently as gases are released from the decayed matter. The bones are blackish-green. Overcome by the stench, one of the men turns away to vomit. Ryabov, in his element as the crime scene detective, identifies the fragments as pelvic bones and vertebrae and demands his audience pause to savour the significance of the moment. More is to come. They go on digging, using their hands now for fear of damaging the contents of the grave, and scoop out the yellowish water with an old bucket and a rusty saucepan which Margarita found when she was searching for firewood. As they bale out the water they can slice off layers of clay with their spade. Then Ryabov gropes around in the muddy water, saying that he can feel ribs and the little tapering bones that form the human hand; but they all know that these are not what he wants to find. Only a skull will authenticate the grave as the Tsar's.

Dispirited, Ryabov shakes his hands clean of the muddy water and moves away from the trench. Air bubbles are bursting all over the surface, and in the soup below there seems to be nothing but gravel and small bones. Frustrated and bombastic, Ryabov starts to berate the others for choosing to dig out this particular corner of the grave. Meanwhile, Vladislav Pesotsky takes his turn. More patient than Ryabov, he sifts the water for fragments of bone, carefully laying them on a bag beside him. He finds a broken piece of pottery, which Ryabov says must come from the ceramic jars that contained the sulphuric acid. Finally, Pesotsky announces that he has found a skull and brings up, first, a jawbone with teeth – the front two missing – and then a skull which still retains some light-brown hair and the remains of its brain tissue. Ryabov seizes it immediately and goes to rinse off its veneer of mud.

They photograph their find and return to the trench where Avdonin and Gennady Vasilev have a go. They feel what they think are two skeletons lying on top of each other and pull out some vertebrae. Fingering their way along the backbone they come to a skull which they lift out, followed by its jawbone. This one has six gold teeth – two crowns and a bridge. Ryabov immediately voices all their thoughts: if these fillings are made of gold, this must be the skull of the Tsar. They have found what they were looking for. But the facial part of the skull is destroyed, and not even Ryabov dares to compare it with the familiar features of Nicholas II. They take more photographs, then Pesotsky decides to have a last grope in the pit and extracts yet another skull. The others joke that he should have been an archaeologist and not a politics student: he has the luck of Heinrich Schliemann. This last skull, too, is rinsed of dirt. The entry and exit wounds from a bullet fired through the temple are quite visible, and it is rather small – maybe it belonged to one of the Tsar's daughters?

Pesotsky now starts to fret about the legality of what they have done. The Criminal Code prohibits disturbing a burial site without permission. They could be accused of grave robbing. Ryabov, who claims to know about these things, is vociferous in defending their actions. This is not a legal grave: there is nothing to mark it as such. Warming to his theme, he repeats the words that he has used in the past to strengthen Avdonin's resolve. They are morally entitled, even obligated, to undertake the search for the Tsar's grave. If anyone should be accused of criminal action it is Yurovsky and his gang of murderers. Not only did they shoot down the Tsar and all his family and retainers in cold blood, but then they desecrated their bodies by this crude burial. It was no wonder that Sokolov never found the grave, says Ryabov; a man brought up at the turn of the century, in Russia's Silver Age, could not conceive of such horrific treatment as Yurovsky had inflicted upon the bodies of the Tsar and his family. It beggars belief that even Bolsheviks would be so callous as to fling their naked corpses into a pit in the road, and then drive a truck back and forth over the top.

Somewhat shaken, but elated by their discovery, the six 'finders' eat lunch and spend the afternoon wrapping up their work. The pit is carefully backfilled with earth, and the railway sleepers replaced. They replant some bushes on top. Then they take more photographs, of the three skulls together and of the smaller bones. They decide that Avdonin will keep one rib-bone and the skull of the Tsar with its gold dental work, while Ryabov will take the other two skulls back to Moscow. The smaller bones are mostly returned to the earth in a bag, although Vasilev asks to keep a vertebra from the Tsar's skeleton and the piece of pottery. They decide to write a letter describing what they have done, and place it in the grave inside a small metal cylinder as a marker to future 'finders'. The task takes them back to their Komsomol childhoods in the 1930s when they used to bury time capsules marking the golden days in their humdrum lives: a pin with Lenin's likeness, a newspaper cutting about the Polar Aviators, a booklet of Pushkin's poems distributed to schoolchildren for the centenary of his death. Feeling that the occasion warrants something more ceremonial than these Komsomol games, Ryabov proposes that they drink to the memory of those buried in the backfilled pit. The vodka is poured and they raise their glasses solemnly, for it seems inappropriate to chink them. Then someone begins to sing the old Tsarist anthem, *Lord, Save the Tsar!* The men's voices deepen and swell with the falling cadences, but nobody knows the words beyond the first line imploring God to 'Save the Tsar, Strong and Mighty!', so they hum the rest.

Back in Moscow, Ryabov tried to have the skulls identified. In Sverdlovsk he had been so sure that as a well-known writer and a researcher for the Interior Ministry he could pull strings at the famous Gerasimov Institute. He expected that the ethnographers there would make for him plastic reconstructions of the skulls and magically re-create the features of the Tsar's children, either Alexei or Anastasia from the smaller of the two skulls, he thought, and probably Tatyana, the second daughter, from the larger. But no one would help him. There seemed to be a tacit pact between all the forensic institutes of Moscow to thwart him.

In July 1980 Ryabov retrieved the skulls and bones from the safety deposit box where he had stored them and returned to Sverdlovsk. Avdonin, growing increasingly uneasy about the skull lying in a box under his bed, was keen to return all three skulls to the grave. He was afraid that given Ryabov's contacts in the Interior Ministry the KGB would come to hear of their discovery. His wife Galya, moreover, had become nervous about why Ryabov had encouraged them to keep the skull with the gold teeth – proof that this was the Tsar's grave – in Sverdlovsk, and hadn't taken it with him to Moscow.

Ryabov has brought the stuff for making plaster casts of the skulls before they return them to the earth. They make the castings at the Avdonins's dacha, a basic wooden hut out in the countryside. They melt the formoplast resin in a bucket over a bonfire and pour it over the two larger skulls, placed in separate bowls. When they ease the skull bones free of the rubbery substance they notice that they have changed colour, taking on some of the amber pigment of the formoplast. The casts turn out somewhat crude but they will still be mementoes of their enterprise, and far less incriminating ones than the skulls themselves.

Avdonin and Gennady Vasilev have already been back to the burial site to retrieve the time capsule and the bag of bone fragments that they buried there the previous June. Now they put a polythene lining inside a wooden box that Avdonin has knocked together from varnished planks supplied by Vasilev, and place the three skulls inside it. The other bone fragments and some teeth that have come loose from the skulls in Ryabov's possession are also wrapped up and placed inside. Finally, Ryabov adds a simple copper icon: their find has awakened latent religious sentiment in him and he has started referring to the bones as 'relics'. On the back of the icon he inscribes a verse from St Matthew: 'Those who endure to the end will be saved' and the dates: 'Taken 01–06–79. Returned 07–07–80.'

They close up the box, which is about the size of a small suitcase, and catch the *elektrichka** from Sverdlovsk. They are the same group that they were a year ago, but more subdued on this occasion. It is already late, about 10.30 in the evening, but the sky is still light, just as it was when Yurovsky hid the bodies all those years ago. Avdonin guides them to the site. He wants to bury the box just where he and Vasilev extracted the time capsule two days previously. This will be quicker and it won't disturb the main grave. Ryabov objects strongly: still playing police detective he wants to find more forensic evidence, particularly bullets. As usual, the others defer to him and begin to dig where they think the edge of the grave lies. By lantern light they make a long, narrow trench about five feet deep, but find neither bullets nor bones. Standing in this trench, they burrow sideways through the soil towards the grave. Avdonin finds a skull. Its

---

* Network of local trains that link cities in Russia with their rural hinterland.

crown is towards him, and he pulls it out for a closer look. It is large, with some dental work of grey metal less ornate than the gold crown and fillings of the Tsar's skull that they are about to return. Ryabov thinks it must belong to Anna Demidova, the family's maid, and they put it back. Then they place the box in the trench and start to backfill it with earth, adding branches and brushwood to make it harder for anyone else to dig down. Avdonin has the idea of manoeuvring a large boulder on top of the box so that if anyone does excavate directly above it they will strike rock. They do their best to conceal the digging, replacing the turf, clearing away the remaining dirt, scattering branches over the trench. The *frisson* of the previous summer's excavations has evaporated, and this time there is no singing and no vodka; but they stand silently for a moment beside the grave, heads bowed with the enormity of their find.

In 1976, when Ryabov had first proposed looking for the Tsar's grave, they had not considered what they might do if they actually found it. At first, Avdonin had been very circumspect about their chances. His caution was understandable. The unexpected evening visit to his apartment by a celebrity like Geli Ryabov had been somewhat disconcerting, all the more so since Ryabov had been introduced by Colonel Ivan Korlykhanov of the MVD,[†] who was also head of the political department in the local soviet. Ryabov was in Sverdlovsk on business, presenting a screening of his popular television thriller – *A Girl Born to the Revolution* – to the Sverdlovsk police. Like most VIP visitors to the city he had asked to be shown the Ipatiev House, which was now closed to the general public. It was, after all, an infinitely preferable alternative to the tour of Sverdlovsk's industrial enterprises that had been arranged by the welcome committee.

The way Ryabov later told it, he had experienced a kind of epiphany in the basement room where the Tsar's family had been shot. This hardened police detective-turned-thriller-writer felt a shiver from the ghosts of the past in the execution chamber and knew that it would be his mission to tell the truth about what had happened to the Romanovs, a cathartic narrative that would make amends for all the cataclysmic cruelties subsequently visited upon Russia. At the very least the story would make a wonderful television mini-series.

When Ryabov started questioning his MVD minders in the Sverdlovsk welcome committee about the Ipatiev House and the events of July 1918, Colonel Korlykhanov had offered to introduce him to Aleksandr Avdonin. A brainy geologist with bottle-bottom glasses, the man was known as a source of local lore and something of a history buff. At first Avdonin's answers to Ryabov's interrogation had been stilted, for he was wary of drawing the MVD's attention to his interest in the Romanovs. But once

---

[†] Interior Ministry, in charge of the police force.

Korlykhanov had left, Ryabov had managed to get the geologist to open up a little. Avdonin, a native of Sverdlovsk, said that he had even interviewed some of the witnesses to the ex-Tsar's death who still lived in the city. Ryabov was fascinated: the man was a gold-mine of information. Trying to pique his interest, he had proposed that they look for the Tsar's grave together, but Avdonin, still cautious, said that any burial site would by now be masked by railway lines and houses. In any case, they would need archival documents to find it. Now Ryabov had his lure: the archives were not a problem, he had access to the *spetskhran* – the collections on restricted access – through his close contacts with Interior Minister Shchelokov himself, who could also protect them from any disagreeable consequences that a search might unleash. Avdonin was hooked and promised to help Ryabov look for the grave, if the secret documents unearthed any clues to its whereabouts.

When he returned to Moscow, Ryabov started his investigations. Shchelokov was as good as his word and produced the magical *spravka* that opened the special collections of the Lenin Library. There Ryabov found books deemed too sensitive for the ordinary citizen: the records of the White Army's 1919 investigation into the Tsar's murder, memoirs by tsarist officials, articles from the émigré press. After a while, however, Ryabov began to doubt that there even was a grave. The White investigators had been convinced that the Bolsheviks had burned all the bodies at the open-cast mine in the forest, near the place called Four Brothers. The Whites had found traces of a large fire at this site, and all the other sources seemed to follow their assumption that the bodies had been burned and not buried. Perhaps there were no remains.

Ryabov took heart from Mayakovsky's poem, 'The Emperor'. In 1928, Mayakovsky – a famous writer, just like him, on a visit to Sverdlovsk – had asked to see where 'Bloody Nick' was buried. The chairman of the Sverdlovsk Soviet had taken the celebrated poet 'nine *versts*'[‡] beyond the river Isetsk, 'with its mines and steep slopes, where the wind whistled'.

> 'Was it here?'
> 'Not here. Further!'
> Here a cedar is marked by an axe,
> Chips through the bark to the roots,
> By the roots, under the cedar, a road,
> And in it – the Emperor is buried.

These lines in Mayakovsky's poem confirmed for Ryabov what Avdonin had told him was in the first book-length Soviet account of the Tsar's death,

---

[‡] One verst = 1.06 kilometres.

The Last Days of the Romanovs, published in Sverdlovsk in 1926. Pavel Bykov, its author, who had been a member of the Ekaterinburg Soviet in 1918, had plagiarized much of his narrative from the versions published by the White investigators but he differed from the Whites' conclusions in one key respect. The bodies, he wrote, had been taken some distance from the open-cast mine at Four Brothers (where the Whites believed that they had been cremated), and had been 'buried in a bog'. *Buried*. Bykov had even used the same word as Mayakovsky – *zaryt'* – the Russian verb implying a hasty, scrabbled burrowing, like an animal rooting in the earth, not a dignified burial or even an archaeological excavation. Avdonin the geologist, who knew that it is impossible to bury anything in a bog, thought Bykov may have meant a damp declivity in the ground, probably near the road that led through the forest from Koptiaki village to the city of Sverdlovsk and which went past the Four Brothers mine.

Letters between Ryabov and Avdonin flew back and forth from Moscow to Sverdlovsk in the flimsy printed envelopes of the Soviet postal service. Ryabov's missives described glittering soirées and mourned the vanished refinements of pre-revolutionary Russia. Avdonin, meanwhile, continued to amass oral reminiscences. These evanescent sources, the recollections of frail old people who had been part of the events of 1918, were the last living link to that night in July when Russia had lost her Tsar. In the summer of 1977 Ryabov again made the day-long train journey to Sverdlovsk and spent a fruitless couple of days wandering the Koptiaki forest road with Avdonin, looking for possible burial sites. Then he met one of Avdonin's sources, the 90-year-old Gennady Nikolaevich Lisin, a former reporter on the *Urals Worker* newspaper that had published the announcement of the Tsar's 'funeral' in 1918. As a teenager Lisin had helped the White investigators search for evidence; later on he had met Mayakovsky on the famous poet's visit to the city. Still with a journalist's feeling for a good story, Lisin suggested that Ryabov should look up Rimma Yakovlevna Yurovskaya, the daughter of the Tsar's executioner Yakov Yurovsky. She lived in Leningrad.

Ryabov's Interior Ministry contacts were not just useful for getting into libraries. The MVD knew everyone's whereabouts, which saved him a lot of time in tracking down Rimma Yurovskaya to a tiny apartment in one of Leningrad's new districts. As usual, Ryabov disguised his real interest with the partially true cover story that he was writing a film script. Rimma Yurovskaya was hostile; now a heavy old woman of nearly 80, she had been a model Komsomolka[§] in the 1930s but, inevitably, had been caught up in the purges and spent many years in a labour camp. She did not want to discuss her father. She said that he had simply been carrying out orders

---

[§] Female member of the Komsomol (the Young Communist League) – the youth wing of the Soviet Communist Party.

when he executed the Tsar and that was the end of the matter. But Ryabov's persistence paid off when she put him in touch with her brother, Aleksandr Yakovlevich Yurovsky.

Another tiny apartment in Leningrad's urban hinterland, this one even more shabby than Rimma's. Aleksandr, a retired admiral of the Soviet Navy, was more forthcoming about their father, hinting that he had been ashamed of what he had had done in July 1918. Then Aleksandr gave Ryabov the key – Yurovsky's own account, as dictated to Soviet historian Mikhail Pokrovsky in 1920, of the Tsar's execution and burial. The famous 'Yurovsky note'. In graphic detail, Yurovsky recounted how he had eventually hidden the eleven bodies of the Tsar and his family and servants. Two of them, he wrote, had been burned; the other nine had been flung into a pit dug in the forest track, they had been doused in sulphuric acid, and railway sleepers had been bedded down in the track to disguise the grave.

The crime scene[2]

On a drizzly July morning in 1991, officials from the Sverdlovsk regional prosecutor's office began arriving in the clearing near the old Koptiaki forest road with instructions to investigate a report received the previous day about the discovery there of human remains. The prosecutor had rapidly rounded up a team of eight experts – two police officers, two forensic experts, two epidemiologists, two archaeologists – 'two of everything, just like Noah's Ark', as the senior archaeologist later put it. She was Ludmila Koryakova, who later went public with her criticism of the excavation, giving interviews to the *Sunday Times* and *Vanity Fair* and writing her own pieces for the local Urals newspapers. At the time, however, there was little she could do to restrain the over-enthusiastic exhumation of bones that everyone knew belonged to the last Tsar and his family. An excavation that should have taken any serious archaeologist two months to complete was carried out in an unseemly two-day race to extract the bones and carry them away for identification.

Also present at the exhumation was Aleksandr Avdonin whose official statement about the discovery of human remains had precipitated the search. Avdonin was angry. The pact of secrecy that he and Geli Ryabov had sworn to maintain had been broken. The man whom he had helped to find a hidden grave in the trackless forests of Siberia had given interviews to the media boasting of his discovery. Was it Ryabov's vanity that had made him do it, or was it the money he thought he could make from his film script about the Romanovs? Since publishing his first article in the history journal *Rodina* in 1989, Ryabov had talked up the mystery of the bones, glorifying his own audacity and persistence in having discovered them, without a single mention of Avdonin or the others. What was more, he had refused to reveal their whereabouts until they were promised 'a proper Christian burial'.

For two years after this the forest had been invaded by Romanov obsessives on their summer vacations, digging around for the bones of the Tsar. Now, in 1991, as the Soviet Union creaked and toppled, its authoritarian structure undermined by Gorbachev's reforms, Avdonin had decided to take matters in hand and had approached Eduard Rossel, the powerful chairman of the Sverdlovsk region Soviet, to announce that he could identify the Tsar's grave. Seeing the chance for self-aggrandizement as the boss of the region where the Romanovs' bones would be found, Rossel had had a word with his predecessor in Sverdlovsk and obtained the invaluable support of Boris Yeltsin, now President of Russia, who was steering his country towards a head-on collision with the dying Soviet Union. The Romanovs' remains might do Yeltsin some good as well, if they could be found. They would be a symbol of Russia's cultural and political autonomy, and their discovery would also exculpate the President for having had the Ipatiev House demolished back in 1977. Given the go-ahead by Rossel, Avdonin had gone to the police.

It had been eleven years since Avdonin and Gennady Vasilev – who had also been 'invited' to help with the excavation – had reburied the three skulls in their little box. Now they tried to recollect the precise spot. The first excavation trench revealed no remains. When a second, adjoining trench was dug, however, fragments of railway sleepers were seen. Koryakova marked out the trenches in a grid pattern according to standard archaeological practice. Under the first layer of soil they located the pit dug by Ryabov and Avdonin to rebury their findings and unearthed the wooden box they had made for the remains. It disintegrated as it was removed, but the polythene bags inside were intact and so were their contents. The three skulls were still there, including the one with gold fillings that Ryabov had confidently attributed to Tsar Nicholas II. Now the skulls were placed in new polythene bags, labelled, sealed, and packed in an army box with the label 'Material Evidence. Box No.1'.

On the second day, they uncovered the rest of the Ryabov–Avdonin diggings. It was clear that their efforts had damaged the edge of the original grave, and there was evidence of yet another disturbance: along the western edge of the grave a power cable had been laid about two-and-a-half feet down, churning up several small bones, so that their provenance would be hard to determine. As the top layers of soil were removed skeletons began to emerge. Skulls first – their domed shape making them protrude above the other bones bedded into the earth – then entire skeletons. When the whole grave was uncovered, it measured some six-and-a-half feet by five and was very shallow, barely four feet at its deepest point. Koryakova, who had opened many prehistoric graves in her professional life and had seen countless human remains, was shocked by the damage that these bones had sustained. She just had time to sketch the skeletons lying in the pit (again, standard archaeological practice) while the policemen and prosecutors took photographs and videos of the site. But now that she had

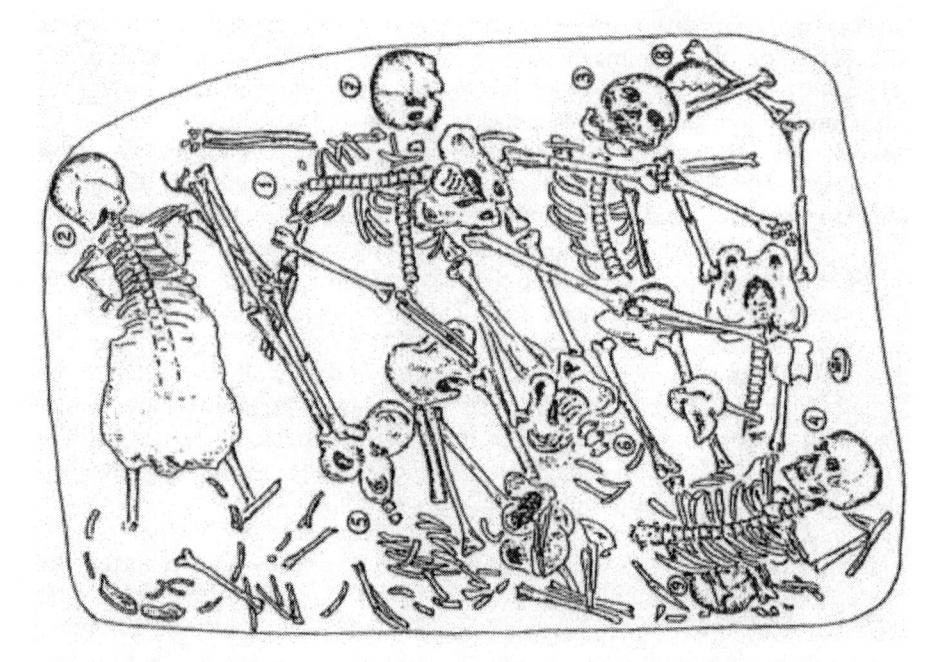

Figure 2.1 Diagram by archaeologist Ludmila Koryakova of the bones found in the mass grave outside Sverdlovsk (Ekaterinburg). Skeleton no. 4 (bottom right) was later confirmed to be that of Nicholas II.

located and opened the grave her expertise was unwanted. There was no time, the prosecutor's representative explained, for the formalities of an archaeological dig. Koryakova's knives and brushes were not required to clean and lift the skeletons bone by bone. They knew what had happened here: now the remains had to be taken away for identification.

As the bones were lifted, the skeletons' remaining integrity was destroyed. Koryakova objected vociferously and tried to walk off the dig in protest, but she was overruled. Everyone joined in the excavation, whether or not they had any archaeological training. The prosecutor was adamant: it was clear that there were nine skeletons. All that was needed now was to put them into separate polythene bags, and then reconstruct them somewhere warm and dry. As the remains were pulled from the ground, hips and skulls fragmented and some bones disintegrated entirely. After a few such catastrophes they began to lift the fragile ribs and vertebrae still encased in their clods of earth, in order to prevent them from breaking apart. In the end, twelve ammunition boxes were filled, locked and sealed. Nine of them contained the individual skeletons exhumed from the common grave; another held the three skulls and other bones extracted in 1979 and later returned. There was a further box with an assortment of soil samples, shards of pottery and fragments of rope; and a final box for the sundry bones that could not obviously be attributed to any skeleton.

Lastly, they examined the base of the empty pit. It sloped north to south. At the shallow, northern end the bedrock lay just over three feet below the surface. The bodies dumped here in a single layer had barely been concealed by earth. At the southern end the bodies had been piled two or three deep, and the acid had pooled around them causing significant corrosion to the bones at the bottom.

At 12.40 p.m. on 13 July 1991, the investigation was declared complete.

An investigation at the mercy of politics

Nine sets of human remains had been found in a shallow grave in the forests outside Sverdlovsk. All bore evidence of violent death. This was now an official crime scene and the bones were taken into custody by Lieutenant Colonel Pichugin of the Upper Isetsk Sverdlovsk police department, who had signed off the official record of the excavation.

The forensic examination of human remains aims to establish the identity of the deceased and the cause of death. In this case, the working hypothesis was that the bodies in the mass grave belonged to nine out of the eleven people who had disappeared from the Ipatiev House on the night of 16 July 1918: Nicholas, Alexandra, their five children (Olga, Tatyana, Marie, Anastasia and Alexei), Doctor Botkin, and three servants (Trupp, Kharitonov and Demidova); that they had all been shot or stabbed to death; and that two bodies out of this group of eleven had been hidden elsewhere. Over the next seven years a battery of experiments was carried out to test this hypothesis and the results of every test indicated that these bodies were indeed those of the Romanovs and their suite, minus two individuals: the 14-year-old Alexei and one of the four daughters.

The investigation, though, was messy and incoherent. Post-Soviet Russia reinvented itself during the 1990s in a massive upheaval, cultural as much as political, and the examination of the 'Ekaterinburg remains' – as they became known – reflected this upheaval.[3] A conflict that emerged early on in the investigation stemmed from the tensions arising between central and local government. In 1991 the city of Sverdlovsk resumed its old name of Ekaterinburg, abandoning the commemoration of Bolshevik revolutionary Yakov Sverdlov in order to celebrate once again Empress Catherine the Great. In 1993 the region of Sverdlovsk (which confusingly had retained its name despite the change in nomenclature of its principal city) made a brief attempt unilaterally to upgrade its status to that of an autonomous republic within the Russian Federation. The new 'Urals Republic' lasted only until November that year, when Yeltsin abolished it, dissolved its regional soviet and dismissed the soviet chairman Eduard Rossel. Yet Rossel – a political survivor at least as canny as Yeltsin –

staged a come-back in 1995 when he became governor of Sverdlovsk region in Russia's first direct local election. Throughout these political shenanigans the 'Ekaterinburg remains' lay in a morgue in the city, where they provided Rossel with a source of income and prestige, and he was reluctant to part with them. He obstructed their removal from the city so successfully that the bones remained in Ekaterinburg throughout the entire investigation, and only left it when they were reburied in St Petersburg in 1998.

Lack of funding, institutional rivalries and competing jurisdictions, not to mention wounded national pride, pressure from the Russian Orthodox Church, and the political imperative to organize a ceremonial reburial drove the investigation of the remains way beyond the control of any single authority. As more and more agencies became involved, rivalries proliferated. Moreover, everyone concerned in the forensic investigation was hampered by the hierarchical jealousies and bureaucratic obstructionism that had permeated the culture of Russian officialdom since well before even Nicholas II.[4]

The office of the Russian prosecutor general appointed a commission in August 1991, under the Russian Federation Public Health Ministry's chief forensic medical examiner Vladislav Plaksin. The commission was ordered to investigate the 'forensic-medical and medical-legal' aspects of the remains. But lines of authority were immediately confused with the simultaneous appointment of a second commission under the Russian Federation Ministry of Justice's Urals Central Forensic Research Laboratory, which was ordered to carry out a 'forensic-criminalistic, physical-chemical and physical-technical examination' of the remains.[5] Altogether, around fifty Russian scientists took part in the forensic tests, each of them with a specific area of expertise in human decay (bones, blood, teeth, hair) or in physical trauma (wounds from shooting, stabbing, smashing). A second search of the grave site in October 1991 turned up over three hundred bone fragments and thirteen loose teeth which the first exhumation had missed.

Foreign experts were also invited to participate, but competing jurisdictions again produced confusion as a group of US government scientists, gathered on the orders of Secretary of State James Baker in response to a request from Eduard Rossel, were beaten to Ekaterinburg in July 1992 by a group of scientists from Florida who, having got wind of Rossel's request for assistance with the Romanov bones, had gone straight to the Sverdlovsk authorities offering their services. This group was led by the forensic anthropologist William Maples, who had gained a reputation as a consultant in intriguing historical cases such as the remains of conquistador Francisco Pizarro and of the 'Elephant Man' John Merrick.[6]

The Romanov case provided Maples with plenty of additional publicity, generated mainly after he challenged the Russian scientists' conclusions over which of the four daughters was missing from the grave. On the basis of skeletal and dental development, Maples insisted that the missing girl must be the youngest daughter, 17-year old Anastasia, thereby contradicting the Russian scientists' conclusions which were based on the controversial technique of cranio-facial photographic superimposition and which had suggested that the missing skeleton was that of the third daughter, Marie, who had turned 19 just three weeks before she was shot. The question may never be resolved. The four Grand Duchesses were close to one another in age, ranging from barely 17 to just 22 at the time of their deaths; late adolescence, moreover, is a period when the standard markers of development vary considerably from person to person. Maples's conclusions that the missing body was that of Anastasia were awkward principally because they breathed new life into the notorious case of Anna Anderson. The claims of this eccentric woman to be Anastasia were finally scotched by posthumous DNA tests in 1994 which proved her to have been born, not a Grand Duchess, but Franziska Schanzkowska, the daughter of a Polish farm worker. But when Maples asserted that Anastasia's bones were not among the 'Ekaterinburg remains', he gave a new lease of life to her claims.[7]

Final proof that the remains belonged to the Romanovs (minus two members) and their servants presented itself in 1993 with the results of the DNA tests carried out in the UK. Final proof, that is, for all but the most obdurate conspiracy theorists. In the early 1990s the testing of DNA extracted from old human tissue was at the outer limits of scientific knowledge, and few laboratories in the world had the facilities to perform it. Molecular biologist Pavel Ivanov, head of genetic analysis under chief forensic medical examiner Plaksin, therefore went on behalf of the Russian federal authorities to the UK Home Office's forensic science service at Aldermaston, carrying sections of the femurs from the remains. Here DNA extracted from the bones was compared with DNA from living descendants – albeit distantly related ones – of Nicholas and Alexandra. The results proved positive, with certainty odds of 70 to 1 that these were the Romanov bones. Taken together with the anthropological and circumstantial evidence, the odds were calculated at between 700 to 1 and 8.4×10^5 to 1.[8]

Yet once again the status of the results was marred by rivalries between Ekaterinburg and Moscow, for while the experiments were being run in Aldermaston under a bilateral agreement between the Russian and British governments, the local authorities in Sverdlovsk had permitted William Maples to remove teeth and bone samples from the remains for DNA testing at the University of California, Berkeley. Maples's action, compounded by his unguarded criticism of the Aldermaston test results – he swore an affidavit alleging contamination of the bone samples – tarnished the DNA test results obtained at Aldermaston without justification.[9]

For the scientists at Aldermaston, however, a more significant problem than institutional jealousies had been that of finding a DNA match for the putative bones of the former Tsar. Opposition from obscurantist Russian religious nationalists, both émigrés and home-grown, made it impossible to test the bones against DNA from the Tsar's closest living relative, his nephew Tikhon Kulikovsky-Romanov (born in 1918 and the son of Nicholas II's sister Olga Alexandrovna), or from his closest deceased relative, his brother Grand Duke Georgy Alexandrovich (who had died of tuberculosis in 1899). The Russian religious nationalists objected both to the involvement of foreigners (the British scientists) in carrying out DNA tests on Russia's history, and to the sacrilegious opening of Grand Duke Georgy's tomb. Apparently convinced that the Russian state which had authorized the Aldermaston tests was an equally godless successor to the Soviet Union, Tikhon and his wife Olga pursued a virulent campaign against the investigation and particularly against Pavel Ivanov, whom Olga described as 'a diploma-holding adventurist'.[10] In the end, the Aldermaston team had to look for two more distant living relatives of the Tsar who would agree to supply blood samples for DNA comparison.

In an attempt to regain some control over the 'Tsarist affair', Russia's prosecutor general in August 1993 instituted a formal criminal investigation – 'On the circumstances surrounding the demise of members of the Russian Imperial House and persons from their suite in 1918–1919' – under senior prosecutor Vladimir Soloviev. By channelling the forensic investigation of the bones into evidence in a criminal case, the Russian government aimed to put pressure on the quarrelling scientists and the recalcitrant Sverdlovsk authorities. To put even more momentum behind the investigation, in October 1993 the Russian government formed a 'Commission On the Identification and Reburial of the Remains of Russian Emperor Nicholas II and Members of His Family', to which Soloviev's criminal investigation was to report. The Commission's composition reflected the various forces in Russian society with a stake in the 'Ekaterinburg remains'. Chaired by a deputy prime minister, it included a metropolitan from the Russian Orthodox Church (ROC), as well as scientists, historians, archivists, writers and Sverdlovsk politicians. Not surprisingly, this attempt at inclusivity delayed resolution of the case. When Soloviev declared the criminal investigation completed on 18 September 1995, the Holy Synod of the ROC responded by requesting the government Commission to order further tests on a number of points which became known as 'The Patriarchate's Ten Questions'. The Commission complied, and the prosecutor general told Soloviev to reopen the case.[11]

The 'Ten Questions' reflected the suspicions permeating the Russian nationalist communities (émigré and domestic) that the 'Ekaterinburg remains' were a hoax, the bones of someone other than the ex-Tsar, planted in the grave by the Bolsheviks after 1918 to mislead those who would worship the Tsar's mortal remains as holy relics. A particularly absurd scenario was energetically promoted by Vadim Viner, the head of a 'Research Centre on the Demise of the Romanov Family' in Ekaterinburg. Viner hypothesized that a family of doubles had been murdered in place of the Romanovs as a decoy, and that the descendants of the wider Romanov family wanted the remains swiftly identified in order to stake their own claim to the fabled fortune of Nicholas II still held in foreign banks.[12] National patriotic circles in Russia and émigré associations such as the 'Russian Expert Commission Abroad' – founded by émigré aristocrats in 1989 to 'establish the fate of the remains of the Russian Imperial House' and 'to restore legitimate government in Russia' – firmly believed that the White investigators in 1919 had been right: all the bodies had been burned. One of the hypotheses proposed by the Whites had stated that the absence of teeth among the ashes of the bonfire must mean that the Bolshevik executioners had decapitated their victims and taken their heads to Moscow as proof of their deaths. It says much about the persistence of this belief in the Russian nationalist mind that the last two of the Patriarchate's Ten Questions posed to the government Commission were these: Was the killing of the Tsar and his family a ritual murder? and: Had the Tsar been decapitated after his death?

To these questions, senior prosecutor Soloviev responded that there was no evidence in support of the heads having been severed from the bodies or of the murder having been 'ritualized'. In any case, he said, 'ritual murder' was not a concept recognized in law. Even so, nothing in the accumulation of evidence affirming that the 'Ekaterinburg remains' were those of the ex-Tsar and his entourage could shake the belief of the national patriots that the bones were a hoax. And although Soloviev tried to present his criminal investigation as a legitimate successor to that of the Whites in 1919, his fundamentalist opponents had only to see the serial number assigned to it – 18/123666–93, encoding the 'number of the Beast', 666 – to know that Soloviev was a servant of the forces of darkness.[13]

Like the hero of a detective novel, Soloviev was beset by conspiracies and vested interests. He was even challenged over the decapitation issue by one of the scientists from the investigation, Professor V. Popov of St Petersburg, a professor of forensic odontology, who stated that since two of the loose teeth found in the grave belonged to an adolescent male, this must be Alexei, whose body was missing, and that the grave must therefore have been disturbed. Popov discussed in the press whether the family's heads had not, therefore, in fact, actually been severed and taken to the Kremlin. After all, was not Hitler's skull preserved in the Soviet Central Committee archives? The government Commission later overturned Popov's attribution of the teeth to Alexei, and concluded that they belonged to Anastasia; Soloviev, meanwhile, was so irritated by this publicity for the severed heads story that he publicly accused Popov of manufacturing sensationalist rumours in order to increase the sales of the two books he had written about the investigation.[14]

By the middle of 1997, the investigation of the remains had lost momentum. The government Commission had held only two meetings since December 1995 and had twice changed its chairman. In June 1997, however, a new chairman was appointed. This was Boris Nemtsov, Russia's new First Deputy Prime Minister, a young, liberal figure who had constructed a careful image as a man untainted by the Soviet past. Although initially very reluctant to get involved in the 'Tsarist affair',[15] Nemtsov brought to the Commission a subvention of two billion roubles for additional scientific tests and sufficient impetus to force a conclusion. He also decided to make public the Commission's work. The resulting collection of selected documents came out in 1998, entitled *Repentance*.[16] Further tests were carried out and the existing work was summarized in a form that answered the 'Patriarchate's ten questions' of 1995. The final sitting of the Commission, held in January 1998, determined that the bones were indeed those of Nicholas II and his entourage, and resolved that they should be buried in the Cathedral of Sts Peter and Paul in St Petersburg on the eightieth anniversary of the Romanovs' execution, 17 July 1998.

Faced with this resolution, the Holy Synod of the ROC found itself in a delicate position. To endorse the Commission's conclusion that the 'Ekaterinburg remains' were authentic would put the Russian Orthodox Church–Moscow Patriarchate on a collision course with the Russian Orthodox Church Outside Russia and with national patriotic forces at home, which were an increasingly important constituency in its parishes. Yet to oppose the Commission would threaten the Church's cosy relationship with the Russian government. The ROC's representative on the Commission, Metropolitan Yuvenaly of Krutitsky and Kolomna, thus appended a special statement to the Commission's final resolution. It was a masterpiece of equivocation, a technique that the Church had honed over years of existing under the Soviet system. Yuvenaly recognized that the 'Ekaterinburg remains' should be buried, 'for it is immoral to persist in refraining from consigning them to the earth'; but he maintained scepticism about the proof of their identity: 'the history of science bears witness that what today in science seems completely final, precise and reliable, tomorrow may seem antiquated, imprecise and mistaken.' The Church was therefore proposing a compromise: the 'Ekaterinburg remains' should be buried in 'a symbolic grave-monument until all questions of authenticity have been resolved'.[17] The idea was rejected and the state burial went ahead in July 1998. But the Church still would not acknowledge the bones and its senior members boycotted the state ceremony, staging instead a national service of remembrance for the Tsar, his family, and 'all victims' of the 1918 to 1921 conflict.

The science of identification

The discipline of forensic anthropology emerged from the techniques developed during World War II to identify the remains of US servicemen killed in the Pacific theatre, where bodies decayed rapidly. In order to restore individual identity to a set of skeletal remains, the forensic anthropologist poses questions that become increasingly specific. Starting with: 'Is it bone? Is it human? Is it modern?', he goes on to ask: 'What is the sex, age, race, and stature?' and, finally: 'What are the individual characteristics?' – such as diseases or healed fractures – that might assist identification.[18]

When they received the ten army ammunition boxes of human bones that had been hastily extracted from the common grave in July 1991, the Russian scientists had to reconstruct the remains into coherent skeletons and restore to three of them the skulls and other small bones removed eleven years earlier by Avdonin and Ryabov. After the reconstruction, which was basically completed by October 1991, the sex, age, height and race of the skeletons could be determined. This produced a profile of a group of nine individuals (four men and five women) that exactly matched that of the nine people thought to be buried in the grave, except for the dispute about which of the two younger girls was absent.

Of itself, this evidence was more circumstantial than conclusive, but a relatively new branch of forensic science – the testing of the chemical building blocks of the human body, its DNA – promised to provide definitive proof. DNA analysis produces an individual 'fingerprint' of the deceased that can be matched with tissue taken from living relatives. DNA occurs in two varieties: nuclear and mitochondrial. Nuclear DNA, from the chromosomes in the nucleus of the cell, is inherited equally from father and mother and can be tested to determine family relationships. At Aldermaston, the first tests to be carried out determined that, of the nine skeletons in the grave, three were the female children of two of the others, and that the other four skeletons were unrelated both to this family group and to each other. This pattern of relationships also matched that of the Romanovs and their suite. To prove the identity of these individuals, however, DNA matches would have to be found with their living relatives (or their deceased ones if tissue could be found) using the DNA from the mitochondria of the cells. Mitochondria are structures found in the cytoplasm of each cell and they too contain DNA, but in much smaller quantities than is found in the nucleus. Mitochondrial DNA (mtDNA) is unique because it passes unchanged through the maternal line. It is therefore possible to match DNA from subjects who are several generations apart, provided that they share a common female ancestor through unbroken matrilineal descent.[19]

At Aldermaston, the scientists searched for living relatives of Nicholas and Alexandra, descended from their maternal ancestors exclusively through the female line. In the case of the Tsarina this was relatively straightforward: the mother of Alexandra was Princess Alice, second daughter of Queen Victoria, who had married into the house of Hesse. Another of Princess Alice's daughters, Alexandra's sister, Victoria of Hesse, was the maternal grandmother of Prince Philip, the Duke of Edinburgh, making him the

Tsarina's great-nephew and descended, like Alexandra, through unbroken female line from Princess Alice. The mtDNA sequences obtained from a blood sample provided by the Duke of Edinburgh were an identical match with the mtDNA sequences obtained from the bone samples of the putative Tsarina Alexandra. Naturally, these mtDNA sequences also matched those obtained from the three young female skeletons in the grave, the Tsarina's daughters. DNA testing could not determine which of the four daughters were present in the grave, however, because they had no descendants: their genetic line had ended with their deaths.

Finding a match for the Tsar proved more difficult. Rebuffed by Tikhon Kulikovsky Romanov and faced with the obduracy of the Russian Orthodox Church over exhuming the body of Grand Duke Georgy, the Aldermaston team sought more willing living relatives of Nicholas II to provide a blood sample. Provided these individuals were of unbroken matrilineal descent from a common female ancestor with the Tsar, they would share his mtDNA. Two sources were found: the Tsar's maternal grandmother had been Louise of Hesse-Cassel, and Louise's great-great-great-granddaughter, Countess Xenia Cheremeteff-Sfiri, offered to co-operate. Xenia Cheremeteff-Sfiri's mother had been Irina Cheremeteff, and her mother had been Irina Yusupova (wife of Prince Felix Yusupov, one of Rasputin's assassins), and Irina's mother had been Nicholas II's sister Xenia Alexandrovna (who of course shared with Nicholas Louise of Hesse-Cassel as maternal grandmother). Xenia Cheremeteff-Sfiri's mtDNA matched that taken from the bones belonging to the putative Tsar. The mtDNA from a blood sample presented by the great-great-grandson of Louise of Hesse-Cassel also matched that of the putative Tsar. This person wanted initially to be anonymous, but was later named as the Duke of Fife, the grandson of Queen Alexandra, wife of Edward VII. Alexandra had been Nicholas's aunt, the sister of his mother Maria Feodorovna and the daughter of Louise of Hesse-Cassel; she was also the mother of his cousin and near double, George V.[20]

The results seemed conclusive, apart from one small discrepancy. Comparisons of mtDNA are made by looking at a specific segment of base pairs (the interlocking double chemical component of DNA) of around 500 bases long. It has been found that this 'control region', also known as the hypervariable region, differs widely between individuals because the DNA within the segment contains many mutations. The DNA of the hypervariable region appears not to control any vital functions within the body and so it can accumulate mutations which do not die out. When mtDNA is tested, it is this hypervariable region which is compared against a reference sequence (produced in 1981 when the first mtDNA was sequenced) and variations from this reference sequence are noted.

The blood samples provided by the two descendants of Louise of Hesse-Cassel for testing against the mtDNA of the presumed Tsar matched one another exactly at all points in the hypervariable region of their mtDNA, despite their being very distant cousins to one another. When they were compared against the mtDNA of the putative Tsar, the sequence was also an exact match at all points of the 782 base pairs tested, except for one single nucleotide (chemical) at position 16169. Here, the presumed Tsar's mtDNA presented a mixture of two chemicals, C (cytosine) and T (thymine), in a ratio of approximately 4:1, while the two comparison samples had thymine alone. This phenomenon of combined chemicals is known as heteroplasmy and occurs when a new mutation in the mtDNA is being established. In 1993, however, when the tests on the Ekaterinburg bones were being carried out, the phenomenon of heteroplasmy had not been extensively studied and its rate of incidence in the general population was disputed.

Two years after the results of the Aldermaston tests were published in the discipline's leading journal, *Nature Genetics*, more mtDNA tests were performed, this time using bone samples from the Tsar's brother, Grand Duke Georgy, whose exhumation had finally been permitted by the ROC. The tests were carried out this time by Pavel Ivanov working with US colleagues in the laboratory of the US Armed Forces DNA Identification Laboratory in Maryland. MtDNA extracted from bone samples of the presumed Tsar Nicholas II was compared with mtDNA from the remains of his younger brother, and with more blood supplied by Countess Cheremeteff-Sfiri. The results confirmed the earlier findings: the heteroplasmy observed in the presumed Tsar's mtDNA at position 16169 was seen at the same position in Georgy's mtDNA, but not in the mtDNA of Xenia Cheremeteff-Sfiri. Both brothers showed a mixture of cytosine and thymine, although in different proportions. The article summarizing the research hypothesized:

> The previous discrepancy between the putative Tsar and these relatives [Countess Cheremeteff-Sfiri and the Duke of Fife] is due to heteroplasmy [the mixture of two chemicals] that was apparently passed from the Tsar's mother Maria Feodorovna to her sons Georgij and Nicholas, but which segregated to homoplasmy [a single chemical] in the course of more extended intergenerational transmission.

The scientists calculated, in conclusion, that they were 1.3×10^8 more likely to have obtained this mtDNA data from the Romanovs' remains than from those of a family unrelated to them.[21]

Further evidence that heteroplasmy was the probable cause of the discrepancy came from research carried out by Mary-Claire King at Berkeley. King had tested the samples that William Maples had controversially removed from the 'Ekaterinburg remains' in 1992, and she reported verbally to *Nature Genetics* that her group 'found C and T nucleotides at several sites in the DNA allegedly from Nicholas consistent with heteroplasmy, sequence background, or contamination'.[22]

Yet more mtDNA evidence confirming the identity of the Tsar's bones was produced, eventually, from tests on the blood of Tikhon Kulikovsky-Romanov. Although adamantly opposed to Pavel Ivanov and his work, Tikhon did leave provision in his will for a sample of his blood to be tested, and his widow eventually allowed tests to be performed by a scientist whom she had got to know personally. This was Evgeny Rogaev, Director of the Laboratory of Molecular Brain Genetics at the Russian Academy of Sciences, who was a visiting professor at the University of Toronto, the home of Olga Kulikovskaya-Romanova.[23] The results of the mtDNA tests on Tikhon's blood were presented to the Russian government Commission at a sitting in September 1995 which was attended by both Kulikovskaya-Romanova and Rogaev, but it was not until late in 1997 – as the Commission was trying to wrap up its work – that Rogaev received instruction from senior prosecutor Vladimir Soloviev to analyse mtDNA from the putative Tsar's bones for comparison. In 1998, the journal *Nature* reported Rogaev's results in its 'News-In-Brief' section under the headline 'Independent DNA analyses by Russian scientists confirm UK/USA tests'.[24] Rogaev's results replicated those produced by Pavel Ivanov on the bone samples of putative Nicholas and of his brother, finding a mixture of C and T (predominantly C) at position 16169. Tikhon's blood sample exactly matched the sequence of the putative Tsar, except for being entirely C at position 16169, which suggested that the mutation observed in the Tsar's mtDNA had not been established in his nephew. Rogaev concluded that the results 'did not contradict the hypothesis' that the bones belonged to Nicholas II.

These results were conclusive. However, two further sets of DNA tests carried out after the state reburial of the Romanovs in 1998 produced minor waves in Russia because they suggested that the bones were not, in fact, those of Nicholas and Alexandra. The results of the tests are problematic because they used suspect source material and they were performed by scientists whose attitude to the bones was not impartial. Nevertheless, they were seized upon by those who wanted to believe that the 'Ekaterinburg remains' were a hoax.

In 2001 a group led by Tatsuo Nagai from Japan's Kitasato University challenged the identification of Nicholas's bones. The group included Vyacheslav Popov – the forensic odontologist from St Petersburg who had clashed with senior prosecutor Soloviev over the suggestion that the bones in the grave might not be those of the Imperial Family. Nagai extracted mtDNA from three sources – sweat from Nicholas II's clothes; Tikhon Kulikovsky-Romanov's blood; and hair, nail and bone tissue from Grand Duke Georgy Alexandrovich – and compared it with the mtDNA sequences from the bones, reported in the first tests in 1993. Nagai's principal finding, which he reported at two international forensic science conferences, was that there was no heteroplasmy C/T at position 16169 in any of the three samples he had tested. In an interview with the Russian newspaper *Izvestiya* in June 2001 Nagai also claimed to have found 'five substantial differences' – upon which he did not elaborate – between Ivanov's results and his own tests.[25]

Nagai's claims produced an ill-tempered spat in Russia. This time, however, opposition to the involvement of foreign scientists in the 'tsarist affair' came from groups that had previously courted it; and it was the national patriots – who earlier had claimed that no test performed by foreigners could be unbiased – who welcomed the Japanese scientists' results with jubilation. Aleksandr Avdonin's Discovery [*Obretenie*] Foundation, established to support the identification of the 'Ekaterinburg remains' as the bones of the Romanovs, called Nagai's experiments 'blasphemy by foreigners and their stooges who have been grubbing around in the holy tombs of our Fatherland and stealing historical relics from our museums'. Meanwhile, Vadim Viner's 'Research Centre on the Demise of the Romanov Family' and the Russian Expert Commission Abroad – both of which were still claiming that the 'Ekaterinburg remains' were fakes – took it upon themselves to apologize publicly to Nagai for *Obretenie*'s rudeness.[26]

Common sense alone suggests that the value of Nagai's findings was highly dubious. The provenance of Nicholas's sweat-stained clothing and Grand Duke Georgy Alexandrovich's tissue was unclear; the partisan involvement of Vyacheslav Popov was suspect; and the tests suggested, at most, that the Aldermaston results needed clarification. Even Lev Zhivotovsky, a Russian scientist who had criticized Ivanov's research in the past, said that Nagai 'at present has no grounds for making any sensational announcements'.[27]

Further research carried out after the reburial queried the identity of the skeleton identified as that of Alexandra, but this, too, was suspect. In 2004 *Annals of Human Biology* published a paper by a Russian-US group which had tested the mtDNA allegedly extracted from the remains of Alexandra's older sister, Elisabeth (Ella), who was also a Romanov by her marriage to Nicholas II's paternal uncle, Sergei Alexandrovich, in 1884. The paper was co-authored by Professor Lev Zhivotovsky, who in 1999 had published an article, also in *Annals of Human Biology*, which queried the chain of custody between the exhumation of the 'Ekaterinburg remains' and the 1993 DNA tests. In his article Zhivotovsky had cited highly tendentious sources to support his allegations, including authors whose main thesis was that the Romanovs had escaped and that the bones were decoys. He also acknowledged assistance in his research from groups such as the 'Russian Expert Commission Abroad' which were far from impartial about the question of the bones' authenticity.[28] In the 2004 article that compared the mtDNA from both the putative Alexandra and the tissue allegedly from her sister Elisabeth, the research group found four discrepancies between the mtDNA of Elisabeth and the Ivanov–Gill 1993 sequence reported for Alexandra. However, the provenance of the piece of Elisabeth's tissue that the group tested was highly questionable. It came from Elisabeth's finger, which had been removed from her body and preserved as a relic by Bishop Anthony Grabbe in New York. Elisabeth – who after her husband's assassination in 1905 had joined a Russian Orthodox convent – had been killed along with several other members of the wider Romanov family at Alapaevsk, north of Ekaterinburg, in July 1918. Her remains were allegedly buried in Jerusalem in 1920 and, after the grave was opened in 1982, Bishop Anthony had come into possession of the finger as a holy relic. The chain of evidence for the tissue allegedly from Elisabeth's finger was weak and many of the sources cited were highly tendentious, yet the publication of this research in an academic journal gave it a spurious air of authenticity.

When the first DNA tests on the 'Ekaterinburg remains' were performed in 1992 to 1993, the use of DNA for forensic purposes was barely a decade old. By 2003, the thirteen-year human genome project to map the entire human genetic code was complete. During the same period, accumulated data from several DNA tests on the 'Ekaterinburg remains' had positively identified the bones as those of Nicholas and Alexandra and their children. Nevertheless, opposition to recognizing the identity of the remains continued, with ever more specious explanations about whose bones had been found. For if the grave were, in reality, a hoax, the close mtDNA matches between its contents and the tissue of Romanov descendants would have to be explained. One rather desperate hypothesis was that the remains of close relatives had been placed in the Ekaterinburg grave instead of those of the Imperial Family; or possibly that the Tsar's body alone had been replaced by that of his brother, Grand Duke Michael Alexandrovich (killed by the Urals Bolsheviks in June 1918), whose mtDNA would be identical with that of Nicholas and whose remains have never been found. If the contents of the grave were, in fact, a decoy, it has never been explained which other relatives supplied the bones of Alexandra and the children, or of Dr Botkin and the three servants. In any case, this absurd scenario relies on a level of co-ordination among the Urals Bolsheviks quite at odds with Yurovsky's testimony about that chaotic night. It also disregards the anthropological findings that identify 'Skeleton No. 4' with the Tsar's known physical characteristics.

Yet more specious challenges to the DNA evidence have focused on the statistical probability of finding similar mtDNA matches among the local population. Lev Zhivotovsky, for example, claims, correctly, that DNA evidence identifying the bones of Nicholas II with a 99 per cent certainty means that one in a hundred individuals could be him, which statistically is the equivalent of claiming that the remains could belong to tens of thousands of people in Ekaterinburg province at the turn of the twentieth century.[29] Statements like this are legalistic trickery. DNA has acquired a talismanic quality because of its ability to identify an individual from the smallest piece of evidence. Taken in isolation, the DNA evidence on the 'Ekaterinburg remains' could be open to challenge: certainly a good defence barrister would argue that the chain of evidence was so corrupted in the botched exhumation and identification process that the DNA results from it were inadmissible in court. On the other hand, common sense would argue that these bones must be those of the Romanovs. Repeated tests have produced identical results; the DNA results tally with the anthropological and historical evidence. Who else could be in the grave? Statistically speaking, the possibility of false identification stands not at 1 per cent, as Zhivotovsky spuriously argues, but – on a conservative calculation – at the unimaginably miniscule chance of one in 1,300,000,000.[30]

Restoring the personhood of the bones

DNA analysis had produced a positive identification of the 'Ekaterinburg remains'. At the same time the bones remained a set of badly damaged skeletal fragments. The techniques of forensic anthropology, however, can restore individuality to these unpromising vestiges of a human being. Looking at the set of bones labelled 'Skeleton No. 4' through the eyes of a forensic anthropologist, they become once again the physical person of Nicholas Alexandrovich Romanov, last Tsar of All the Russias.

'Skeleton No. 4' was a mature male, around 50 years old, of medium height and build, with proportionately rather short legs. At some point he had suffered a fractured rib which had knitted together leaving a callous on the bone. The way that the balls of the thigh-bones had thickened betrayed many hours spent on horseback. The fusion of some of the bones in the left lower back (the left sacro-iliac joint) showed also that in later life this person had suffered back pain.

In this way, the skeleton confirms what we know from historical sources: that Nicholas was a keen horseman, who had broken a rib in a riding accident in his youth, and that from about 1912 – as we can see from film footage – he began habitually to stand with his right hand resting on his hip and to limp on his right leg like someone suffering with backache.[31] Judging from the bones, the Tsar also suffered from severe toothache. There were no fillings in any of the remaining seven teeth of 'Skeleton No. 4', which were 'worn to gray nubbins', and there was evidence of decay in the lower jaw-bone. This is a sign of periodontal disease which causes the teeth to fall out: the Tsar had lost at least nine teeth during his lifetime, judging from the dental remains. Why Nicholas had allowed his teeth to deteriorate so badly remains something of a mystery. The decay in the teeth and jaw-bone also suggests that he would have suffered from chronic halitosis – an unpleasant symptom of periodontal disease – but not, unsurprisingly, something that is mentioned in the historical record.[32]

Forensic odontology has revealed other things about the dental condition of the Tsar's family and their servants. Avdonin and Ryabov had assumed that the skull with gold dental work which they had extracted from the grave must have been that of Nicholas: only a Tsar would have gold teeth.

Forensic examination proved them wrong. The skull had belonged to a middle-aged woman, and the gold teeth were, in fact, 'a gold bridge of poor workmanship'. There were two middle-aged female skeletons in the mass grave, and the other one – 'Skeleton No. 7' – had 'exquisite dental work' with platinum and porcelain crowns and 'wonderfully wrought gold fillings ... extremely costly and cunningly contrived'. This turned out to be the skeleton of Alexandra, who had enjoyed the most advanced dentistry available, whereas the skull with gold teeth that Ryabov had rushed to assign to the Tsar in fact belonged to the maid, Anna Demidova. The three young women in the grave, meanwhile, had numerous amalgam fillings, all of the same type, suggesting both that they were 'fond of sweets' and that they had been 'treated by the same dentist' – as sisters would be.[33] One more skeleton, that of a middle-aged man, had 'ante-mortem loss of all teeth in the upper jaw'.[34] This belonged to Doctor Evgeny Botkin, whose false teeth had been found by the White investigators in 1919.

Other special techniques can return the humanity to skeletal remains. Facial reconstruction is one of the most dramatic, since it restores the features of an individual person to the blank skull. This may be done by building up the face through clay modelling, and in 1995 casts taken from all nine skulls underwent plastic reconstruction. The results were impressive in the sense that the Imperial Family's features re-emerged upon the skulls, but were perhaps not definitive proof of the skulls' identity. All the skulls had been so badly damaged that the skeletal basis for reconstruction was very patchy.[35]

Facial reconstruction may also be achieved through a technique called 'craniofacial superimposition'. This involves 'creating a photographic image of the skull that can be superimposed on an ante-mortem photo of the person'.[36] When it came to the 'Ekaterinburg remains', forensic anthropologist Sergei Abramov developed a new technique of mathematical modelling to assist recognition. Abramov was the head of the new technology section under Russia's chief forensic medical examiner Plaksin, whose department was initially responsible for identifying the bones. Abramov's technique used photographic superimposition to compare fixed points on the skulls with identical points on facial photographs of the hypothetical victims. The well-photographed Romanovs could supply numerous portraits taken from all sides that could be used for this technique. Two photographs of the children were used extensively in the photographic superimposition technique, since they showed them with their heads shaven after an attack of the measles, and were taken from both front and back views. The photographs had been taken for fun by the children's tutor, Pierre Gilliard, and showed their five heads protruding above a black sheet as though decapitated. The resemblance to five skulls in Gilliard's macabre visual joke had a black irony during the attempts to identify the remains of the Tsar's children.

However, there were bitter disputes over this technique too. Abramov was viciously criticized by William Maples for his photographic superimposition and for what Maples said was a clumsy reconstruction of the badly damaged skulls. Abramov, portraying himself as the heroic lone scientist in a battle against underfunding and lack of recognition, claimed that his mathematical modelling set his methods apart from the usual 'craniofacial superimposition', and canvassed the support of an eminent German craniofacial forensic scientist.[37] The dispute between Abramov and Maples centred on which of the daughters was missing from the grave, Abramov claiming – on the basis of photographic superimposition – that it was Maria, and Maples insisting – on the basis of conventional anthropology – that the missing girl was Anastasia. In the end, and perhaps as a reflection of jurisdictional divisions rather than scientific ones, every official document of the government Commission agrees with Abramov.

Means, motive, opportunity

The investigation of any crime scene tries to establish how the victims died. In this case, the historical record of shooting and stabbing was also borne out by the forensic evidence. The White investigation had found thirty-two bullet holes in the walls and floor of the execution chamber. When the bodies were exhumed in 1991, the excavators found a total of twenty-five bullets which had become dislodged from the bodies as the flesh decayed. The bullets that the White investigation had found were identified as having been fired from four makes of hand-gun – a 7.63 mm calibre Mauser, a 7.65 mm calibre Browning, an 11.43 mm calibre Colt and a 7.62 mm calibre Nagant revolver. In the 1990s, Soloviev's investigation found bullets consistent with these types of Nagant, Mauser and Browning guns among the grave materials. The latter investigation was also able to match the bullets with the actual Mauser, Colt and Browning pistols that had been used by Ermakov and Medvedev-Kudrin, who had presented the weapons with which they claimed to have shot the Tsar to state museums.[38]

None of the bullets, and none of the damage caused by them, were identified as having come from a rifle. It must therefore be the case that the Latvian *Strelki* [sharpshooters] who formed part of the execution party used their weapons either not at all, or only for bayoneting the victims. Yurovsky's accounts and other testimony suggest that side arms (not rifles) were distributed to all members of the firing squad. The number of bullets and bullet holes is also significant in assessing how the victims may have died. The execution party appears to have fired between fifty and sixty bullets at their victims, about four or five bullets per man, although some of the accounts describe certain members of the execution party wildly firing off many more rounds than this. Does this mean that some of them fired no bullets at all?

42   True crime

The skeletal remains bore evidence of bullet and stab wounds. It is impossible to say with certainty how the fatal blows were inflicted in each case, since if a bullet passes through soft tissue it may kill its victim but leave no trace on the skeleton, while a bullet which damages bone might not be fatal. The 'Ekaterinburg remains' were far from complete skeletons since several rib-bones were missing, making it even harder to determine the precise cause of death. That said, the bones did produce some evidence of how the Romanovs and their servants died. 'Skeleton No. 4', for example, showed multiple gunshot wounds to the chest: according to eyewitnesses most of the executioners fired first directly at the ex-Tsar. The bodies of the other three men – Dr Botkin, the valet and the chef – also show multiple gunshot wounds. Does this indicate that the executioners were squeamish about shooting the women and preferred to direct their fire towards the male victims? Or perhaps that the three men, who were standing near the former Tsar, received some of the bullets intended for him? The skulls showed that two of the three daughters were definitely shot in the head. This tallies with the historical accounts which describe how two of the girls, found crouching against a wall when the shooting stopped, were executed at point-blank range with bullets to the temple. Finally, the facial bones of most of the skeletons had suffered extensive damage to the area between eye-sockets and jaw, damage caused by blows from 'massive, blunt, hard objects with a relatively small surface area', a fair description of a rifle butt. Furthermore, all the bodies bore signs of other trauma, possibly caused by rough handling post-mortem.[39]

Conclusions

The commonly accepted legal burden of proof – to dispel 'reasonable doubt' – has been met many times over in the case of the 'Ekaterinburg remains'. The one remaining mystery in this 'true crime' story of the Tsar's bones is that of the two missing bodies. Yurovsky's explanation is problematic. He claims in his accounts that he decided to burn two bodies while the grave was being dug and that he chose Alexei and Alexandra, but he burned the maid, Demidova, by mistake. He gives no reasons for choosing the son and wife of the ex-Tsar for cremation. Yet the missing bodies are not Alexei and his mother, but Alexei and one of his sisters: either Anastasia or Marie. Could it be that the bodies were already so decayed that Yurovsky mistook a teenage girl for her middle-aged mother, or even her maid? Perhaps his instructions to burn the Empress were misunderstood? More problematic still is the question of whether it would be possible to burn two bodies almost to ash in the space of a few hours. The Russian government Commission reported that it would take between twenty and fifty hours completely to burn a body in the open air, far longer than the period that Yurovsky reports spending at the burial site.[40] Is it possible that some of his assistants were left to supervise the cremation after the rest of the party had gone? If so, Yurovsky's report elides this, since he states that during the digging of the grave the remnants of the cremated bones were dug into the earth and another fire lit on top to hide the remains. Moreover, no traces of ash or bones have been found near the mass grave. On the other hand, the searches for these remains have been completely unsystematic and may well have missed or even destroyed the evidence. Besides, as already mentioned, Yurovsky could have blurred the time sequence in his account. Or, more likely still, the fire did not have time completely to burn the bodies, but the remaining charred bones were so thoroughly smashed and dug into the ground that nothing has been found since.

Would-be Romanov descendants have bolstered their claims to authenticity with the fact that the bodies of two members of the family were never found. The missing bodies have also inspired several novels with plots more plausible than any of the survival stories of these alleged Tsar's children. An anonymous informant presented in Edvard Radzinsky's *The Last Tsar* as the Romanov investigation's own 'Deep Throat' hints at the children's survival. According to this man, Yurovsky's account of the double cremation was a complete fabrication, intended to conceal his incompetence at having allowed two of the children to escape.[41]

Until more credible evidence than this comes to light, however, the matter comes down to probability. Is it likely that two teenagers – one of them a haemophiliac – could have survived the shooting in the cellar? The eyewitness accounts concur that those victims not killed in the fusillade were finished off by bayonet thrusts or bullets fired at point-blank range. Alexei was shot in the head. Even if the two children had, by mistake, been left alive – and people do sometimes survive massacres, although usually massacres on a much larger scale – it is not likely that they could have slipped unnoticed from the truck, and still more improbable that they survived afterwards.

The bald conclusions are these. Bodily remains show that a person was once alive: without them, there is no ultimate proof of death. Sentimentally, we would like to believe that two children survived the carnage: reasonable doubt sways us to accept that they died. The remains of the parents, sisters and servants of the absent pair have been found and minutely scrutinized: what happened to the bodies of the two children may never be known.

3 The many deaths of Nicholas II

(And does history repeat itself, the first time as tragedy, the second time as farce? No, that's too grand, too considered a process. History just burps, and we taste again that raw-onion sandwich it swallowed centuries ago.)
(Julian Barnes, *A History of the World in 10½ Chapters*, 1989)

To any writer with a good imagination all memoirs are false. A fiction writer's memory is an especially imperfect provider of detail; we can always invent a better detail than the one we remember. The correct detail is rarely exactly what happened; and the most truthful detail is what could have happened, or what should have.
(John Irving, *Guardian*, 13 August 2005)

In 1927 some of the men who had executed Nicholas II approached Stalin for permission to publish their collected reminiscences. They wanted to mark the tenth anniversary of the night of 16–17 July 1918 when Russia's last Tsar – together with his wife, his children and their servants – had been killed in the basement of the Ipatiev House in Ekaterinburg. Stalin's characteristically brusque response was this: 'Not another word about the Romanovs!'[1]

Did that really happen? Did Stalin really say those words? The only irrefutable evidence is that no such volume of executioners' reminiscences was published in 1928. Whether or not the story is apocryphal, the futility of Stalin's injunction is all too apparent today. In 1918 the execution of the ex-Tsar and his family was no more than an item for 'news-in-brief, a non-event'.[2] Some eighty years and many Romanov books later, Nicholas and Alexandra are iconic figures in contemporary Russia and beyond, the manner of their deaths still inspiring history, popular fiction, movies and websites. Narratives about the Imperial Family's death have mutated and multiplied. From fragments of evidence, writers have fashioned contrasting tales of revolutionary justice and ritual murder, of death and survival. And new evidence has not subdued the old narratives. After all, as writers in Soviet Russia defiantly insisted: 'Manuscripts don't burn.'[3]

Bodies are not so easy to obliterate either. When human remains were exhumed near Ekaterinburg in 1991 new narratives challenged the version universally accepted until then: that the Romanovs' bodies had been burned in the forest. Until these bones were unearthed, no bodies had ever been found for the Imperial Family, and it had still been possible to believe that some of them may have escaped from the Ipatiev House. When the grave was opened in 1991, the escape theorists felt vindicated, since two bodies were missing. The Romanov family – Nicholas, Alexandra, their four daughters and their son – had been imprisoned in the Ipatiev House in Ekaterinburg, with their doctor and three of their servants, from April until July of 1918. On the night of 16–17 July all had disappeared. Yet the grave held only nine bodies, and when the remains were reconstructed by forensic anthropologists it became clear that the bones matched the age, sex and stature of the Romanov family and their suite, but that the bodies of a teenage boy and girl were missing. Of itself, this did not necessarily mean that the grave was that of the Romanovs (although the circumstantial and anthropological evidence was compelling). But when genetic tests were carried out on the remains a new genre of Romanov literature emerged, consisting of the intricate strings of DNA sequential analysis and the convoluted genealogical tables of Europe's royal families.

Despite the DNA evidence, which – coupled with anthropological and historical proofs – made it inconceivable that the remains were *not* those of the Romanovs, a persistent myth holds that the bones are a hoax. In Russia, despite all the forensic evidence, the Russian Orthodox Church (ROC) has never accepted the bones discovered in 1991 as those of the Imperial Family. Instead, the Church maintains that the White Russian investigation of 1919 into the family's disappearance revealed the truth about the murder of the Romanovs. Nikolai Sokolov, the magistrate who carried out this investigation, published his conclusions in France in 1924.[4] Sokolov stated that the Bolsheviks had burned all the Romanovs' bodies to ash in a massive bonfire, the traces of which had been discovered by the White detectives in the forest outside Ekaterinburg in 1919. In fact, the Whites had found the remains of the bonfire in which the Bolshevik burial party had burned the Romanovs' clothing, and they never thought to dig beneath the little bridge of railway sleepers which they had found in the forest road.

It was in this spot that the bones were exhumed in 1991. The discovery overturned the standard version of the fate of the Romanovs' bodies, which had been based on Sokolov's investigation. But the Church and its Russian nationalist allies could not accept this. Even as forensic tests carried out upon the bones seemed to prove beyond doubt that they belonged to the Romanov family, another slew of publications appeared which challenged the bones' authenticity and reiterated the White investigators' version of the family's death. There were new editions of Sokolov's and others' accounts from the 1920s, as well as completely new works along the same lines.[5] Many of these repeated the rumour which circulated among the

Whites that the Bolsheviks had decapitated the Tsar after shooting him, and removed his head to Moscow as proof that he was finally dead. Ironically enough, given his own profound anti-Semitism, Nicholas II's death was interpreted in these versions as a Jewish ritual murder and an attack on Russia itself by the Jewish-Bolsheviks. Russian émigré readers of the inter-war period found here a satisfying explanation for the cosmic significance of the Bolshevik Revolution and the diabolical nature of Soviet power. Similarly, after 1991, this anti-Semitic narrative suggested to Russian nationalists a way of coming to terms with the collapse of the Soviet Union – the entity which had supplanted the Russian Empire in their eyes.

Another fantastical version of the Romanovs' deaths emerged from the discovery, in 1991, that two bodies were missing from the mass grave. This prompted a surge in the steady stream of 'Romanov survivors' that has kept speculation alive since the family was killed in 1918. Russian playwright Edvard Radzinsky, the most prominent contemporary exponent in Russia of the Ipatiev House narrative, regularly receives letters beginning: 'My name is Romanov and I have begun to think that I am a descendant of the Tsar.'[6] In addition to the survival narratives by would-be Romanovs that infest the internet and occasionally make it into print, books are still being published that purport to tell the true story about the family's escape from the cellar death chamber. It is a well-established genre, which began with a pair of hoax 'diaries' published in 1920 as *Rescuing the Czar*. The 'diaries' have given rise to some very silly books about the 'secret rescue' of the Romanovs, in which their escape is usually orchestrated by square-jawed gentlemen spies on the clandestine instructions of a secret network of European royalty concerned about their Romanov cousins.[7]

In 2000, the ROC made Nicholas II and his family saints. Canonization implied that they were more than historical characters, that their deaths were a moral and eschatological turning point for Russia. The fashion sweeping Russian Orthodox parishes for new Romanov narratives – stories about weeping icons, miraculous healings and supernatural appearances by the martyred members of the Imperial Family – swayed the Holy Synod's decision to canonize them, and place them firmly in the Russian historical tradition of 'martyr princes'.

However, there is another post-Soviet Russian perspective on the Romanovs, which is also the prevalent narrative in Anglo-American culture. It is a story of cosy domestic bliss, tragically violated by the intrusion of politics. This version of Nicholas's death romanticizes the Romanovs. It idealizes their family relationships and emphasizes their paradoxical ordinariness, despite their glamorous lifestyles. It uncritically reproduces the propaganda produced by Nicholas himself, and both in Russia and the West it has created a rosy misinterpretation of the late Imperial period in which the members of the Imperial Family appear as innocent, misguided victims. The saccharine narrative lends itself particularly well to a photographic portrait of Nicholas II and his family and to costume dramas about them. To meet a demand for books about the romance of pre-revolutionary Russia, the contents of the Russian archives – private photographs, diaries and letters – have been plundered, and ever more obscure family members have become the subject of biographies.[8]

Myth or history

The prominence in the Romanov narratives of survivors' stories and tales of the romantic family does not merely indicate an inability to distinguish fact from fantasy. It represents a way of explaining an event which would otherwise be too random, cruel and painful to accept. This does not make the stories true in the sense of 'what really happened', but it makes them explicable. How, then, can we convey 'what really happened'? For history-writing is itself a constructed narrative, albeit one which should be grounded in verifiable evidence. 'We all know objective truth is not obtainable,' declares Julian Barnes:

> that when some event occurs we shall have a multiplicity of subjective truths which we assess and then fabulate into history, into some God-eyed version of what 'really happened'. This God-eyed version is a fake – a charming, impossible fake, like those medieval paintings which show all the stages of Christ's Passion happening simultaneously in different parts of the picture.[9]

Barnes's solution, as a novelist, is to shape the 'objective truth' through fiction. Some historians, too, openly acknowledge that they cannot achieve objective truth, and that the very act of writing – the choice of words, of structure and of genre for the narrative – shapes the events (the 'mini-narratives') being described.[10] Manipulating historical narrative in this fashion, some historians have abandoned writing history within the traditional paradigm of the 'realistic' nineteenth-century novel and the omniscient narrator, choosing instead to make their readers aware of the essential artificiality of this convention. The result is intriguing histories, which explore – in Simon Schama's words – 'the teasing gap separating the lived event and its subsequent narration'. In his *Dead Certainties*, for example, Schama includes a section called 'The Many Deaths of General Wolfe' (I confess stealing his title) in which he consciously reveals that gap by experimenting with contrasting ways of retelling a particular incident.[11]

What did 'really happen' to the Romanovs was told in the previous two chapters, which detail the manner of their deaths and the discovery of their remains. However, these are the most 'fictionalized' chapters of the book in terms of their presentation. The narrator of 'Cruel Necessity', for example, is an anonymous member of the execution squad, a composite figure whose 'recollection' of the event is rooted in the existing fragments of eyewitness testimony and forensic evidence. This account of Nicholas's death is as accurate as any written in a conventional form, in the sense that it is based on the same sources, tested with the same rigour. Yet it questions the false certainties of traditional narrative history, which can never produce a perfectly objective version replicating the events of the past but which is always 'doomed to be forever hailing someone who has just gone around the corner and out of earshot' (Schama again).[12] Why not, then, admit the essential artificiality of 'objective' history writing and attempt, within the parameters of historical accuracy, to imagine the experience, the sensations of that dramatic event, as they might have been lived by one of its participants?

The chapters that follow, on the other hand, explore the different myths about the death of Nicholas Romanov or, rather, about what became of him – of his body and his image – after his death. Far-fetched as these myths might be, they matter because they speak to contemporary concerns about Russia's past and future, and because they interweave themes of universal significance: death and the body, love and the family, spirituality and science. Put another way, these narratives make – or have the potential to make – good stories.

The history so far

In Western academic history, the way in which the 'mini-narrative' of the Romanovs' 'execution' – or their 'murder': the choice of word is vital – is told depends upon how the historian chooses to present the broader narrative of the Russian Revolution. For E.H. Carr, for example, the execution of the Imperial Family is merely an historical footnote to the momentous story of shifting social forces.[13] After all, by 1918, the ex-Tsar and his family were just an awkward minor irritant to the Bolsheviks. Having abdicated the throne for himself and on behalf of his son, the Tsarevich, in February 1917, Nicholas Romanov began to live as a private citizen – albeit under comfortable house arrest – with his family in the Alexander Palace outside Petrograd. Tsarism finally expired when the next in line to the throne, Grand Duke Michael Alexandrovich (Nicholas's younger brother), immediately also abdicated, handing power to the Provisional Government with the face-saving proviso that should a Constituent Assembly vote to reinstate the monarchy he would (re-)ascend the throne.[14] Of course, by the time a Constituent Assembly did convene, in January 1918, the Bolsheviks were in power and virtually all members of the Romanov family were facing either arrest or exile. But the personal tragedies of the Romanovs had little effect on the course of the revolutionary process in Russia.

Conservative Western historians such as Richard Pipes, on the other hand, see a more sinister meaning in the murders. They represent not just the Bolsheviks' essential inhumanity, but also a qualitative shift in the immorality of power. The decision to kill the Romanovs, writes Pipes, 'carried mankind for the first time across the threshold of deliberate genocide', because it represented ideological revenge upon innocent people.[15] Spokesmen of the post-Soviet Russian national patriotic movement, such as Oleg Platonov, echo this reasoning. Platonov describes the murder of the Imperial Family as 'the most terrible and evil crime of the twentieth century', and claims that 'the Gulag system began in the Ipatiev House, and without the Gulag it is impossible to understand Hitler's camps'.[16]

Meanwhile, Orlando Figes, one of the younger generation of historians of the Russian Revolution, takes a legalistic approach. He focuses on the decision to abandon the idea of a public trial of Nicholas II in favour of his secret execution as evidence of the Bolsheviks' illegitimacy as rulers. Whereas Charles I and Louis XVI had at least the semblance of legal representation and due process of law prior to their executions, writes Figes, Nicholas II – with his family – was precipitately assassinated in a sordid cellar. By killing the former Tsar rather than putting him on trial – a trial which would have admitted at least 'the *possibility* of his innocence' – the Bolsheviks 'passed from the realm of law into the realm of terror'.[17]

As explanations of why the Romanovs were killed, approaches such as these are constrained by their ideological perspective. The alternative is to avoid grand politicized narratives in favour of the banalities of circumstance. The Bolsheviks' execution of the former Tsar and his family in fact depended more on the vagaries of telegraph communication and train timetables than upon a considered decision by the Soviet government to eradicate the Russian monarchy.[18] The precise sequence of events around the shooting remains murky, despite enormous efforts by researchers to decide whether the order to kill the Romanovs originated in Moscow or whether it was a more *ad hoc* verdict by the Urals Bolsheviks. For while public statements spoke only of the ex-Tsar's execution (his wife and son, it was affirmed, had been 'sent to a secure place' and nothing was said of the fate of his daughters and servants), Sovnarkom – the new Russian government – knew that all the Romanov prisoners had been executed. A coded telegram from the Bolsheviks in Ekaterinburg on 17 July 1918 had informed Sovnarkom that 'the entire family suffered the same fate as its head'.[19] This telegram suggests, however, that the Bolshevik leaders in Moscow had not intended to wipe out the whole family. A diary entry by Trotsky supports this hypothesis. Remembering that he had asked Sverdlov whether the family had been killed along with the ex-Tsar, Trotsky records Sverdlov's chillingly casual response:

'All of them?' I asked, clearly with some surprise.
'All of them!', answered Sverdlov. 'So what?'[20]

Sverdlov's careless cruelty horrifies modern sensibilities, but if we want to understand why the entire family was summarily killed, we have to look more closely at the context. The Bolsheviks certainly considered putting

Nicholas II on trial, naturally with the consummate political orator, Trotsky, in the role of public prosecutor. It would have been a show trial: Nicholas would not have been found innocent, any more than were Charles I or Louis XVI. However, since popular sympathy for the former Tsar had largely evaporated, his prosecution could only increase support for the new regime. Trotsky, reminiscing from exile, recalled how he had proposed:

> a public trial which should lay open the entire reign (the policy towards peasants and workers, national and cultural policy, two wars and so on); the progress of the trial should be broadcast on the radio (?) throughout the country; reports of the trial should be read out daily with commentaries in all the volosts.[21]

It was practical rather than ideological reasons that prevented the staging of the trial of the ex-Tsar. Lenin had been in favour of the idea, Trotsky records, but, ever the pragmatist, had warned that 'there may not be time'.[22] Moreover, once the Romanovs had been transferred from Petrograd to house arrest in Tobolsk in the Urals in August 1917 – a precautionary measure ordered by Kerensky, head of the Provisional Government – it had become virtually impossible for the Bolsheviks to bring them back to Moscow for trial. Moving the Romanovs and their suite securely during the chaos of the Civil War was enormously difficult. Moreover, not only were communications severely disrupted over the 1,100 miles between Moscow and Ekaterinburg, but the structure of command in Russia was also extremely friable and the Bolshevik leadership in Moscow had little effective control over Bolshevik members of the Urals Regional Soviet. Indeed the Romanovs only ended up in Ekaterinburg because they were, in effect, hijacked by the Urals Bolsheviks. In Moscow, the Bolshevik leaders were so concerned about the threats their radical colleagues in the Urals were making against Nicholas and his family that they dispatched an envoy to try and escort the Romanovs back to the capital. Special Commissar Vasily Yakovlev arrived in Tobolsk, where the Imperial Family was confined in the governor's mansion, in April 1918. He embarked on the return journey to Moscow escorting just Nicholas, Alexandra and their second daughter Marie; the other girls remained with Alexei who was too sick to travel. The Urals Bolsheviks succeeded in diverting Yakovlev's train through Ekaterinburg, where he was forced to relinquish his charges to the Urals Regional Soviet. Three weeks later, the rest of the family and servants also arrived in Ekaterinburg, and the Romanovs and their retinue were reunited in the requisitioned mansion of Nikolai Ipatiev.[23]

Any chance of staging a trial in Ekaterinburg itself was thwarted as the summer wore on by the approach of White anti-Bolshevik forces, which had been strengthened by the rebellion of the Czech Legion in May. This was a force of some 35,000 Czech and Slovak POWs and defectors from the Austrian army, who were aiming for Czech independence from the Austro-Hungarian Empire, and had fought alongside Russia during World War I. They were supposed to be leaving Russia to rejoin the war in Europe, travelling eastwards through Siberia and embarking from Vladivostok. But when, after minor disputes between the Czechs and local Soviet authorities, the Bolsheviks ordered the Czech Legion to be disarmed, they rebelled, went over to the anti-Bolsheviks, and began to take the cities along the Trans-Siberian railway. The Czechs posed a real threat to Ekaterinburg and its Bolshevik commissars, who feared that they had a potential rallying point for the White forces in the person of Nicholas. (Ironically, the Bolsheviks were probably wrong: the Whites were by no means all monarchists; and even those who supported a restoration of tsarism preferred a more imposing figurehead than the discredited Nicholas.[24])

It was, therefore, practical considerations that dictated the decision to kill the Imperial Family, rather than the Bolsheviks' need to 'spill blood to bind their wavering adherents with a bond of collective guilt', as Pipes melodramatically puts it.[25] Ultimately, during the desperate months following the October Revolution, a public trial of the ex-Tsar was a political luxury that the Bolsheviks could not afford as their fledgling regime fought for survival. Instead, in July 1918, the Bolsheviks in Ekaterinburg followed the conventional course taken when a city was about to fall to the enemy: that of shooting all political prisoners. A reading of the telegrams exchanged between Moscow and Ekaterinburg shows that Sovnarkom in Moscow sanctioned the executions, but probably only after the event and under pressure from the militant Urals Regional Soviet. Liberal historians may construe the shooting of the ex-Tsar's family, his defenceless and blameless wife and children, as a cruel and immoral deed, a 'political crime' that placed the Bolsheviks in a class of their own.[26] But, as Trotsky indicates in his diaries, the dynastic principle of tsarism meant that Nicholas's family were political prisoners: Alexandra or one of the children could – in the Bolsheviks' eyes – conceivably have become regent in the event of a White victory. Moreover, their deaths were not atypical of the time. The Bolsheviks' security force, the Cheka, killed the families of many of their prisoners, especially when a city was about to fall to the enemy.[27] (The Whites, of course, were no more humane.) The execution of the Imperial Family actually reveals more about the methods of the Cheka in 1918 than about the Bolsheviks' attitude to the ex-Tsar and his entourage. Ultimately, they were eleven among thousands of prisoners who fell victim to the exigencies of the time. Interpreted this way, the Romanovs' deaths cannot be dismissed as historically insignificant, but nor do they offer an opportunity for anti-Soviet grandstanding.

The Soviet years

In Soviet Russia, the story of the last Tsar's execution was soon shunted aside with something resembling embarrassment, at least after the initial explanations had been stumbled through. The first public announcement of Nicholas's death appeared in a leaflet published (probably) on 18 July 1918 by the All-Russian Central Executive Committee of Soviets (VtsIK, formally the supreme body of state power). It stated that 'the Crowned executioner' Nicholas Romanov had been shot and that his wife and son 'are in a place of safety'. The following day, *Pravda* editorialized: 'Nicholas Romanov was essentially a pitiful figure. But . . . he became the inescapable symbol of a brutal regime of blood and violence against the people . . . a regime in which the brothel and divine worship were both elevated to the throne.'[28]

From the very start, false stories circulated about the last Tsar's death, which created confusion about who had been responsible. In September 1918, the *Urals Worker* newspaper told its readers – possibly as a piece of deliberate disinformation, possibly in genuine error – that Nicholas's corpse had been exhumed by the White army and was to be reburied in Omsk 'in a zinc coffin encased in lavish wooden paneling of Siberian pine'.[29] In April 1922, Chicherin, the Commissar for Foreign Affairs, claimed that 'the fate of the young daughters of the Tsar is at present unknown to me. I have read in the Press that they are now in America.' Chicherin told this blatant lie during an interview with the *Chicago Tribune* at the Genoa conference convened to establish normal diplomatic relations between Soviet Russia and the other Great Powers. Probably, he meant to deflect the lingering distaste of his new diplomatic partners at the rumours that the Bolsheviks had killed the Romanov children. His remarks had the additional effect of confirming 'sightings' of the 'Romanovs' as far afield as New York and Vladivostok.[30]

Meanwhile, in Soviet Russia, it was admitted that the entire family had been executed. The first full account was written by Pavel Bykov, a member of the Ekaterinburg Soviet at the time of the execution who later became chairman of the Urals Regional Soviet. Bykov's sketch from 1921, 'The Last Days of the Last Tsar', was included in a collection of articles published for local consumption in the Urals to mark the fourth anniversary of the October Revolution. A few years later, when the Romanovs had slipped from international public attention, more reconstructions of the Imperial Family's execution were published in Soviet Russia. In 1926 Bykov brought out an expanded version of his account, now called *The Last Days of the Romanovs*. (This was translated for a left-wing British publisher in the 1930s as *The Last Days of Tsardom*.) Bykov denounced Nicholas as 'a tyrant, who paid with his life for the age-old repression and arbitrary rule of his ancestors over the Russian people, over the . . . impoverished and blood-soaked country'. Only now, with Red victory in the Civil War, could the Tsar's execution be properly appreciated, claimed Bykov, for at the time the Ural proletariat, preoccupied with defending the Revolution, had barely noticed it.[31]

The many deaths of Nicholas II 53

Two years after Bykov's expanded account, on the tenth anniversary of Nicholas's execution, the journal *Red Virgin Soil* published extracts from the memoirs of Aleksandr Avdeyev, the first superintendent of the Ipatiev House. Avdeyev described the ex-Tsar as a rather pathetic figure, too dim to be much bothered by his captivity. Avdeyev's explanation of why Nicholas posed a threat was rather different from Bykov's. It was not because Nicholas was a tyrant that he had to be killed, but because in order 'to guard the pitiful remnants of tsarism' from rescue by their 'Black Hundredist friends'* valuable fighting men were being kept from the front. Once the decision had been taken to shoot the ex-Tsar, wrote Avdeyev, 'with those close to him (who had refused to abandon him), three hundred workers employed as guards heaved a sigh of relief and hurried to the front to help their comrades beat back encroaching capital and strengthen the conquests of October'.[32]

To mark the tenth anniversary of the October Revolution, Yakov Yurovsky – the commandant of the Ipatiev House who had organized the execution – and his deputy, Grigory Nikulin, donated the weapons with which they claimed to have shot the ex-Tsar to the Museum of the Revolution in Moscow. Military Commissar Ermakov also donated a weapon to the Museum of the Revolution in Sverdlovsk (the new name of Ekaterinburg), claiming likewise that he had shot the ex-Tsar with it. Yurovsky and Ermakov became star speakers at local gatherings of Young Pioneers† and Bolshevik Party members, where they related the events of that night. Ermakov's accounts were highly exaggerated, to judge by the interview he gave to a credulous American journalist in the 1930s.[33] Yurovsky's more sober retelling was recorded on at least three occasions. In 1920 he dictated the story of the Romanovs' execution to the leading Soviet historian Mikhail Pokrovsky, and this document – lodged in Moscow's Museum of the Revolution – became known as the 'Yurovsky note'. He also wrote a personal memoir in 1922; and in 1934 a stenographer recorded the speech that Yurovsky gave to a meeting of Old Bolsheviks‡ in Sverdlovsk. All these documents were held in Russian archives until after the Soviet collapse, and subsequently crept into publication.[34]

The Romanovs' execution was also commemorated for a while in Soviet Russia's cultural landscape. The Ipatiev House was turned into a Museum of the Revolution, where visitors could see artefacts from the Romanovs' captivity, including Ermakov's gun and an intercepted letter from Nicholas responding to an escape proposal (this was the letter which had been

---

* The Black Hundreds were extreme right-ring groups, supporters of autocracy prior to the Revolution.
† The Soviet Youth Movement, founded in 1922, similar to the international Scout Movement, but with a different ideology.
‡ 'Old Bolsheviks' was an unofficial term for Bolshevik Party members who had joined the party before 1917. Most were liquidated in Stalin's purges of the 1930s.

forged by the Ipatiev House guards as though from 'an officer of the Russian Army').[35] In the Museum there also hung a huge canvas by V.N. Pchelin, 'Handing over the Romanovs to the Ural Soviet' (1927), which was reproduced as a souvenir postcard. Intourist's *Pocket Guide to the Soviet Union* of 1932 informed foreign visitors about 'the Revolutionary Museum, housed in the very building in which Nicholas II and his family were shot', but hardly encouraged them to make the detour. Tourists who did visit the site and who sensed the Museum's 'heavy atmosphere of grief and terror' had missed the point.[36] The Ipatiev House Museum was meant to lionize the Bolsheviks, not to incite sympathy for the Romanovs. Underlining this, Resurrection Square on which the Ipatiev House stood was renamed Square of the People's Vengeance.

The execution was also marked in Soviet literature. Superstar poet Vladimir Mayakovsky wrote his poem 'The Emperor' after a visit to Sverdlovsk in 1928, when he had asked to be shown the site where the Tsar's remains were buried. Mayakovsky's poem was a clue to the location of the grave. Indeed, those few Soviet accounts of the Romanovs' execution to mention what had become of the bodies did not support the White investigators' conclusions that they had all been burned. But the fate of the Romanovs' bodies was dropped from subsequent Soviet histories.

The Museum in the Ipatiev House was closed in the late 1940s, and Square of the People's Vengeance was again renamed, to become the anodyne Komsomol Square. After victory in the Great Patriotic War (World War II), the Soviet Union had a new founding myth, and there was little need to retell the death of the old regime. Many witnesses to the Romanovs' captivity and execution had died, a few from natural causes, more during the purges of the 1930s in which thousands of Old Bolsheviks perished. However, popular interest in the Romanovs was rekindled in the 1960s and 1970s, when Russian intellectuals began to ride a wave of nostalgia. Russian nationalism regained cultural respectability. The 'village prose' of writers such as Valentin Rasputin and Vasily Shukshin eulogized the vanishing *mores* of rural Russia. Painter Ilya Glazunov staged monster exhibitions of his kitsch paintings, crowded with figures from Russia's past. And the *Pamiat'* [Memory] organization, which was originally a cultural preservation society and only later became an extreme Russian nationalist group, demonstrated the first cracks in the Soviet political monolith.[37]

Part of this vogue for the clichés of Russia's pre-revolutionary history was a growing interest in the Romanovs. The last two survivors of the execution squad – one of whom was Grigory Nikulin, Yurovsky's deputy – recorded their memories for Moscow State Radio in 1964, although their words were never broadcast. The impetus behind these recordings had come from Mikhail Medvedev, the son of another member of the execution squad, Mikhail Medvedev-Kudrin. The younger Medvedev had already persuaded his father to write down his account, and this document, with the transcripts of the radio interviews, was deposited in the archives.[38] In 1972 an historical novella about the last Tsar's death, called *Twenty-three Steps Down*, was serialized in the journal *Zvezda*. It was published in book form in 1978 and reissued in 1982. In 1975 the director Elem Klimov made a feature film about Rasputin, in which the character of Nicholas II was sympathetically portrayed alongside a debauched Rasputin. However, the film, *Agoniya*, was not released until 1984. For the first time academic historians also began to publish works about Nicholas's death.[39] This trickle of creativity about the death of the last Tsar – although miniscule in comparison with the output of late and post-Soviet writers and film-makers – alerted the Politburo to the fact that the Romanov story had found new narrators and a new audience. There were even reports of pilgrimages to the Ipatiev House where flowers were left for the murdered Tsar. Aware that the sixtieth anniversary of the execution was approaching in 1978, the Politburo issued a secret instruction in 1977 to demolish the Ipatiev House, and the Sverdlovsk Party Committee was told to assume public responsibility for the decision.

Some twenty years after this, 'history just burped' and the man who, as First Party Secretary of Sverdlovsk, carried out the Politburo's instruction, found himself as President Boris Yeltsin of Russia attending the ceremonial reburial of the Romanovs' remains in St Petersburg.[40]

Monarchists and nationalists

How much does this story matter in post-Soviet Russia? The *tsarskoe delo* (the 'tsarist affair': in essence, the controversy over the remains) has featured regularly in the press since 1989. The exhumation of the remains of Nicholas II and his family in 1991 from their hidden grave was just one of the numerous upheavals that Russia experienced during the post-Soviet period. It was not the most far-reaching of these developments, yet the death of the last Tsar assumed profound significance in post-Soviet Russia, where the political and cultural resonances of the story were felt more sharply than in Anglo-American culture. Indeed, the actual remains of the last Tsar – the bones discovered in the mass grave and identified by DNA analysis – as well as the ubiquitous physical representations of Nicholas – statues, icons and photographs – were at the centre of the cultural turmoil that followed the demise of the Soviet Union.

Dead bodies are invested with particular significance at times of change. A political transformation is frequently marked by some form of manipulation of the body: for example, decapitating the monarch, embalming the dead leader, or reburying a statesman's corpse in a more suitable location. Dead bodies are linked with the concepts of life and death, with the emotions of kinship and empathy, and with notions of identity and self-identity. The very corporeality of dead bodies gives them a symbolic weight which contrasts with abstract notions like patriotism. 'Dead bodies, in short, can be a site of political profit.'[41] Nicholas's remains were thus constantly present in the new Russia, in the reassertion of Russian Orthodoxy in popular culture, the rivalry between federal and local government, and the re-evaluation of the Soviet regime.

On the whole, the Russian media portrayed Nicholas II in a positive light, which failed to illuminate his errors of political judgement, his obscurantism and his obstinacy. 'What really mattered was that he was a good man and not that he was a bad politician.'[42] This attitude coloured media coverage of the ceremonial reburial of the remains in 1998, when for the majority of Russians the Romanovs seemed to represent 'a yearning for the bourgeois family ideal, for the genteel and decent life the Romanovs enjoyed but the common Russian people never had'.[43]

For a small minority, the Romanovs' deaths also symbolized the criminality of the Soviet regime contrasted with the monarchist ideal. It is important to recognize, however, that the discovery of Nicholas II's body did not lead to a resurgence of pro-monarchist sentiment in Russia. Monarchist groups remain politically weak, very fragmented and wholly eccentric. Moreover, even were autocracy to be revived, a Romanov restoration is hardly credible, since the clan's members remain bitterly divided. The majority, led by the senior member of the family Prince Nicholas Romanoff, pursue various careers from their comfortable European residences and interest themselves in Russia at the level of charity work.[44] They also disdain the sole branch of the Romanov family which openly proclaims its right to the non-existent throne. Settled in Spain and headed by the redoubtable Maria Vladimirovna, this part of the family is actively scheming to make Maria's son, 'Grand Duke George of Russia' (born in 1981), Russia's next tsar. The rights of this Romanov offshoot are hotly disputed. Their claim dates back three generations to Maria's grandfather Kiril Vladimirovich, a first cousin of Nicholas II. However, morganatic (unequal) marriages and the insertion of a woman (Maria) into the traditionally all-male line of succession have meant that George's self-proclaimed status is recognized by only a handful of supporters, even though Maria has insisted that these include the Russian Orthodox Church and the Russian presidency. In any case, it is rather doubtful whether George is up to the task: his plans to go to Russian naval academy were quietly dropped for fear of his being bullied, and the late Dmitry Likhachev, Russia's most eminent historian, was distinctly uncomplimentary about Georgy's behaviour during a guided tour of the Hermitage: 'The pudgy little fellow ran right over to the throne and tried it out for size. No, he won't do at all.'[45]

Yet while monarchists gained little from the post-Soviet resurrection of Nicholas II, it was vitally important to the Russian Orthodox Church. With the demise of the Soviet Union, the ROC became a focus for the ambitions of religious Russian nationalists. The religious extremists had little overt representation in secular politics – there was no religious party of any significance, for example, just as there was no monarchist party –

The many deaths of Nicholas II   57

but nationalists were extremely powerful within the Church, and the Church has a huge cultural influence upon contemporary Russia. To understand some of the myths about Nicholas II, we need to understand why the ROC has fallen so heavily under the influence of the conservative nationalists, or 'national patriots' as they call themselves.[46]

The ROC establishment had settled into a *modus vivendi* with the Soviet state, largely as a survival mechanism against sometimes harsh persecution, but an opportunity for Church reform emerged in 1988 with the ROC's millennium celebrations. These coincided with the start of Mikhail Gorbachev's reform of the Soviet system. As the Church became bolder in its activities, so did secular democratic activists who wanted to push Gorbachev towards faster political change. Yet this potential alliance between the democrats and the Church was never sealed; the democrats alienated the ROC hierarchy by continually berating the Church for having collaborated with the Soviet state. Democratic activists regularly made sensational claims that bishops, metropolitans and even the Patriarch had been KGB informers, without ever really investigating the different levels of co-operation and conformity that had been required of Church leaders.

Treated with suspicion by the democrats, the ROC hierarchy swung towards the national patriots. There were institutional and ideological reasons for this, too. Groups within Russian Orthodoxy were competing with the Moscow Patriarchate (the official establishment of the ROC in Russia) for the allegiance of its parishes. The Union of Orthodox Brotherhoods was one such group, a network of laypeople that claimed to defend the purity of Russian Orthodoxy. Another was the Russian Orthodox Church Outside Russia (the ROCOR, also known as the Karlovtsy Synod) which had been established by Russian émigrés in 1922 and maintained ever since a pathological hatred of all things Soviet. The ROCOR canonized Nicholas and Alexandra in 1981. With the demise of the Soviet Union, the ROCOR stepped up its activity in Russia to the extent that the Moscow Patriarchate began to fear defections by its own parishes to this rival denomination and had to adopt the ROCOR's attitude towards the Tsar.[47] Another reason for the national patriots' influence in the ROC is that the Church has preserved a religious fundamentalism, a pre-Enlightenment way of thinking that is contrary to Western secularism and matches the nationalists' own anti-modernist views.[48]

The institutional and philosophical cohesion between the Russian national patriots and the ROC was strengthened by the Church's cultural conservatism. The ROC has very little tradition of evangelism or reform, meaning that its predominant ethos is backward-looking. Some would suggest that herein lies its strength, in that it has been able to preserve its traditions in the face of a hostile ideological environment and increasing secularism. There are parish priests within the ROC who urge reforms, such as using modern Russian in church services rather than old Church Slavonic, in order to bring the Church into the contemporary world. They suggest that the ROC is a victim of its own 'incorrect practice' in having relied too heavily on tradition and ritual instead of developing a new theology. The Church hierarchy, however, insists that reform must be gradual because its parishioners are emotionally reliant upon the familiar rites and traditions. Certainly the enormous popularity of advice literature stipulating the correct forms of behaviour in and around the Church suggests that, for most churchgoers, cultural norms are more significant than theology.[49]

When it came to the 'tsarist affair', then, the ROC positioned itself firmly with the national patriots. And this, as we shall see, meant that the myths about the 'ritual murder' of Nicholas II or about the 'miracles' performed by the canonized Tsar had wide currency in Russia.

The many deaths

This book is not trying to get at just 'what really happened' in the cellar of the Ipatiev House: it is experimenting with ways of conveying the past. It deals with a multiplicity of competing narratives about the death of Nicholas II. Some are verifiable; some are patently false. Even the latter are important, however, because of what they say about the beliefs of those who accept them. This is not to say that they are 'true', in the sense of being historically accurate, but that they deal with issues which continue to have resonance in contemporary Russia: anti-Semitism, Russian Orthodoxy, fractured domesticity, paternalism and authority.

The different narratives about the Tsar show both his 'many deaths', and also his many lives. In Chapter 1, Nicholas Romanov is the remembered victim of a composite fictionalized narrator, whereas in Chapter 2 he is the 'silent witness' in a forensic investigation. In Chapter 4, Tsar Nicholas II becomes the victim of a ritual Jewish murder, while in Chapter 5 the Romanov dynasty continues in the guise of some of the numerous false Tsarevich Alexeis: 'The Tsar is dead. Long live the Tsar!' Chapter 6 discusses Nicholas, the Holy Tsarist Martyr; Chapter 7, however, sees him as a family man, a tragic private individual forced to play the role of Tsar.

For the record, let me state my own position on some of the controversies surrounding the death of the last Tsar. I have used the verifiable evidence to imagine what a member of the execution squad experienced in July 1918 in the cellar of the Ipatiev House and later in the forest, as Yurovsky and his men killed the Romanovs and then attempted to conceal their bodies. When those remains were exhumed seventy-three years later, modern forensic science positively identified them as those of the Romanovs and their suite. I believe that the remains are genuine, and I do not believe that any one of the eleven victims survived; yet two bodies are missing from the mass grave, one of them Alexei's. Despite this, and whatever did happen to his body, I do not believe that any of the claimants whom I discuss was Alexei. The canonized Tsar and his family have performed 'miracles', which can all be explained by chemistry, physics or psychology. In my view, the Imperial Family were not and will not be Russia's salvation. Nor were they a perfect family, or even in any way an 'ordinary' one. They were actually a group of self-absorbed, over-sheltered and highly privileged individuals, of no exceptional abilities, and harmless in and of themselves, were it not for the immense responsibilities carried by them as the representatives of Russia's autocratic ruling dynasty.

Away from academic history, and judging by the tone of most biographies and the numerous websites devoted to the family, there remains an unresolved sense of outrage about the story of the Tsar's death. It is easy to believe that we know the Romanovs, because we have access to so much of their personal material. We have read their diaries and their letters; we have watched dramatizations of their lives; we have seen innumerable family photographs, some posed and official, others simple snapshots of family life. We have traced the children as they grow from angelic infancy to adolescence; and it seems inconceivable that the four little girls with tumbling curls and their toddler brother, identically dressed in sailor suits, could die horribly in a dingy basement swimming in blood and gore. We feel a pang for their mother, Alexandra, prematurely aged by worry for her haemophiliac son and by guilt that she has transmitted the disease to him. Seduced by these emotions it is easy to be blind to the extreme pragmatism of the Bolsheviks in choosing to kill the Romanovs. Instead, we search endlessly for greater meaning in their deaths because of their historical role and because we know so much about them from their own obsessive self-documentation. In contemporary Russia, the Romanovs have additional currency because they offer a number of choices – a menu of 'Russias' derived from the narratives of the Tsar and his family – from which a society rediscovering its past can choose. This is one good reason for studying the Romanov narratives. Another reason is that they make good stories.

So here, and without apology to Stalin, is an experiment in writing history that might say 'another word about the Romanovs'.

4 Gothic horror

> Rumour who loves to spice big bowls of the false
> With a pinch of the true,
> And who, gulping her own confections,
> Grows from nearly nothing to fill the whole world.
> ('Hercules and Dejanira', Ted Hughes, *Tales from Ovid*, 1997)

> My attention was fixed upon every object the most insupportable to the delicacy of the human feelings. I saw how the fine form of man was degraded and wasted; I beheld the corruption of death succeed to the blooming cheek of life; I saw how the worm inherited the wonders of the eye and brain. ... I collected bones from charnel-houses; and disturbed, with profane fingers, the tremendous secrets of the human frame. In a solitary chamber, or rather cell, at the top of the house, and separated from all the other apartments by a gallery and staircase, I kept my workshop of filthy creation: my eyeballs were starting from their sockets in attending to the details of my employment.
> (Mary Shelley, *Frankenstein*, 1818)

In 1921 Nikolai Nikolaevich Breshko-Breshkovsky published yet another of his potboiler romantic thrillers with the Presse Franco-Russe. In *The Tsar's Diamonds* [*Tsarskie brillianty*] Grand Duke Michael, the younger brother of Nicholas II, returns in triumph to save Russia from the vile Bolsheviks, and the Romanov dynasty is restored when he ascends the throne as the second Tsar Mikhail Romanov, thereby bringing to an end Russia's second 'Time of Troubles'.* As usual, Breshko-Breshkovsky was aiming at a Russian émigré readership whose predominant mood was one of 'vague, sentimental' monarchism.[1]

The opening scene of the novel sees a train arrive in Moscow from Ekaterinburg. Among its passengers are the Tsar's executioner Yakov Yurovsky, and Yurovsky's lover, the vampiric Dora Spevak. In a small

---

* The first Tsar Mikhail [Romanov] was chosen in 1613, founding the Romanov dynasty, at the end of the Polish invasions of the 'Time of Troubles'.

Gothic horror 61

leather suitcase they bring with them the severed heads of Nicholas and Alexandra to show to the Bolsheviks. Yurovsky is a crude *nouveau riche* dressed in an expensive leather coat, 'red faced, with a bullish neck, broad-shoulders ... A butcher'. Dora, with her black hair, green eyes and red lips, is 'a striking and peculiar combination of '*rusalka*† and vampire'. Their train pulls into Moscow and they take their suitcase, with its terrible contents, to the Kremlin. The deeper Yurovsky and Dora go inside the fortress, the more acutely they sense 'the presence of the red tyrants, the cruellest, most bloodthirsty that ever walked the earth'. Eventually, they are shown into 'a small vaulted chamber' where they await the arrival of their Bolshevik masters. Then comes the scene where the severed heads of the Tsar and Empress are revealed. [Translation mine.]

> The door swung open. Yurovsky's legs gave way. This was not the one for whom he was waiting with such quivering anticipation. But even this individual – a personage in a threadbare, greasy jacket with a dirty scarf wound about his neck, thick lips; a straggly moustache and beard – was the senior Soviet dignitary behind Trotsky and Lenin. Sverdlov, the chairman of the Central Executive Committee; Sverdlov, one of the most disgusting and gloomy figures in the rabble of Soviet loutocrats.‡
>
> Yurovsky recognized him from his photographs. Yes, this was Sverdlov, the son of a master watchmaker. ... To what heights had he risen! Sverdlov, with whom Germany's ambassador Count Mirbach had conducted negotiations to bring the Tsar's family out of Russia. Sverdlov, who had given his word, all the while planning what had now come to pass.
>
> He turned to Yurovsky with a single word:
> 'Proof?'
> 'Here!', answered Yurovsky, patting the suitcase, as he remembered that he had left his rubber gloves in the inside pocket of his overcoat. Never mind, he'd do it without his gloves. ...
> 'In a moment Comrade Trotsky will be here, and we will inspect your "proof" together'.

Trotsky enters the chamber in theatrical style, preceded by two tall adjutants dressed like tsarist guardsmen and then four Cossacks in full regalia. Finally:

---

† Water sprite: in Russian folklore *rusalki* were sinister and dangerous creatures, despite their beauty.
‡ The Russian is *khamoderzhets*, a pun on *samoderzhets* – autocrat; *kham* means a lout or uncouth person.

The door was opened by some unseen hand and there entered the awesome ruler of all Russia, Leon Davidovich Bronstein – Trotsky.

Dora had seen him once before at a rally in Petrograd during the Kerensky regime. He had been receiving deputations of sailors in the Tauride Palace.[§] But what a difference between that Trotsky and this! At the time, exploiting the collaboration, and even the protection, of that cowardly nonentity Kerensky, Trotsky had been building up his power, buying the allegiance of the dregs of sailor society with bald flattery. And at that time he had been the complete toady in his democratic civilian suit. The predator hid his claws until the moment came, caressing his stupid dull prey with velvet paws. . . .

Now he was the proletarian Attila or Gengis Khan, who had raised his bloody banner over the sanctuaries of the Kremlin. An unruly shock of wavy hair stood up above the smooth forehead. On the prominent chin twisted a tuft of beard that was truly Satanic. The glint of the lenses in his pince-nez could not dim or soften the malevolent gleam of his eyes.

In place of the democratic suit in which he had appeared before the sailors in the Tauride Palace, he wore a service jacket, riding breeches and yellow gaiters. Without looking at anyone, he went up to the monumental throne of Tsar Alexei Mikhailovich[**] upon which lay the suitcase and, like Sverdlov, pronounced a single word, this one even shorter:

'So!'

In the railway carriage, Yurovsky had boasted of his strong nerves. But now they deserted him, although for quite a different reason. Trotsky blinded him, dazzled him with his haughty magnificence. The key trembled in his fingers and he could not make it fit into the lock. This elicited another exclamation, more impatient than the last:

"So!"

Trotsky dismisses the adjutants and the Cossacks, and the climax of the scene arrives as Yurovsky finally opens the suitcase.

In it lay something wrapped in a thin cambric sheet, with a crown embroidered in white silk.

Comrade Yurovsky, with his butcher's physiognomy, had now regained his composure and, like a merchant-peddler who knows that

---

[§] The Tauride Palace was the original site of both the Petrograd Soviet and the Provisional Government, which was led from July 1917 by Alexander Kerensky. In September 1917, Trotsky became chairman of the Petrograd Soviet, which was soon to overthrow the Provisional Government in the October Revolution.

[**] The second tsar of the Romanov dynasty, father of Peter the Great, and favourite tsar of Nicholas II.

his wares will please a wealthy patron, was standing with his back to the audience busily unwinding the sheet. And suddenly – now a merchant no longer, but the court executioner of an Asiatic despot – Yurovsky swiftly turned around, holding in each hand a severed head, one male one female. He raised the terrible, blackened heads with their cold greenish pallor by the hair. Dim glassy eyes. Half-opened, parched, blackened lips. ...

Now Yurovsky felt himself to be in control of the situation. His hands no longer trembled. His voice was firm.

'What further proof could you ask for? What? Here is Her Imperial Highness. Here is His Imperial Highness! And they bow down at the feet of Comrades Trotsky and Sverdlov!' And Yurovsky lowered the severed heads to the ground.

Both autocrats had awaited this moment in agony.... How incredible it was! The heads of the couple who had ruled the country that they now ruled; the heads of the pair who, twenty-five years before, had been ceremonially crowned within these very Kremlin walls – these same heads were now lying in the dust before two exiles with a dark criminal past, and an even more criminal present. Was this not the greatest victory there could be? Was this not a triumph that could never pall? And Sverdlov's thick lips spread wider and wider into a smile; and Trotsky's eyes behind the pince-nez burned with a Satanic flame more malevolent than ever.[2]

The scene is pure Gothic horror. Breshko-Breshkovsky incorporates all the classic elements of the genre: mysterious locked chambers, a vampiric female, the flavour of the mysterious Orient in the guise of the Cossacks and the comparisons with the court of an 'Asiatic despot', graphic description of the severed body parts that reveal a horrific crime, and foreign villains: in this case Trotsky and Sverdlov, who are portrayed through a crude codified anti-Semitism (Sverdlov's 'thick lips' and Trotsky's 'wavy hair') and who are also demonized by Trotsky's 'Satanic' beard and malevolently burning gaze.

Breshko-Breshkovsky's novel played to its émigré readership's dream of a 'White Tsar' (Grand Duke Michael) who would reclaim the Russian throne from the Bolsheviks. Dealing in historical figures, the novel blurs the lines between fact and fiction, reality and imagination. For the scene quoted above, in which the severed heads of the Tsar and Tsarina are laid at the feet of Trotsky and Sverdlov, was actually Breshko-Breshkovsky's embellishment of a rumour about the fate of the Tsar that circulated during the 1920s among the Russian émigrés of Paris, Central Europe and America. Many of Breshko-Breshkovsky's readers were convinced that the Bolsheviks in Ekaterinburg had shot the Imperial Family, and then cut off their heads and taken them to Moscow as proof that the Tsar was dead.

64   Gothic horror

From the very start of the White investigation in 1919, a significant narrative thread in the stories about the death of Nicholas II and his family has been this Gothic version of the Tsar's murder and the fate of his body. In post-Soviet Russia this narrative has been consumed primarily within Russia's national patriotic milieu, and it is structured by the world view that the national patriots have adopted: the concept of Russia as a victim of malevolent global forces, embodied in the Jews. The Tsar's murder is interpreted as a pivotal point in this struggle. The national patriots have exhumed stories – not bodies – from the early émigré texts about the Tsar's murder. These stories are presented as historically verifiable fact, but they are written with all the stylistic features of the genre of Gothic horror.

The reasons why Russia's national patriotic writers (from the 1920s and the 1990s) have chosen to adopt the Gothic genre horror will be discussed later in this chapter. First, let us find out what happened to the heads that Yurovsky and Dora brought to Moscow.

Around the time that the putative remains of the Imperial Family were being exhumed from the forest outside Ekaterinburg in 1991, the right-wing weekly journal *Literaturnaia Rossiia* published an anonymous text relating what had happened to the Tsar's head. The journal introduced the text as a translation into Russian of an article that had first appeared in 1928 in a German newspaper, the *Hannoverscher Anzeiger*. The Russian translation had been discovered, according to *Literaturnaia Rossiia*, in the Russian archives. Some ten years after *Literaturnaia Rossiia* published the article, historian Oleg Platonov included the same story in his *History of the Tsar's Murder* – a volume in his series *Russia's Crown of Thorns*. As the title suggests, Platonov's books adopt an extreme right-wing stance and are profoundly anti-Semitic, yet they follow all the formal conventions of history-writing (footnotes, references, equivocations). Platonov even casts mild doubt on the severed heads story, while relishing it as a description of the Bolsheviks' depravity.

What follows is my translation of the text of the anonymous article published in 1991 in *Literaturnaia Rossiia*. Like Breshko-Breshkovsky's novel, the text contains all the hallmarks of Gothic fiction. It is set in a castle (the Kremlin) with ancient passages and gloomy chambers, the stormy weather conspires to increase the tension, a heinous crime is concealed, women faint, and there is plenty of gore.

> Everyone knows that the bolsheviks killed Emperor Nicholas II together with his entire family on July 18, 1918, in Ekaterinburg. I believe it to be a less well-known fact that the instigators of this evil deed were Trotsky and Zinoviev. In Germany nobody knew until now what the bolsheviks did with the head of the murdered Sovereign; I can now reveal the precise details of this. . . .†† The news of the murder of the

†† Platonov starts his version here.

Tsar's family was received in Berlin on July 18. No one in Berlin believed this rumour. On July 19 a Moscow radio station picked up a radiogram from Berlin to one of the leading newspapers in Vienna which contained the following information: 'The Tsar and his whole family have been taken by their supporters[‡‡] to a place of safety.' This radiogram unsettled the bolsheviks to such an extent that Trotsky demanded Beloborodov give more details and material proof of the Sovereign's death. His telegram read as follows: 'Require precise information whether Russian tyrant met fitting punishment.'

In reply to this telegram, a sealed leather suitcase was received on July 26, containing the head of the Sovereign. They could not have sent more weighty material proof. On July 27, at Lenin's command, the supreme figures in the bolshevik dictatorship were summoned, and shown the 'package' from Ekaterinburg. It was formally recorded at this meeting that the head of Emperor Nicholas II was contained in a glass vessel in a leather suitcase, and a protocol was drawn up, signed by all the bolsheviks present: Lenin, Trotsky, Zinoviev, Bukharin, Dzerzhinsky, Kamenev, Kalinin and Peters.[§§]

At this meeting Kamenev raised the question of what to do with the head of the murdered Emperor. The majority of those present felt that this head should be destroyed; only Zinoviev and Bukharin proposed preserving it in alcohol and placing it in a museum for the edification of future generations. This proposal was defeated, and it was resolved to destroy the head of the Sovereign, in order – as Peters put it – that it should not become a holy relic for undesirable elements and sow confusion in simple minds. Trotsky was charged with implementing the decision.

On the night of July 28, that is, ten days after the murder of the Tsar's family, the incineration of the Sovereign's head was to take place.

The article continues with a description of the actual incineration, allegedly 'from the words of an eyewitness':

'At the appointed time I was at the gates of the Kremlin. . . . It's spitting with rain and we can see a fire burning beyond the River Moscow. The Kremlin fire engine sweeps past us, the church bells are sounding the alarm. Krylenko*** whispers: "The shades of old Russia are mourning their former ruler." There is a thunderclap, a flash of lightning, and I see that one of those present makes the sign of the cross. Krylenko exclaims: "Devil take it. I am not responsible for this

---

[‡‡] Platonov has 'with their supporters'.
[§§] Platonov lists them as Lenin, Trotsky, Zinoviev, Kalinin, Peters and Bukharin.
[***] Nikolai Krylenko, Commander-in-chief of the armed forces.

ill fortune." The Kremlin Commandant opens the entrance to the outbuilding, and we find ourselves in a small chamber, dimly lit by a burning stove and a kerosene lamp. Now I can see the other people present better – there were about twenty of them. Among them were Eiduk, Smirnov, Bukharin, Radek with his sister, and several others. A little later, Peters and Angelica Balabanov turn up; Alexandra Kollontai, Latsis, Dzerzhinsky and Kamenev follow them. It became so stuffy in the little room that we could barely breathe. Everyone was very nervous and excitable, only Kollontai (who later became Soviet ambassador to Oslo and Mexico) seems more reserved. She moves closer to the burning stove and starts picking at a stain from her dress. Last to appear is Trotsky. Once he arrives, a square suitcase is placed on the table. Trotsky greets everyone, looking at them searchingly and, having consulted with Dzerzhinsky and Bukharin, orders the suitcase to be opened. It is immediately surrounded by a crowd of curious people, and I am left outside the circle, unable to see what is happening.

One of the women is taken ill, and leaves the table. Trotsky laughs sardonically: "Female nerves". Krylenko echoes him. Dzerzhinsky, with exaggerated courtesy, tries to assist Kollontai, and helps her to a bench by the wall. Now I can see what is inside the leather suitcase. It contains a thick glass vessel with a red liquid inside; in the liquid floats the head of Emperor Nicholas II. I am so overcome that I am barely able to recognize the familiar features. But there can be no doubt: before us lies the head of the last Russian Tsar – proof of the dreadful deed committed ten days ago in the foothills of the Ural mountains. All the others experience the same feelings of horror. Some of them proffer remarks. Bukharin and Latsis express surprise that the Tsar has gone grey so young; indeed his hair and beard are white, perhaps as a result of the war, the revolution and his long imprisonment. Trotsky orders those present to sign a statement of what they have witnessed. So the second protocol is compiled. Kollontai has disappeared, but yet more curious people have taken her place. Among them I recognize Krestinsky, Poliakov and several sailors. Before signing the protocol everyone examines the glass vessel one more time, and I can see from their faces that they feel unwell. Bukharin, trying to dispel the heavy mood, tries to say a few words that will illuminate the affair from a revolutionary perspective but he soon breaks off and falls silent. Even the emotionless Latsis is nervously fingering his sandy beard and casting sideways glances at the table. Trotsky orders the vessel brought to the burning stove. All bow their heads, involuntarily falling back, but only for a moment: real communists cannot betray their inner turmoil.'[3]

The use of an eyewitness account is characteristic of Gothic fiction, where it is deployed to heighten the atmosphere of terror. Who is this 'eyewitness' to the Bolsheviks' incineration of the Tsar's decapitated head? Oleg Platonov names him as the monk-priest Iliodor. This infamous character had a life as colourful and encrusted with legend as his more famous friend and benefactor, Rasputin. He was a radical monarchist, who in the years before the Revolution led a popular movement in the Volga provinces that preached a primitive Slavophile vision of Tsar and people united against the evils of modernity. In 1911 he turned against Rasputin, demanding that he sever relations with Nicholas and Alexandra because his debauchery was bringing the imperial couple into disrepute. In response, Rasputin engineered Iliodor's downfall: the monk-priest was defrocked and sent into exile. He continued his campaign against Rasputin, writing a damning exposé entitled 'The Holy Devil'. This was published in Russia after the Revolution, and when Iliodor later emigrated to the USA it was published there as *The Mad Monk of Russia*. Iliodor's life after the Revolution is obscure: some believe that he returned to Russia and joined in the persecution of the Church that had sided with the Tsar and Rasputin against him.[4] He is thought to have died in poverty in the USA around 1952.

Before his death, Trufanov produced another sensational manuscript called 'The Head in the Kremlin'. It seems to be this shadowy source that is cited in several versions of the Gothic horror narrative of Nicholas II's decapitation, including the one above. It has cachet because it is written by a real historical figure, although of course Iliodor's motives as an 'eyewitness' are highly suspect. As an example of how Iliodor's manuscript fed the Gothic narrative, we turn now to a biography of Nicholas II published in German and English in the 1930s by Mohammed Essad-Bey. This author, an émigré from the Russian Empire just after the Revolution, converted from Judaism to Islam and, exiled in Germany, produced biographies of Stalin and Nicholas II. Under the pen-name Kurban Said, he also wrote the engaging romantic novel *Ali and Nino*.[5] Essad-Bey's biography of Nicholas II is blatantly partisan, romanticizing its subject as 'the bearer of a mystical faith' whose 'radiant features' may be recognized 'only from the exalted height of irrational feeling'. The following extract (taken from the English translation of 1936 by Paul and Elsa Branden with the melodramatic title *Nicholas II: Prisoner of the Purple*) deals with the fate of the Tsar's body, and relies on Iliodor's manuscript for evidence. There is madness, haunting, exoticism and horror in Essad-Bey's narrative, all characteristics of Gothic fiction.

> The Four Brothers Mine is situated twenty-four *versts*[†††] from Ekaterinburg, amidst wild, primeval forest. Gloomy tales, told by peasants, surround that haunted spot. Deserted for more years than the people can remember, men and beasts have kept away from the pit in abject fear. Phantoms peer from the underbrush and will-o-the-wisps

---

[†††] 1 *verst* = 1.06 kilometres.

dance across the swamps. The entire neighbourhood abounds with fearsome visions and fantastic sagas. . . . The only visible and tangible clue to the fate of the Czar does not lead to the Four Brothers Mine, but to the Kremlin, in the gold-domed city of Moscow. In this connection, Priest Illiodor reports:

'I had to go to the Kremlin to see Kalinin and talk to him about some important church reforms. Passing through a dark corridor my guide suddenly opened the door to a small secret chamber. I entered. On a table, under glass, lay Nicholas II's severed head, a deep wound over the left eye. I was petrified.'

In the long, blood-curdling story of the Last of the Czars, no statement is more uncanny than Illiodor's. It conjures up the severed head of Nicholas II guarded by the spirits of his forebears in a secret chamber of the old Kremlin. According to rumours the severed head was brought to Moscow at the orders of the Ural Soviet by the prostitute Gusseva, paramour of one of the alleged murderers. The journey with the head of the Anointed One proved too much for the woman. She lost her mind. Barefoot, her clothes in tatters, her hair flying wildly, she strode through the deep snow of Moscow and, in a babbling voice, told people congregating around her that she had brought back the head of the Anointed One to the holy city of his coronation. Eventually she was shot and her story perished with her.[6]

Essad-Bey treats Iliodor's fantasies about the head in the Kremlin as a reliable source, and the 'Priest' – although Iliodor had been defrocked by then – seems to have included just enough semi-facts to be convincing. Iliodor passes himself off as an adviser to the Bolsheviks, although it is patently absurd to suggest that Kalinin – at the time the chairman of the Central Executive Committee (in effect, head of state) – would consult Iliodor about 'important church reforms'. The 'deep wound' over Nicholas's left eye is a reference to the wound sustained by Nicholas during his tour of the Far East in 1891 before he ascended the throne. In Otsu, Japan, a fanatical policeman had attacked him, wounding him on the forehead, but the scar when it healed was barely visible, let alone a 'deep wound'. Iliodor's influence in this story spreads beyond his claims to have seen the Tsar's head. 'The prostitute Gusseva', who Essad-Bey says brought the Tsar's head to Moscow, was, in fact, one of Iliodor's followers – a woman called Khionia Guseva who had been a prostitute before turning to religion. When he fell out with Rasputin, Iliodor had encouraged Guseva to assassinate his enemy, and in 1914 she almost succeeded, stabbing Rasputin in the stomach.

Together, Iliodor and Essad-Bey create an atmosphere of pure Gothic terror in relating the horrific fate of the Tsar's head. Not all émigré authors were so easily duped, however. The historian Sergei Melgunov included the story of the Tsar's head in his 1951 study (in Russian), *The Fate of*

Emperor Nicholas II after His Abdication, but he makes it clear that it is just that, a story. Melgunov notes that the legend of the 'head in the Kremlin' is linked with Captain Paul Bulygin, a monarchist officer who had been a faithful assistant and bodyguard to Nikolai Sokolov, the White investigator of the Tsar's death.[7] This is Melgunov's discussion of the legend of the 'Tsar's head' [translation mine]:

> Let us note one such fantastic 'true story', which has its origins in the gossip of the local inhabitants and serves as a kind of epilogue to the Ekaterinburg drama. It is worth mentioning because it is linked with the name of Captain 'B' who helped Sokolov to conduct the investigation – or at least, it is to him and his authoritative evidence that the author of a 1929 article in the Parisian *Russkoe vremia* referred when this apocryphal tale first appeared in the pages of the émigré press. The story goes, no less, that among the material evidence brought to Moscow connected with the murder in the Ipatiev House was a special 'leather bag' containing a glass bell-jar filled with a red liquid, in which floated the head of the executed Emperor!
>
> In 1921 in Berlin, the article's author claims, Captain B(ulygin) had told him that this fact 'definitely took place'. At the time the author was sceptical about the Captain's words, but at the end of 1928 in the *Frankf. Kur.* newspaper of 20 November he read an article entitled 'The Fate of the Tsar's Head' from the pen of a certain Pastor Kurt-Rufenburger, who related from the words of 'an eyewitness' how in July 1918 the bolsheviks had burned the 'terrible cargo' they had received from Ekaterinburg. Some were of the opinion that the head of Nicholas II preserved in alcohol should be kept in a museum for the edification 'of future generations', but in the end they resolved, as Peters proposed, to destroy it in order to prevent the head of the former tsar from becoming a 'Holy relic' in the eyes of 'stupid people'. The 'eyewitness' observed the process of incineration which took place in the presence of almost the entire bolshevik council. The 'head' of Nicholas II preserved in alcohol was also seen by Iliodor – in 1919. The 'sensation', for which the former monk-priest was paid $1,000 by the American press and which even seemed plausible to the *Poslednie novosti* paper, was not news at all by then, for one of the same organs of the Paris émigré press had reported it three years earlier.[8]

Melgunov is clear that this story of the Tsar's head in the Kremlin is supported by no authentic evidence. He makes its apocryphal status even clearer by framing it as a (lengthy) footnote, and linking it with other apocryphal stories about the Tsar, such as the numerous escape and survival narratives. Russian national patriotic publications from the 1990s, however, cite Melgunov in support of their claims that Nicholas's head really did end up in Moscow. They exploit Melgunov's status as a respectable academic

70 Gothic horror

historian, disingenuously omitting to mention that he only discusses the 'head in the Kremlin' story in the context of myths about the Tsar.[9] The rumour that the Tsar's head had been preserved in the Kremlin surfaced from time to time in the Russian media during the 1990s, including on at least one occasion during a television programme for the NTV channel in 1996.[10]

A particularly vivid version of the 'head in the Kremlin' legend – which I translate below – comes from the writer and researcher V. Rodikov, who took part in the 1996 NTV programme. In an article published as early as 1990 in an obscure Moscow weekly, *Inzheneraia gazeta* – after the news that the Tsar's grave had been found, but before his bones were exhumed – Rodikov claimed to have hard 'evidence' that Nicholas's head had been preserved in the Kremlin.

> About two years ago the historian N. Borisov[‡‡‡] told me what he had come across during one of his research trips. He was in Prague at the time, working in the Slavonic Library. During breaks from his research, he used to leaf through the émigré press. And apparently in *Novyi zhurnal* he stumbled over a strange admission. He does not remember the article's author – the theme was not relevant to his research – he just skimmed the piece and thought no more about it. The story was told by an acquaintance of Kuibyshev,[§§§] who later escaped abroad. Apparently, Valerian Vladimirovich once told this acquaintance that a vessel with the head of the Emperor preserved in alcohol had been kept in one of the safes in the Kremlin right up to 1924. They came across it by chance, opened it up, and – my God, there was the head, moustache, beard and all! They set up a commission to identify it, which included Stalin and Kuibyshev, then they summoned prisoners from the OGPU. And these men, if the story is to be believed, immured the head somewhere in the Kremlin Wall.[11]

This modern version of the story of the Tsar's head descends from Gothic horror into Soviet bathos. There is no ceremonial opening of the case containing the head, no sinister passages or secret chambers: just one of the Kremlin's – presumably numerous – safes. Nicholas's head is reduced to a caricature of moustache and beard, rather than being distinguished by the noble wound over his left eye. In true Soviet bureaucratic fashion, a commission is formed to discuss what to do with it, and it was decided to

---

[‡‡‡] Nikolai Sergeevich Borisov, historian of early modern Russia, whose works include biographies of Ivan III (2000) and Sergei Radonezh (2002).
[§§§] Valerian Vladimirovich Kuibyshev (1888–1935), chairman of Gosplan 1930 to 1934. Died, officially of heart failure, after failing to carry a motion in the Politburo demanding a Central Committee investigation into Kirov's death.

destroy the Tsar's severed head not by incineration at midnight before the leaders of the Bolshevik Revolution, but by ordering condemned political prisoners from the secret police to hide it in the wall around the Kremlin. The generation of Russians who remembered Khrushchev's deStalinization campaign would realize that being immured in the Kremlin Wall can be an ambiguous end: not only are Soviet heroes commemorated there, but after Khrushchev had the mummified body of Stalin removed from the Lenin Mausoleum it was discreetly hidden – at night – in the Kremlin Wall.

As Sergei Melgunov hinted, the origins of the 'head in the Kremlin' myth are to be found not in the émigré press but in the very first accounts of the Tsar's death, written by the White investigators. These versions, of course, were passionately anti-Bolshevik and, as censorship dissolved and the fate of the Romanovs became a fashionable topic in late Soviet Russia, the national patriots seized on these early versions of the Tsar's death to push their own agenda – the portrayal of Russia as the victim of a Jewish plot. In the early 1990s, the national patriotic media republished the accounts of the White investigators for a new readership that, only a decade earlier, would have been unable to see such texts at all unless – like Geli Ryabov – they had the connections to gain access to the restricted collections of the Lenin Library.

One such account was the lengthy 1922 book by General Mikhail Diterikhs, *The Murder of the Tsar's Family and members of the House of Romanov in the Urals*. In the introduction to its re-edition in 1991, the publishers write that Diterikhs's book was hitherto known only to a narrow circle of specialists in Russia with access to the special archives.[12] General Diterikhs had been the White officer in charge of the area when Ekaterinburg was captured by the Czech Legion, a few days after the execution of the Tsar. Dissatisfied with the progress of the various investigations into the disappearance of the Romanovs, in February 1919 Diterikhs appointed special investigator for the Omsk regional court, Nikolai Sokolov, to head the search. After the defeat of Admiral Kolchak's forces in Siberia late in 1919, Diterikhs and Sokolov retreated to Russia's far east, taking with them the evidence they had managed to collect. This included small items of jewellery and metal fastenings, fragments of animal bones, part of Botkin's false teeth, and a severed finger. In exile, Diterikhs began his account of the Tsar's death, which was published in Vladivostok – an outpost of the White movement – in 1922.

On the basis of Sokolov's dossiers of evidence, Diterikhs composed a horrific reconstruction of the events as he believed them to have occurred. A crucial scene in his narrative was the severing of the imperial head and its transport to Moscow. Diterikhs marshals his evidence around the a priori argument that the Tsar's murder was a Jewish plot against Russia. He gives the starring role to Philip Goloshchekin, military commissar of the Ural Regional Soviet, whom Diterikhs calls by his given name, Isaac,

72 Gothic horror

to emphasize his Jewish origins; he does the same for Yakov Sverdlov, whom he renames Yankel. My translation of extracts from *The Murder of the Tsar's Family* shows Diterikhs's eagerness to use the most unsubstantiated pieces of evidence to support his vision of Jewish ritual murder. First, Diterikhs relies heavily on rumour:

> After the murder of the entire Tsarist Family, when Isaac Goloshchekin visited Yankel Sverdlov, bringing three heavy boxes of some kind, a rumour spread through the city that Isaac Goloshchekin had brought barrels containing the heads of all of the Members of the Tsarist Family, preserved in alcohol. The intelligence service reported that some minor secretary or other from Sovnarkom,**** who was particularly bent on moving abroad as soon as possible, rubbed his hands and said gleefully: 'Well, we're set up now; we can go to America and show off the Romanovs' heads in the movie theatres.'

Second, Diterikhs bends the evidence to fit his theories. Among the evidence found at the site of the Four Brothers Mine, he lists the following:

> On the 'doctors' plot',†††† pages of a medical textbook were found, which could only have been used by a doctor. They show that the operation to hide the bodies required the presence of a medical man. His help may have been needed either to supervise those handling the acid, or for some kind of surgical operation on the bodies. ... The savage operation to chop up the bodies for greater ease of burning did not, of course, require the presence of a doctor. But if, before this, the heads really were severed from the bodies of Isaac Goloshchekin's unfortunate victims, if the three mysterious iron barrels taken back to town on carriages really did contain alcohol in which to immerse the severed heads, then a doctor was most certainly needed for such an operation. ... However disfigured the bodies may have been, Isaac Goloshchekin understood perfectly that for a Russian believer it is not just the physically complete body that has significance, but also its most trivial remains which become holy relics of the bodies whose souls are immortal and cannot be destroyed by Isaac Goloshchekin or other fanatics like him from the Jewish people.

Having aired his speculative use of the evidence, Diterikhs proclaims his definitive conclusions about the decapitation of the Imperial Family.

**** The Council of People's Commissars – Soviet government.
†††† *Polianka vrachei.* 'doctors' plot' is my pun. Diterikhs uses the local name for the area where the pages were found, which could be translated as 'doctors' field/patch/plot'; the 'Doctors' Plot' was a conspiracy fabricated by Stalin in 1952 in which Jewish medical staff treating the Soviet leaders were accused of trying to murder them. Only Stalin's death prevented a new purge.

In answer to his own rhetorical question: 'What did the fanatic Isaac Goloshchekin do with the bodies of his victims?', he writes:

> First of all, Isaac Goloshchekin severed their heads. I mentioned above the rumours that spread through Moscow among the Soviet functionaries with the arrival there after the murders of Isaac Goloshchekin and in connection with his taking three disproportionately heavy boxes to Yankel Sverdlov. What do the investigators of the site have to say about this? First of all the pieces of lace or chain worn around the neck bear the traces of having been cut, which may have happened when the heads were severed from the bodies by a sawing or chopping implement. Furthermore, during the operation to sever the heads from the bodies some rather large, heavy icons worn around the neck rolled away; they were flung into the grass of the pit, to the left of mine no. 7, and were not found in the fire. Finally, teeth burn worst of all; however, despite all the care taken in the search, *not a single tooth was found* anywhere, in the fires, in the soil or in the scatterings from the mine.
>
> It is the view of the commission that the heads of the Members of the Tsar's Family and those dear ones murdered together with Them were preserved in alcohol in the three iron barrels brought to the forest, packed into wooden boxes and carried away by Isaac Goloshchekin to Yankel Sverdlov in Moscow as incontrovertible proof that the orders of the fanatics at the centre had been carried out to the letter by the fanatics on site.[13]

Diterikhs's fantasies about the posthumous decapitation of the Imperial Family reveal the deep anti-Semitism that runs through this version of Nicholas II's death, and which we saw surface in Breshko-Breshkovsky's novel. The same anti-Semitic logic was also articulated by Robert Wilton, an associate of Diterikhs and Sokolov and the correspondent for the London *Times* in Russia during the Revolution. Wilton also used Sokolov's material for a book on the fate of the Tsar. In *The Last Days of the Romanovs* – a book written by an Englishman horrified at Russia's withdrawal from World War I and fearful of his own country's fate – the Tsar's death is presented as a ritual murder carried out by the Jews at Germany's instruction in order to destroy Russia. Nothing here is down to chance; the killing of the Tsar is premeditated and meticulously planned. Sinister forces of black magic execute the plot: 'the occult powers of the Ekaterinburg *chrezvychaika*' [Cheka] and 'the Jewish camarilla', as Wilton puts it.[14] But the murder of the Tsar is only a small part of the Jewish plan. Wilton's peroration is a model of the anti-Semitic rationalization of the Bolshevik Revolution which was prevalent among certain segments of inter-war British society:[15]

74 Gothic horror

> The Germans knew what they were doing when they sent Lenin's pack of Jews into Russia. They chose them as agents of destruction. Why? Because the Jews were not Russians and to them the destruction of Russia was all in the way of business, revolutionary or financial. The whole record of Bolshevism in Russia is indelibly impressed with the stamp of alien invasion. The murder of the Tsar, deliberately planned by the Jew Sverdlov (who came to Russia as a paid agent of Germany) and carried out by the Jews Goloshchekin, Syromolotov, Safarov, Voikov and Yurovsky, is the act not of the Russian people, but of this hostile invader.[16]

Post-Soviet Russia's national patriots, who have republished Diterikhs and Wilton for a new readership, focus on the Tsar's 'murder' as a 'Jewish plot'. Oleg Platonov's works about Nicholas II's death have all the academic apparatus of footnotes and references while fantasizing a dark world of Gothic horror. Platonov conjures up a mysterious rabbi, who visits the Ipatiev House a day before the murders and apparently directs the whole 'ritual'. This figure embodies the national patriots' anti-Semitic paranoia that Russia is the victim of Judaism. He seems to have appeared first in a very brief description in Wilton's book of 'two young men, one of them a Jew', who arrive at the Ipatiev House after the murders to collect 'seven pieces of baggage, among them being a black leather trunk covered with seals'. Wilton implies that the baggage contained the artefacts, and the heads, of the Tsar's family.[17] Out of this brief phrase, Platonov constructs a sinister figure – described variously as 'a "Jew" with a beard as black as pitch' or 'a person in black clothing like a Jewish Rabbi' – who directs the 'ritual' of the Tsar's death.[18]

Platonov also uses this invented 'Jew' to explain the infamous 'inscriptions' that the White investigation found on the walls of the death chamber. These graffiti, which considerably puzzled the White investigators, consisted of two lines in German misquoted from Heine's poem 'Belsazar', and four indeterminate marks. The lines from Heine read: 'Balthasar was killed by his servants that very night' – an apt commentary on the events in that room, especially as they punningly misrender the German 'Belsazar' as 'BelsaTZAR'. The four 'indecipherable marks' were harder to interpret, since they seemed to form no coherent system of notation. Indeed, a casual observer might see them merely as idle scribbles. Nothing daunted, in the 1920s a Russian émigré called Mikhail Skariatin published a pamphlet under the pseudonym Enel, in which he decoded the inscription as a series of marks denoting the letter 'L' in Greek, Hebrew and Aramaic. Using a pot-pourri of esoteric knowledge, including the Cabbala, numerology and ancient languages, Skariatin claimed that the mysterious inscription read: 'Here, on the order of the forces of darkness, the Tsar was sacrificed for the destruction of the State. Let all the peoples hear this.'[19]

Gothic horror 75

Enel's pamphlet gained notoriety and credence in post-Soviet Russian national patriotic circles, and was reprinted in its entirety in a xeroxed periodical called *The Tsar Bell* [*Tsar Kolokol*] that is one of the most viciously extremist anti-Semitic publications of the 1990s. The intoxicating mix of Skariatin's occult learning rendered his particular narrative of Russia's victimhood enormously attractive to the national patriots. Platonov cites 'Enel' extensively and establishes Enel-Skariatin's credentials beyond reproach: not only was he a colonel in the Tsar's Horse Guards Regiment who then spent twenty years in Egypt translating papyrus about magic, writes Platonov, but he was also 'Orthodox, a deeply religious person, an elder in the Orthodox Church in Cairo and the director of the Russian Department of the Egyptian Interior Ministry'.[20] In his *History of the Tsar's Murder*, Oleg Platonov presents the shooting as an occult ritual intended to destroy Holy Russia, which was performed by the unknown Jew and attested to by the mysterious inscriptions on the wall of the death chamber. I have retained in my translation all Platonov's equivocations – 'maybe', 'perhaps' – and his deliberately academic style, as well as his vicious anti-Semitism. Platonov intercuts a standard narration of the execution – the arrival of the lorry, waking the family, taking them downstairs on the pretext of unrest in the town – with fanatical claims that the execution was an anti-Christian ritual act. (Platonov's repeated assertion that Yurovsky was the grandson of a rabbi is unproven, although it is an article of faith for the national patriots.[21])

> The rabbi's grandson [Yurovsky] led the members of the Tsarist Dynasty of the Russian Orthodox Kingdom through the door set in the western part of the room and spread them out in a pre-arranged order opposite the east and partly the south walls. The altar of a Christian Church faces East. The antichrist moves towards the East from the West. It was the plan of the organizers of the bloody ritual that the Russian Tsar, the lynchpin of the Christian world, should fall along the axis of the altar of a Christian Church. They were not dealing with an ordinary man, but with the Lord's anointed and his spouse, his heirs, and his faithful servants. They must all die, sprinkling one another with splashes of their blood.
>   ... After the regular firing squad had left the place where the ritual had been carried out, other people entered the room. Probably these were the rabbi (whose name I do not know), Yurovsky – the grandson of a rabbi – and the Hassidic Jew Goloshchekin. What ritual dances they performed on the site of the deed we do not know but, after they left, on the south wall where the Tsar's family perished and which faces the Temple of Solomon there were two inscriptions that explained the meaning of the ritual performed there. The inscriptions were made, most probably, by the rabbi and Yurovsky, for they clearly understood the role of the Tsar and Tsarist power in Russia; they were aware of

the consequences of their crime: the collapse of the millennium-long spiritual foundations of Russian statehood. The criminals rejoiced at the fall of historical Russia. One inscription, written in German, drew a historical parallel between Russia and Babylon, Nicholas II and the Babylonian King Belshazzar (Balthasar). ...

The other inscription, consisting of four cabbalistic signs, bears witness to the ritual nature of the murder and was a kind of key to understanding the entire ritual performed in the Ipatiev House.

... There are witnesses to yet one more horrible detail of the ritual tsar-murder. For the Jewish leaders who organized it, the mere fact that it had been carried out was not enough. The cruel Jewishness boiling in their blood demanded material proofs of the evil deed. Some researchers are convinced that the leaders of the Jewish Bolsheviks demanded the severed head of the Tsar as proof of the fanatical ritual.[22]

The authors of this particular story about Nicholas II's death – the post-Soviet national patriots like Platonov and the early twentieth-century émigrés like Breshko-Breshkovsky – have adopted a particular style for their narrative: that of Gothic horror. The motifs of Gothic fiction are everywhere in these tales of the Tsar's severed head: locked chambers in a castle (Kremlin); thunder and lightning at climactic moments; severed body parts; sinister villains such as Diterikhs's demonic doctor and Platonov's black-bearded rabbi; female insanity and hysteria.

Why should the genre of Gothic fiction have been selected to express the myth about the Tsar's head? To answer this we need to focus on the impelling incident of this particular narrative about the death of Nicholas II, and ask why the severing of the king's head from his body during an act of revolutionary regicide should have become so enveloped in Gothic motifs.

In both the English and the French Revolutions, the decapitation of the monarch was redolent with symbolism. The separation of the nation's head of state from the body politic, which represented the revolutionary destruction of the old political order, was played out literally and symbolically in the severing of the king's head from his body. The head was then displayed to the masses as proof that their liberation had been achieved. In the 1790s in France the image of the severed head of Louis XVI held aloft by his executioner became iconic. Louis's head, depicted in rather serene profile with blood dripping from the neck, became a design classic; indeed, so fashionable was it that the Sèvres factory produced a porcelain cup with the image painted in gold so that French citizens could display their revolutionary enthusiasm while enjoying their morning coffee.[23]

When it came to the execution of Nicholas II, however, there was no public display. The occasion lacked any ceremony and the executioners strove to conceal rather than show off their work. This would appear to represent a step backwards to a furtive dynastic assassination rather than the imposition of revolutionary justice. In the Gothic horror version of Nicholas's death, however, ceremony is restored and the Tsar's head is displayed, but not to the public – only to the villains and in secret. The Gothic elements in the narrative stem from this secretiveness, for the Gothic genre functions by expressing sublimated desires and fears and by laying bare the horrible. When it first emerged in the early nineteenth century, Gothic fiction gave form to repressed anxieties – often sexual but also political – as its genesis in cultures traumatized by the French Revolution and the fear of scientific and political change indicates. Gothic fiction is distinctive, then, not for 'the spooky claptrap so often thought of as Gothic (gloomy castles, ghosts and graveyards)' – this is more Shakespearian in origin –

> but [for] a particular frame of mind which questioned traditional values of good and evil, of virtue and reward and which sought to challenge and to test philosophical, religious and ethical beliefs through the postulation of a basically uncertain and incomprehensible world.[24]

The émigré milieu in which the narrative of the Tsar's severed head emerged had also been traumatized by revolution, and was facing an uncertain world. The myth of the Tsar's head in the Kremlin thus gave form to the inchoate fear which the displaced individuals of the White emigration felt towards the Bolsheviks. The myth of the Tsar's head, as expressed in Gothic fictional form, perverted the classic themes of regicide. In the Gothic narrative of Nicholas II's death, the Bolsheviks do not stage a public display of the king's head so that the people's liberation from oppression can be joyously confirmed; rather, they demand that the object be brought to them clandestinely as proof of the deed, and then they secrete it within the Kremlin – the heart of the Russian state. The Tsar's head thus becomes an inverted holy relic which is gloated over by the Satanic Bolsheviks.

As well as the severed head motif, other elements in this narrative may be read through the filter of Gothic horror as expressions of the sublimated anxieties of the Russian émigrés, and as dark echoes of earlier versions of revolutionary regicides. The figure of a mysterious doctor, for example, often appears in Gothic novels: think of Dr Frankenstein or Dr Jekyll who, by tampering with nature, create a perverted evil (Frankenstein's monster and Mr Hyde). In the Tsar's decapitation narrative, as Diterikhs tells it, the doctor also perverts his professional duty. Rather than healing, he performs the operation to sever the Imperial Family's heads; rather than certifying that death has taken place, he ensures that the physical proof of death reaches the 'monsters' who ordered the killings. Diterikhs's mysterious doctor figure could also, of course, have been conjured up by association with Dr Guillotin and his decapitation device, which was introduced as a

78   Gothic horror

more humane method of execution but was later turned into an instrument of terror, and which also sliced off the head of Louis XVI.

Another favourite character of Gothic fiction is the exotic foreign villain. In the Gothic horror version of the Tsar's death this role is assumed by the Jewish Bolsheviks, which also gives cosmic significance to the story: the Tsar's death is a crucial moment in the Jewish plot to destroy Russia, yet Russia's mission is to defeat this plot, both for itself and for Christendom at large. The fact that some of the Bolsheviks with 'starring roles' in the narrative (Trotsky, Sverdlov, Goloshchekin) were ethnic Jews is produced as 'evidence' of the 'plot'. Similarly, the rabbi who visits the execution chamber to direct the 'ritual murder' personifies the evil forces that bring down the Russian state. Thus the Tsar is brought face-to-face with his nemesis, as the invented figure of the nameless rabbi supplies the missing drama of confrontation in the story of the Tsar's death. (An apocryphal story from the English Revolution similarly brings Charles I into contact with his enemy. The night after the execution, goes the legend, a mysterious muffled figure visited the embalmed body of the King. He muttered 'cruel necessity', and left. 'The voice and gait were like those of Oliver Cromwell', says the story.[25])

Ironically enough, Nicholas II believed implicitly in this cosmic conflict between Russia and Judaism and fostered the belief that the Jews engaged in ritual murder. Less than ten years before the Tsar and his family were killed in Ekaterinburg, a Jewish clerk, Mendel Beilis, had been put on trial in Kiev for the ritual murder of a 13-year-old Ukrainian boy. The prosecution was brought with at least tacit support from Nicholas and the quite overt interference of the Russian Minister of Justice who packed the jury with peasants in an attempt to get a conviction. Beilis was acquitted, although what appeared to be the triumph of legality over superstition was undermined by the jury's finding that the victim had, nevertheless, been ritually murdered.[26]

At the same time as the White Russian émigré milieu was fantasizing a Gothic version of the Tsar's death, early Soviet culture was formulating a different Gothic expression of sublimated fears. In the 1920s, Soviet hopes for a new future were struggling with the introduction of Lenin's New Economic Policy (NEP). This policy reversal allowed limited capitalism to function again in Russia as a means of economic recovery, but was regarded with extreme suspicion by the supporters of the Revolution. In the cultural sphere, 'NEP Gothic' was the result, in ideological texts as well as in fiction.[27] Just as Gothic fiction arose in the early nineteenth century as an expression of anxiety about the legitimacy of the old social and religious structures in the wake of the French Revolution, so the 'NEP Gothic' of the 1920s expressed radical Bolshevik fears about the return of a phantasmal vampiric past, the 'undead' capitalist society which had supposedly been slain by the 1917 Revolution.

In 1925 a Soviet critic of Breshko-Breshkovsky's novel *The Tsar's Diamonds* (the piece which opened this chapter) interpreted it as a threat from NEP – and by extension from the old regime. I.M. Vasilevsky was analysing contemporary publications by the White émigrés in a book sinisterly entitled *What are They Writing? The Memoirs of the Former People*. Vasilevsky accused Breshko-Breshkovsky of perpetuating his pre-revolutionary 'boulevard' fiction. He ripped into the novelist for continuing to foist upon readers his ersatz 'eternal heroine': 'the countess with her delicate profile', her 'tender, aristocratic face, framed by ash-blonde hair' and her 'fairy-tale, dreamy yet sultry, vague half-smile'.[28] Vasilevsky objects, as might we, to the cliché-ridden prose of *The Tsar's Diamonds*, to its painted-by-numbers characters and its deeply implausible plot. But to whom is the novel addressed, asks Vasilevsky? The novel is written in Russian, so it is not destined for the French *petite bourgeoisie*, who might appreciate its lurid anti-Sovietism; it is not aimed at the newly emerging Soviet citizen, who 'does not yet read such novels'; nor is it meant for an émigré Russian audience, since such readers would not accept 'this astonishing vulgarity'. It is the new breed of the NEPman, concludes Vasilevsky, which is the only readership that could appreciate 'Breshko''s lurid fiction.

The Bolsheviks despised the NEPman – a small trader and businessman – for having adopted with such gusto the petty capitalist freedoms provided by the New Economic Policy; yet they also feared this new type for undermining the idealized figure of the new Soviet man whom the Revolution was to have brought forth. 'No, this White novel is not for the ordinary émigré, nor for French concierges,' writes Vasilevsky.

> The true traitor Breshko-Breshkovsky was destined for the NEPman, for His Excellency the NEPman; born of his tastes, inspired by his interests. Who is he, this NEPman who is becoming ever more clearly defined? It is truly his tastes, his mental and moral level that the genius of Breshko has reflected.[29]

Vasilevsky's critique of *The Tsar's Diamonds* reveals the deep unease in radical Soviet circles about the NEP and the cultural miscegenation that came with it. Vasilevsky despises the novel's 'vulgarity' and sensationalism – characteristic traits of the Gothic to its critics. Yet his critique also suggests that the Gothic horror version of the Tsar's death could have had a cathartic function for radical supporters of the early Soviet government, in that it allowed their fears of resurgent capitalism and the undead Tsarist regime to be expressed in heightened style, and laid to rest. As the Tsar's head is displayed to Trotsky and Sverdlov in the opening pages of *The Tsar's Diamonds*, it represents for them the irruption into the present of the 'undead past' – represented by 'the posthumous vitality of an ancestral presence or artifact'.[30] Yet the head is destined for incineration, the final destruction of the terrifying past.

The re-emergence of the Gothic horror narratives of the Tsar's death in the post-Soviet era is also indicative of sublimated fears felt by the post-Soviet Russian national patriots: the fear that the Soviet past is not dead. The Gothic stories of the Tsar's decapitation by the Bolsheviks suggest the fear that Soviet power might rise from the grave. A post-Soviet readership is particularly receptive to the Gothic horror style in writing about manifestations of Soviet power, because in the post-Soviet era Gothic imagery has commonly been deployed in analysing and describing Stalinism. Since the death of Stalin, and particularly since the Khrushchev 'Thaw', accounts of the late 1930s – the Terror – have frequently 'cloaked themselves in the Gothic, particularly when they have sought to gain emotional and narrative strength from the suggestions that "Stalin" may not, after all, be dead'.[31] Evgeny Evtushenko's 1962 poem 'The Heirs of Stalin', for example, chillingly suggests that the tyrant in the Mausoleum is not dead, only sleeping, gathering his strength for a new assault against Russia. Finally, one of the most popular Russian novels of the late and post-Soviet years, Mikhail Bulgakov's *The Master and Margarita*, is full of Gothic imagery. Written in the 1930s, the novel gained cult status in Russia when it was published in full, just before the Soviet Union collapsed. Much is made in recent Russian criticism of the esoteric and occult aspects of *The Master and Margarita*, but the motif of the severed head is also crucial, both to the plot and to the thematic material.[32]

As a version of 'what really happened', the Gothic horror version of Nicholas's death has no value. Yet as an expression of sublimated fears, it reveals the concerns of the White émigrés, the early Soviet radicals and the post-Soviet national patriots. Eager to believe the most horrific tales of the Bolsheviks' cruelty, émigré writers imagined Gothic scenes in which the severed head of the Tsar was displayed to the Bolsheviks or incinerated in the Kremlin. Fearful of the resurgence of capitalism, meanwhile, the early Soviet radicals despised such stories as fit only for the NEPmen – yet perhaps found them cathartic in the way in which they imagined the final disposal of the remains of Tsarism. For the post-Soviet national patriots, the Gothic horror version of the Tsar's death, with its fabrications about the Jewish ritual murder of Russia's Tsar, expresses their understanding of Russian history as a struggle between good and evil. Gothic fiction suggests an uncertain world, in which morality has gone astray. That it should be such a strong theme in the national patriotic version of the Tsar's death should alert us to the insecurities of that milieu.

5 False Alexeis

'How shall I tell you who I am? Can you prove to me who you are?'
(Anna Anderson/Anastasia, quoted by Michael Gray,
Blood Relative, 1998)

The Cossacks invented 'false Dmitris' by the dozen. But in August, 1607, the second Dmitri appeared. Who he really was is not known. . . . The name of Dmitri provided cover for the operations of a band of plunderers. For all the malcontents of society, however, he was the genuine Dmitri. Even Marina Mniszech [the wife of the first 'false Dmitri'] recognized him as her husband, and bore him a child. The nun Martha declared that he was indeed her child.
(Roland Mousnier, *Peasant Uprisings in Seventeenth Century France, Russia and China*, 1971)

In 1924 the peasants of the remote Siberian region of Barnaul realized that the Tsarevich had come to live among them. A young man named Alexei, from Biisk village, had been recognized as the heir to the Russian throne. From all the miserable hamlets of Barnaul region, the peasants – free men since two generations but Soviet citizens for only seven years – gave thanks for the miraculous survival of the young Romanov and tried to assist the heir. Tsarevich Alexei lived off the succour of these loyal subjects for almost two years, moving from town to town as word about him spread. He found shelter with religious communities, some of them parishes belonging to the Russian Orthodox Church, now under new political masters; others sectarians called Ioannites, who were loyal to the memory of Father John of Kronstadt, a priest venerated by Tsar Nicholas and the scourge of St Petersburg's revolutionaries.[1]

Alexei, the 'Tsarevich', was often seen in the company of his 'sister' Maria and her close friend 'Grand Duke Vladimir'. Sometimes they would be joined by another 'sister' Anastasia. The 'Tsarevich', 'Maria' and the 'Grand Duke' even went to Moscow together in 1926, to try and obtain an exit visa for Maria at one of the foreign consulates now reopened for business.

As the news spread through western Siberia that the heir to the Romanov throne had survived, the OGPU security police began to track the wanderings of the 'Tsarevich' and his associates. Shortly before Easter in 1926, Alexei returned to Barnaul from his unsuccessful trip to Moscow. But his hosts in Barnaul – followers of Father John – decided that he was too risky a guest and forced him to move to a village 200 kilometres away. They were right to be cautious, for later that year, alerted by anti-Soviet leaflets that were disseminating the rumour that the Tsar's children were now living in Siberia, the OGPU finally caught up with Alexei and arrested him.[2]

His real name was Alexei Ivanovich Shitov, and he was a peasant's son. In 1924, when he was discovered to be the Tsarevich, he had been working for the state trade department in Biisk. He had joined the Komsomol, the Communist Youth League, in 1920, making him at least 19 years old in 1924, since the Komsomol admitted young people from the age of 15. In 1924 Alexei would have been a young man of 19 or 20 years old, had he survived.

Shitov's pedigree as Tsarevich Alexei rested on nothing more than a physical resemblance to the boy killed in 1918 and the testimony of Maria, his would-be sister. The first person to recognize Shitov as the heir to the Russian throne had been his landlady in Biisk, Natalia Kusova. The young man had supposed at first that she was fussing over him because she hoped he would marry her daughter. But around Easter in 1924, Shitov had been at the home of a colleague from work, Nikolai Bushuev, whose wife was a friend of Natalia Kusova. The two women began to insist that Alexei Shitov must be his Imperial Highness the Tsarevich Alexei. Holding up a mirror to Shitov, they confronted him with his uncanny likeness to the boy pictured on the postcard photo-portrait of the Tsarevich which was one of their most treasured possessions. Angrily denying his royal birth, Shitov ripped up the postcard and left, swearing never to return. But a few days later he was back, unable to resist the pleading of Bushuev's wife who had visited him to retrieve her torn portrait of the heir. In the Bushuev household once again, he was introduced to a young woman dressed like a peasant who embraced him joyfully as her 'brother'. When Shitov bluntly denied any such thing she became hysterical, weeping and reproaching him for his cruelty. Bewildered and somewhat embarrassed, Alexei decided to humour this pitiful and evidently deranged young woman, whom his friends the Bushuevs called 'Grand Duchess Maria Nikolaevna'. It was a significant mistake. Having acknowledged her as his royal sister, he was to remain her associate until the OGPU arrested him two years later.

Maria Nikolaevna had a psychological hold over Alexei: 'she knew how to influence me, somehow', he later said in his statement to the OGPU. He had apparently come to believe that she really was the Tsar's daughter, even as he constantly tried to convince her that he was not the Tsar's son. Maria was, of course, a practised con-woman. When he was finally arrested some two years later, Shitov realized that the only way out of his predicament was to find Maria Nikolaevna and the man she had introduced to him as 'Grand Duke Vladimir', but by then Maria had disappeared. Although the OGPU eventually arrested her, neither they nor later researchers were able to determine who she really was, for she had no fixed address and used several different aliases adopted from stolen identity papers. The report on the case that the OGPU drew up in August 1927 listed her as 'Evdokia Mikhailovna Kovshikova-Chesnokova, a.k.a. Malyugina, a.k.a. Andrievskaya', but she was named by some witnesses in the case as 'Leonora Yurevna Doiskurdaite'.

Maria Nikolaevna survived on hand-outs from religious communities who thought they were helping the Tsar's daughter, and she seems to have roamed widely across Russia during her frequent absences from Alexei Shitov. It is possible he was not her only victim. As Grand Duchess Maria she skilfully played up what people expected to hear about her treatment at the hands of the wicked Bolsheviks. To the five nuns of the Trinity Convent in Sychevsk near Smolensk, for example (who were followers of Father John of Kronstadt), she told a melodramatic tale of torture and escape. The Tsar's family had fled from the underground room in their Ekaterinburg prison after a sympathetic guard had given Maria his keys, she told them, according to the nun Natalia Feodorovna, another witness in the Shitov case. Maria had been the last to leave through the underground passage, and the Bolsheviks had captured her and sliced off her breasts. She recovered in hospital and was discharged when a doctor put up bail for her. Meanwhile, the Tsar, the Empress and all the others had fled the country, she said, leaving only herself, Alexei and Anastasia in Russia.

This Anastasia – the third impostor in the Shitov case – was a nun from Sverdlovsk who seems to have been another of Maria Nikolaevna's victims. When Anastasia was introduced to her 'brother', Alexei Shitov, each believed that the other was the sibling of Maria Nikolaevna, but neither would admit to being a child of Nicholas II themselves.

It was to communities of Ioannite sectarians like the Trinity Convent nuns that Maria Nikolaevna first took Shitov in his persona as the Tsar's son Alexei. Perhaps she chose these communities because their eagerness to believe that the Tsarevich was still alive predisposed them to accept that Shitov was Alexei. Their traditions of charity also made them easy targets. The news that the imperial children had survived spread through the underground network that John of Kronstadt's followers had developed in order to evade persecution by the official Orthodox Church and the state. Shitov found himself welcomed, with all the respect due to the Tsarevich, by the Trinity Convent nuns and by other Ioannites in Barnaul, who were led by a man called Mikhail Karlenko. Other groups from the mainstream Orthodox Church joined the conspiracy to protect the fugitive Tsarevich. These included the parish of Father Fyodor Toporkov, one of the most popular and respected priests in Barnaul, whom the Ioannite leader Karlenko approached when Shitov had asked him to find a priest to hear his confession. Father Fyodor – also eager to find the Tsarevich alive – was taken in by Shitov, telling the OGPU later that he had 'found the "heir" to be just what he should be'.

Something in Shitov seems to have changed after meeting Maria Nikolaevna. His initial hostility to being recognized as 'Tsarevich Alexei Nikolaevich' softened and he no longer tried to deny that he was her brother. He began to attend church and he left the Komsomol 'because of his religious convictions'. He got used to being hailed as the Tsarevich and – not surprisingly – began to enjoy the adulation that this excited. The OGPU prosecutor reported that between the autumn of 1924 and the summer of 1925:

> All these [monarchist] people, having learned about the 'heir', tried to get to know him, paid him due respect and offered material help, in the hope that in time he would be returned to the Russian throne. . . .
> Shitov, having – as he put it – become accustomed to hearing himself talked about as the heir, kept quiet, paid visits to many people, and received the extraordinary attentions of all of them as his due.[3]

In the end, such adulation cost Shitov dear. In 1927 he was shot, together with 'Maria Nikolaevna', 'Grand Duke Vladimir' and six other people. Thirty-six more of those who had assisted the 'Tsarevich' were sentenced to prison terms or periods in exile ranging from ten to three years. The one person who was never found, strangely enough, was Anastasia.

Why did Shitov come to accept his new role? Was it just that he enjoyed the celebrity status? Or did he perhaps begin to believe that he really was Tsarevich Alexei? In post-revolutionary Russia – a time of fluid identities and status – it was not uncommon for people to transform themselves into someone completely different. This fluidity was encouraged by the Bolsheviks' project for remaking the old, enslaved man into a new being, free from the constraints of the past. The Soviet state in the 1920s established a framework for this through new social organizations, public celebrations and a radical education system which were designed to remould the population.

Like many teenagers in the 1920s Shitov had joined the Komsomol or Young Communist League. The leaders of this preparatory organization for Communist Party membership organized meetings and social events, and even staged alternative rites of passage, such as Red weddings and Komsomol funerals, which aimed to replace the old culture with a new Soviet one.[4] Shitov, however, found himself going in the wrong direction. Instead of becoming a member of the new society, he was impersonating the boy who embodied the old Tsarist ways. As Shitov absorbed the persona of the Tsarevich, he seems to have internalized these old values, even becoming sympathetic towards religion.

In fact, Shitov's resurgent religiosity and his ambivalence towards the Komsomol (which he left in 1926) was not so unusual in rural Russia in the 1920s. The local Komsomol groups were a type of heavily ideologized youth club, but most of the rural recruits just saw it as a way of quitting the village for a new life in the city. The Komsomol's ideological purity was also frequently sullied by the young men (mostly men) in its ranks who saw it not as a transmission belt between the Party and young people but rather as a way of rebelling against traditional forms of authority and as an excuse for socializing and getting drunk. Meanwhile, competing with the Komsomol for youth loyalties were religious associations which involved 'hundreds of thousands of young men and women ... genuine and truly voluntary youth movements that by far eclipsed the Komsomol as a social and cultural presence in the countryside'.[5] These associations were (at least in part) a manifestation of the 'Living Church' – a reformist movement in Russian Orthodoxy which was trying to make the Church more relevant to the people as well as more acceptable to the Soviet government.[6] Views on religion in the Communist Party and its associated organizations were becoming blurred in the 1920s as an influx of new members helped to turn the Party from a band of stringent revolutionaries into a mass movement. There were many new recruits who 'hedged their cosmological bets by accepting the general Bolshevik line but also retaining their religious attachments'.[7]

Remaking oneself in early Soviet Russia did not only mean superficial changes such as joining organizations like the Komsomol. Developing a new way of thinking – forging a 'new consciousness', in the Party's jargon – was also part of the project, a process so radical sometimes as to engender confusion about one's identity. A new consciousness might involve learning a new vocabulary in order to frame new thinking and a new morality: one historian has called this 'speaking Bolshevik'.[8] Yet the reinvention of the self could also be achieved far more simply: sometimes it meant adopting a new persona in order to benefit from the newly ordered hierarchies of Soviet society. Imposture for personal gain – as a way of making a living, in effect – was not uncommon in Soviet Russia in the 1920s and 1930s, not least because the circumstances were so propitious: 'a far-flung country with poor communications, traditional hierarchies upset, and a new elite recently recruited and without long-established ties is one of the perfect settings' in which to be an impostor.[9] Two of the favourite con-tricks in early Soviet Russia were the impersonation of officials and the claim of close kinship with newly famous Soviet heroes.

Of course, pretending to be an important official was not a new dodge in Russia. The plot of Nikolai Gogol's famous 1836 comedy *The Government Inspector* revolves around the mayhem caused in a corrupt provincial town by the arrival of the eponymous official, who is revealed in the end to be a minor clerk. And early Soviet satirical works such as Ilf and Petrov's *The Golden Calf* or Mikhail Bulgakov's early stories suggest that

86   False Alexeis

'there were numerous real-life "brothers of Lunacharskii", "descendants of Prince Kropotkin", and "grandsons of Karl Marx" traveling round the provinces and swindling local officials in the 1920s'.[10] As Shitov's story shows, there were also pockets of early Soviet society in which the impersonation of heroes from pre-Soviet times could be profitable, at least until the police caught up with you. Impersonating the Tsarevich, however, was doubly dangerous: not only was it defrauding one's victims, it also represented sedition of the new political order.

As soon as Nicholas II and his family were reported dead, there were sightings of them still alive. The Empress was said to have become a nun, the Tsar was a stoker aboard an American steamship, the whole family was seen in Moscow, Vladivostok, the Crimea, England and the Riviera.[11] In post-Soviet Russia, it is the self-proclaimed grandchildren of the Tsar – the children of Nicholas and Alexandra's son and daughters – who continue to affirm that the family survived the Ekaterinburg execution, and that – as their direct 'descendants' – they are the heirs to the Romanovs' throne and their reputed vast fortune. There are today enough children and grandchildren of Nicholas II 'clamouring for attention to fill a sizeable nursery', as Robert Harris writes of another survival myth, that of Adolf Hitler.[12]

In the West, the best-known Romanov impostor was for many years Anna Anderson, whose claim to be Anastasia was finally disproved by posthumous DNA tests in 1993, as we saw in Chapter 3. However, for several decades since the 1930s, this Polish peasant had encouraged her admirers and even some distant Romanov relatives in their belief that she was the Tsar's youngest daughter. Her motives are impossible to determine. Perhaps, like Shitov, she decided to humour people's mistaken convictions that she was a Romanov, and eventually came to believe it herself. The Anastasia story has spawned its own corpus of work, including at least two Hollywood movies and even a Disney cartoon in which assorted cuddly creatures rescue the Russian princess from the machinations of a hairy Rasputin.

There is no sign that the stream of Romanov claimants will abate. Playwright Edvard Radzinsky, whose fame as the author of *The Last Tsar* forced him to listen to numerous claims by surviving 'Romanovs', calls them 'a form of madness. Here in Russia,' he told *The New Yorker* journalist David Remnick,

> 'we had no way of knowing about Anna Anderson or the Greta Garbo movie about Anastasia. People wanted a miracle, a fairy tale. So these rumors are out of control, as they were at the time of the "false Dmitri" who pretended to the throne in the seventeenth century.* We are a country of impostors.'

---

* A series of pretenders between 1604 and 1613 (the 'Time of Troubles') who, with Polish backing and some popular support, claimed to be the Tsarevich Dmitri (son of Ivan the Terrible), who had died mysteriously in 1591.

Nicholas Romanov, the head of the (genuine) wider Romanov family's descendants, exclaims with similar exasperation: 'If we were to list all the people who have emerged over the years claiming to be the sons of Tsarevich Alexei, or to be Anastasia herself or her daughters, it would be longer than the telephone directory!'[13]

The most frequently impersonated member of the imperial family has always been Tsarevich Alexei. This was the case even before the mass grave was opened and his body found to be missing. The champion of one would-be 'Alexei' has counted 'at least twenty' Alexeis or children of Alexei currently under discussion in the media, not including his own candidate.[14] Alexei is a prime subject for imposture for several reasons. The impersonator's task was much easier because Alexei was only 14 years old at the time of the execution, meaning that his physical appearance would have altered considerably in later years, and certainly more than that of the other victims. Moreover, if he had survived the massacre, the former Tsarevich's future would have been wide open. His world turned upside-down, Alexei would have been forced to reinvent himself and could have become virtually anyone, meaning that almost any male of approximately the right age could claim to be him.

The impostor claiming to be Alexei also has the most to gain. In the unlikely event of a monarchical restoration in Russia, Alexei or his direct descendants would be the legitimate heirs to the throne. They would also have the best claim on the fabled vast Romanov fortune, huge sums of money and bonds stashed in foreign banks and awaiting their rightful owner. Of course, we immediately run into the problem of separating state funds from personal money: when discussing the Romanov fortune, '"Tsarist gold" all too quickly became shorthand for "Nicholas's own money"'. A careful investigation has suggested, moreover, that the family's private investments in Russia were drawn down to pay for their upkeep in Siberia, and that their personal funds abroad were inherited by Grand Duchess Xenia (Nicholas's sister) in 1933. This left perhaps £100 million (in 1918 figures) of state money in tsarist accounts abroad, most of which was subsequently disbursed by the UK and US governments to tsarism's creditors, and which anyway could only be claimed by a restored tsarist regime. There was, quite simply, no 'tsarist gold' to be claimed – not that this has ever dissuaded impostors from trying.[15]

'False Alexeis' began to pop up in Russia from the moment the Tsar's family disappeared. In 1919 General Diterikhs, who was investigating the Romanovs' deaths, summoned the Tsarevich's tutor of French, Pierre Gilliard, to identify a pretender. The possible Alexei had been found in the Altai region of Siberia, where a few years later Shitov would attract the attention of the OGPU. Perhaps the unfortunate Shitov, when he later appeared, stirred local memories of this earlier impostor. This 'Alexei' eventually confessed to impersonating the Tsarevich, but he bore a resemblance that was close enough at least to the photographs of the

Tsarevich to convince the local peasants. Gilliard, who had known Alexei as well as any person still alive in 1919, was not impressed.

> He [the General] informed me that he wished me to see a young boy who was claiming to be the Tsarevich. I knew in fact that for some time the rumour of the survival of the heir had been spreading at Omsk. He was said to be in a village of the Altai. I had been told that the population had demonstrated in front of him with enthusiasm . . . the schoolchildren had made collections in aid of him . . . and the postmaster had, on his knees, offered him bread and salt. . . . General D. had asked me to come, reckoning that my evidence would be conclusive. The door of a neighbouring room was opened and I could look, without him spotting me, at a young man, larger and stronger than the Tsarevich, who seemed to be about fifteen or sixteen years old. By his sailor's outfit, the colour of his hair, and the way he wore it, he did look a bit, very vaguely, from a distance, like Alexei Nikolayevich, but that was as far as any resemblance went.[16]

Some thirty years later, yet another Alexei was discovered in a psychiatric hospital in Petrozavodsk in north-west Russia. The case only came to light some decades afterwards with the publicity generated by the news of the Romanov grave. In his 1993 bestseller about the Tsar's death, Radzinsky included letters from medical staff at the Petrozavodsk hospital, convinced that they had come across a surviving Alexei. Going by the name of Semyonov, the patient in question had been born in 1904, and had suffered from 'persistent hematuria' (bleeding). When consultant psychiatric Professor Gendelevich was asked to examine the patient, he found him able to answer 'utterly accurately and without the slightest thought' any question about the layout of the Winter Palace, court protocol, the various branches of the dynasty and so on. Gendelevich was shaken to discover that his patient also had an undescended testicle, like 'the dead heir Alexei'. Semyonov had been sent to the hospital after an episode of psychosis during which he had repeatedly cursed 'someone named Beloborodov' (the name of the chairman of the Urals Regional Soviet in 1918). At the time, in the late 1940s, Professor Gendelevich found it safer to recommend returning the patient to the prison camp from which he had been brought to the hospital, since his delusions would have attracted the unwanted attention of the Moscow authorities. Semyonov-Alexei was duly reabsorbed into the oblivion of the camp system, a place where, ironically enough, it was safe to acknowledge his identity. In the camp, as a fellow-prisoner recalled, 'all the prisoners called him "the tsar's son," and they all believed it absolutely'.[17]

What might the motives be for claiming that one started life as Tsarevich Alexei? Shitov – as far as we can judge from the evidence in the prosecutor's report – was deluded by 'Maria' and perhaps, in the culture of remade identities, came to believe the story himself. Semyonov was probably psychologically disturbed. Mercenary motives have been important of course, but not all the 'false Alexeis' have been fortune-hunting impostors. A Freudian explanation might be helpful. The psychiatric condition of believing oneself to be of aristocratic descent – despite one's humble circumstances – was classified by Freud in 1909 as 'family romance'.[18] The patient comes to believe that he or she is really the offspring of royalty or the aristocracy, but has been placed as a foster-child in the humble family in which he or she was brought up. This fantasy of replacing one's parents by people of a higher social standing was, Freud concluded, a neurotic reaction to slights or disappointments, born both of envy and a desire for revenge on a disappointing mother and – especially – father. Combined with the 'quite peculiarly marked imaginative activity [which] is one of the essential characteristics of neurotics and also of all comparatively highly gifted people', the neurosis produces a belief in the patient that his real parents were glamorous or wealthy individuals and not the mundane characters with whom he had grown up. Freud found that people suffering from this condition would often latch on to figures of high standing in their local communities as their real parents. However, the Romanovs also seem to have become a prime target for this delusion, perhaps because they are such well-known figures and their image is surrounded by such romance and glamour.

We only know about Shitov, Semyonov and Gilliard's peasant boy as impersonators of Alexei because of the fluke of historical record. Gilliard realized this: 'Chance had put in my way the first of the innumerable claimants,' he wrote, 'who for many years, no doubt, were to be an element of trouble and agitation in the breasts of the ignorant, credulous mass of the Russian peasantry.'[19] How many other 'Alexeis' faded away unnoticed, unable to articulate their story or find others to tell it? And what is our response to those whose stories we do learn? For without physical proof of identity (and no claimant has been able to provide this), these would-be Alexeis can make an impact only by the way in which their stories are told. We can read Shitov's story, but only in the form of the prosecution evidence prior to his criminal trial which assumes from the start that he is an impostor. Yet were we to have heard the case for Shitov's identity as 'Tsarevich Alexei' made by the con-woman 'Maria Nikolaevna', we might think otherwise about him.

The Alexei narratives produced by claimants or their champions occupy a space between fiction and history. Whether they are genuinely deluded or deliberate liars, they present the narratives as the true record of what happened to the Romanov heir following the massacre in the Ipatiev House. And despite all the tall stories and bogus claims there remains a broad receptiveness to such narratives – if they are presented with sufficient dramatic credibility – because we want to believe in the survival of

90 *False Alexeis*

Nicholas's son. Why should this be so? Perhaps because otherwise the horror of that night would be too great to bear; perhaps because we do not want the romance of the Romanovs' story to have ended. The pretender to the throne has to look right, however. A comment posted on the discussion board of one Romanov website moans: 'Why cant [*sic*] any of the pretenders ever be pretty like the girls were?'[20]

The least convincing claimants may be found on the internet, a refuge for cranks of all kinds. Two bizarre recent examples come from women in the USA claiming to be the daughter, or stepdaughter, of 'Tsarevich Alexei'. The presentation of these web pages alone puts one instantly on guard: they are the equivalent of letters written in green ink. In the first case – above a photograph of her family who appear to be wearing pyjamas – the website's creator alleges that her father, 'Alexei Romanov', was held at 'Area 51', the notorious secret US military facility some ninety miles north of Las Vegas which has become associated with the US government's 'cover-up' of alien visits and UFO sightings. In block capitals, the website screams:

ON JULY 8, 2000, THE LAWLOR FAMILY, WERE BRUTALIZED BY THE LAX AIRPORT POLICE, THE BEVERLY HILLS POLICE, THE DELTA AIRLINES, AND UCLA HARBOR GENERAL HOSPITAL. WE WERE HEADED TO RUSSIA FOR THE SECOND TIME THIS SUMMER. IT HAS COME TO OUR ATTENTION THAT MY FATHER SEQUESTERED IN AREA 51 FOR MANY YEARS, WAS ALEXEI ROMANOV, THE SON OF THE MASSACRED ROMANOV FAMILY.

It goes on to claim that there are '46 Fabergé eggs missing' and US$440 million, which now rightfully belong to the Lawlor family. In case visitors to the site were in any doubt, it also assures them that 'We are now designated the Imperial Russian Romanov Royal Family'.[21]

The creator of the second website claims: 'Alexei Romanov was my step father, my father died when I was 9 months old and my Mother never even dated until she met Alexi [*sic*] when I was around 5 years old.' The site is scattered with black-and-white photographs of Alexei living in Cleveland, Ohio, which is where he supposedly settled after arriving (it is unclear how) in the USA. None – even those of the young 'Alexei' – bears the slightest resemblance to the Tsarevich. This rambling website also alleges a cover-up by the US, or possibly the Russian, government, or possibly both:

You see they were worried that Alexi would be found so officals [*sic*] of that time came up with a great plan.
    They hide his identity in prison by saying he had commmited [*sic*] a murder and was given life, but he was never there only his name.[22]

Before the advent of the internet, would-be 'Alexeis' had to find alternative forms of publicizing their claims. A man in Scottsdale, Arizona, who died in 1986, marketed a brand of vodka named 'Alexis': a 'special distillation to the specification of Prince Alexis Romanov, who is a direct descendant of Tsar Nicholas Romanov, Tsar of All the Russias'. This entrepreneurial charmer used his 'Romanov' ancestry to good effect. He was married five times, and popular in Scottsdale where his social circle maintained that this polo-playing prince, who suffered eleven broken bones for his sport, was the haemophiliac Alexei.[23] Yet another 'son' of the dead Tsarevich, called Nikolai Dalsky, from Noginsk, near Moscow, had himself crowned as Tsar Nicholas III in December 1996 by some Orthodox priests. They were subsequently excommunicated.[24]

Four more 'false Alexeis' follow in this chapter. These have all found champions (in two out of the four cases it is the claimant's son) and have published a book (or in one case a highly professional website) detailing their story. My choice to present these false Alexeis in more detail was, therefore, to some extent self-selecting, because they provide the fullest material. At the same time, none of these pretenders could be said to have a solid claim, and none provides the hard evidence – the positive DNA matches with the bones of Nicholas and Alexandra – that would melt public scepticism. What they do provide, however, are structured narratives rather than bizarre assertions. The stories of these Alexeis open up inventive possibilities for his future life, had he survived. The Tsarevich becomes, variously, a schoolteacher in provincial Russia, an aristocratic playboy in Ireland, a defector from the Polish intelligence service, and an Estonian émigré dancing teacher in Canada. The problem with the stories, however, is that their authors try so desperately to insist upon their heroes' identity as Alexei that their narratives – however well structured – collapse under the lack of evidence.

The Russian Romanov

Alexei barely survived the shooting of the Tsar's family. There was no plot to save him and no rescue attempt, but by chance the corset of jewels he was wearing prevented the bullets from penetrating his body. He lost consciousness as the shooting went on, and the executioners assumed that he was dead, like all the others. He was dumped on to the truck that took the bodies away from the Ipatiev House. He regained consciousness under pouring rain in the back of the truck, tumbled off the vehicle and hid under a bridge. The boy crawled away in the darkness, following the railway line around Ekaterinburg to Shartash station about four kilometres away. As dawn broke, he had to escape a seven-man patrol of soldiers, who began stabbing at him with their bayonets and drove him into the nearby forest. They pushed him into a pit which formed part of a mine-working, but he managed to scrabble into a side passage and escape the shrapnel from the grenades that they threw in after him. He was wounded only in the heel.

About four hours later, salvation arrived. Two of the guards in the Ipatiev House – the Strekotin brothers, Aleksandr and Andrei, who had become fond of the boy – had come looking for him. 'Uncle Sasha' and 'Uncle Andryusha' saved me, he would later recall.[25] Andrei Strekotin had been in the house during the shooting, and had been stationed on guard around the bodies when Yurovsky had called off the guards who were looting them. Strekotin had realized at this point that Alexei was still alive among the pile of corpses that was being taken away on the truck. Later on, the Strekotins slipped away from the Ipatiev House to look for Alexei, as they had learned from Yurovsky that two of the bodies had slipped off the truck. They came across the boy, as they expected, near Shartash station, and pulled him out of the pit. They took him to the dressing station at Shartash, where a doctor decided against amputating the boy's wounded leg. This was probably Doctor Derevenko, who had cared for the Tsarevich throughout his life and was living in Ekaterinburg. Knowing that Alexei had, on several occasions, been close to death yet had pulled through, despite his haemophilia, Derevenko patched him up and saved his leg.

The Strekotin brothers then arranged for Alexei to be taken to the house of their friend, Ksenofont Filatov, a shoemaker, who lived in the town of Shadrinsk, 230 kilometres away. Mikhail Gladkikh took him there. Gladkikh was the brother-in-law of Ksenofont Filatov, and knew the Strekotin brothers. All four, in fact, were good friends from their service in the Imperial Russian Army: they may even have planned to rescue the Tsarevich long before the execution took place, since 'having sworn an oath before the tsar, they were duty-bound at his command to save his son'.[26] They also probably knew the Tsar's children quite well. In 1915, Ksenofont Filatov's brother, Andrei Filatov, had spent some months recovering from war wounds in the hospital at Tsarskoe Selo, where the Tsarina and her two elder daughters sometimes appeared to nurse the wounded soldiers.

In Shadrinsk, Alexei was adopted by Ksenofont Filatov and assumed the identity of Ksenofont's son Vasily, who had recently died of Spanish 'flu. He was about the same age as the Tsarevich, having been born in 1907 (Alexei was born in 1904). The boy's wounds were healed by peasant remedies – raw meat and tinctures from pine trees – and Alexei melted into the anonymity of provincial society in the Urals.

In 1921, Ksenofont Filatov and his wife died, leaving Vasily-Alexei an orphan. Although he registered at the local polytechnical college in February 1921, he never attended classes, since the college was staffed by teachers from Ekaterinburg who might have recognized the youth. Like so many unclaimed children of the time, he moved from orphanage to orphanage all over the Soviet Union. In 1930, however, he settled near Tyumen in Siberia, where he trained to become a teacher. Tyumen had been Rasputin's home town.

In 1953, by now middle-aged, he married his colleague Lidiya Klimenkova (who had been born in 1917). They moved to Orenburg and had four children: a son, Oleg, and three daughters (Olga, Irina and Nadezhda). Every summer Vasily and Lidiya took the children to St Petersburg where they stayed with Lidiya's sister. Oleg Filatov recalls being shown the Cathedral of the Saviour on the Blood, built on the spot where terrorists had thrown a bomb at the carriage of Alexander II; and the room in the Winter Palace where the Provisional Government had sat, paralysed, as the Bolsheviks took power. 'Those people removed the tsar, and it led to civil war', Vasily would tell his son. For his father, wrote Oleg, it was 'as though there were no other place on the earth or in Russia' than the former imperial capital.[27] When he grew up, Oleg himself moved to St Petersburg where he worked for fifteen years in the customs service at Pulkovo airport, and then found employment in a bank.

In 1967, Vasily Filatov retired from teaching, and in 1970 he and his wife moved to the warmer climate of Astrakhan on the Caspian Sea. Vasily had never spoken of his true identity until 1983 when a family reunion was arranged to greet Oleg's new wife Anzhelika. In the garden, with his children around him, Vasily began to talk with his new daughter-in-law about his origins and, eventually, about the terrible night in 1918 when he had escaped the Ipatiev House massacre. At last the mystery of his father began to fall into place for Oleg Filatov. Vasily, the son of a shoemaker, who had become a geography teacher in a village school, knew several European languages and was schooled in classical music. He had tried to convey to his son the riches of Russian culture and tradition, and to give him the skills of statecraft.[28] The scars on his body and his chronic poor health also made sense at last. The secret had to be kept, however, until after Vasily's death, which came in 1988 from heart failure. At that point, and as Soviet censorship began to dissolve, the Filatovs decided to tell their father's story.

The principal motivation came from Oleg Filatov and his wife Anzhelika, to whom Vasily had first opened the secrets of his past. Oleg collaborated with three 'scientists' (a forensic expert, an atomic physicist who had taken holy orders, and a handicapped ski champion) on a book that compared photographs and the handwriting of his father with those of the Tsarevich. The events of that night were reconstructed to prove that Alexei had survived the carnage. The book was published in 1998 in Russia just in time for the reburial of the Romanov remains in St Petersburg, and the English version soon followed, published as *The Escape of Alexei, son of Tsar Nicholas II*.[29]

Through ingenious speculation and pseudo-scientific detective work, Oleg Filatov has managed to turn his father's typical Soviet biography into the miraculous survival of the Tsarevich. When evidence did not fit, the sources about the Romanovs were filleted to support the case. For example, Vasily Filatov's grandchildren were tested in the late 1990s for haemophilia, and all the results were negative, showing with more than 90 per cent certainty that their grandfather did not suffer from the disease either. Oleg Filatov concludes from this that the Tsarevich's haemophilia was a rumour, 'a political intrigue, directed at proving that the Romanov family was dying out and it was necessary to renew it by liquidating its sick members and replacing them by more healthy family specimens'.[30]

The book met a mixed reception. Harry N. Abrams, its English-language publisher, came away from a meeting with Oleg Filatov 'convinced he was a rational being', but others have been less enthusiastic. David Remnick, writing from Moscow for the *New Yorker*, said the book was 'fairly dull and absolutely unconvincing', and Orlando Figes described it as full of 'tedious homely reminiscences'.[31] *The Escape of Alexei* was followed in 2000 by Filatov's own book (in Russian), *The Story of a Soul, or, the Portrait of an Age*. Oleg Filatov has become something of a local celebrity in St Petersburg since making the switch from bank clerk to unacknowledged son of Tsarevich Alexei. With the publication of the books about his father, Filatov has worked hard at media interviews to stake his claim; he appears on the 'Personalities of St Petersburg' website; he has also made sure to change his appearance, abandoning his thick-rimmed spectacles and growing a beard and moustache in the style of Nicholas II.[32] What motivates him to pursue one of the more preposterous Romanov survival stories? Could it be money? When Remnick interviewed him in 1998 shortly before the burial of the Romanov bones, they visited the Cathedral of Sts Peter and Paul together. 'Oleg was quiet for a long time,' writes Remnick, 'and then he started talking about money. He said there were "huge" accounts abroad: twenty-seven billion dollars in the United States, he guessed, six billion in a bank in Tokyo – all money that belongs, by rights, to the Romanov family.' Remnick concluded, however, that it was not the money that had prompted Filatov's obsession: rather, it was his 'fantastic, if mistaken, loyalty to his father'.[33] For Filatov, this loyalty has meant personal loss. He became estranged from his son by his first marriage, because the boy's mother feared 'traumatizing' him with his father's obsessions about his royal ancestry.

The Irish connection[34]

Alexei did not die in Ekaterinburg. He and his family were rescued in a daring aerial mission organized by Lt. Col. Joseph ('Joe') Whiteside Boyle of the Canadian militia. Joe Boyle, of Northern Irish extraction, was the perfect choice to get the Romanovs out of Bolshevik Russia. He was a dashing intrepid hero, a gold-mine millionaire, and the lover of Queen Marie of Romania. The Romanovs' rescue had been set in motion by a clandestine network of European royalty anxious for their Russian relatives, but the only trace of this network is an empty Foreign and Commonwealth Office file in the Public Records Office at Kew labelled 'The Trust of

Kings'. Boyle offered a large bribe to the Bolsheviks – who were permanently short of funds – to get them to release the Romanovs. He then organized their transport by air south from Ekaterinburg to the British base at Kotelnikov in the Caucasus. He was assisted in his mission by Captain George Hill, a British intelligence agent in Russia, and possibly by another British agent, Richard Meinertzhagen, who left in his diary a tantalizing report about a mishandled aerial rescue that had managed to save one of the Romanov girls.[35]

Once the family had been flown out of Bolshevik-controlled Russia, the seven Romanovs had to go their separate ways: as a family group they were too recognizable. Alexei's escape route was on board HMS *Marlborough*, the British warship that sailed from the Crimea in April 1920, taking Russia's aristocracy (including Alexei's grandmother, Dowager Empress Marie) out of danger. On 11 April 1920 the *Marlborough* docked in Constantinople, where Alexei joined the thousands of Russian refugees fleeing their homeland.

Now he received a new identity for his new life from the mysterious figure of Nikolai Couriss, who was at the time manager of the American Red Cross warehouse in Constantinople and who would regularly cross paths with Alexei in the future. Couriss turned Tsarevich Alexei into Nikolai Chebotarev, a young member of the minor Russian aristocracy. The alias was ingenious. The name 'Nikolai' recalled his father the Tsar; and a boy called Grigory Chebotarev had been one of Couriss's closest childhood friends in Tsarskoe Selo outside St Petersburg, where Alexei too had been raised in the Alexander Palace. Grigory Chebotarev was the son of Valentina Chebotareva, a nursing sister in the military hospital at Tsarskoe Selo that the Tsarina herself had founded. By giving Alexei a new identity that was at once both false and genuine, Couriss had ensured that he would have a new background that was familiar to him yet sufficiently distanced from the Tsar's family not to arouse suspicion.

The task of protecting the identity of the former Tsarevich was entrusted to other members of the European establishment. 'Nikolai Chebotarev' received his Nansen passport for displaced persons from London later in 1920 with the endorsement of Sir Percy Loraine. This British diplomat later employed Chebotarev as his private secretary in Egypt, and in 1946 found him a job in the translation service of the new United Nations Organization in New York. Before this could happen, however, Alexei-Chebotarev – who had been 15 when he left Russia – had to finish his education at one of the new schools established in Yugoslavia for the numerous children of Russian émigrés flooding into that country. He moved on to France, staying with aristocratic Russian families in Nice and Paris, spent a year studying science at the Sorbonne, and then worked briefly in a chemist's shop.

In 1929 he was in the Middle East with Sir Percy, and thereafter spent much of his time in Northern Ireland, where he resided permanently from

1939 until leaving for New York in 1946. He lived first at Moyallon, the manor house of Hilda Wakefield Richardson, and then, when Mrs Wakefield Richardson died in 1942, at Croft House in Holywood, residence of the flamboyant Russian émigré Natalie Karaulov Cooke.

Rumours about the true identity of Nikolai Chebotarev had begun to circulate among Russian émigrés in France since at least 1925, and they persisted throughout his time in Ireland. However, the connections between the people who surrounded him there suggest that there was a well-managed conspiracy among them to maintain absolute silence about his true identity. This conspiracy protected him against possible Soviet assassination attempts, and also preserved the reputation of the House of Windsor, which had been instrumental in bringing him out of Russia but had simultaneously appropriated the Romanov jewels that, by rights, belonged to Chebotarev and the other Romanovs who had escaped with him.

Chebotarev's life in Ireland was spent mainly among Russian émigré aristocrats; but the house parties of Hilda Richardson and Natalie Cooke were also frequented by upper-class Englishmen (and Ulstermen) with extreme right-wing sympathies. Among them was the ubiquitous Nikolai Couriss, who had opened a Russian language school in the 1940s in Collon, just over the border from the residences of Mrs Richardson and Mrs Cooke. In the 1930s Couriss moved easily between the worlds of the pro-fascist English upper class and the Republican Irish, and it is quite possible that he was working simultaneously for the British, the Soviets, the Nazis and the IRA. His language school was staffed by the eccentric Russian émigrés who populated such establishments in the days before the formation of Russian language departments in Britain's universities, and its alumni included the Cambridge quartet of Soviet spies.

Natalie Cooke's house also provided Chebotarev with a safe place for meetings with the love of his life. This was Princess Marina of Greece, daughter of Princess Helen of Russia and Prince Nicholas of Greece. When they were children (Marina, born in 1906, was some two years younger than Tsarevich Alexei) there had been an understanding between their parents that they would one day marry. Their fathers were personal friends; more importantly, Marina was of royal descent and Orthodox, both prerequisites for any Romanov bride. In the 1920s, Marina and Chebotarev had belonged to the impoverished Russian aristocracy in Paris. However, with Chebotarev unable to reveal his royal identity, his intended bride contracted a different dynastic union in 1934, marrying the Duke of Kent, younger brother of Edward VIII and George V. It was not a happy match. Yet despite three attempts by Marina to divorce the bisexual transvestite Duke, the marriage lasted until 1942 when he was killed in a plane crash, leaving her free to return to Chebotarev. Their assignations had to be secret – the Windsors were not about to relinquish the Duke's widow to the 'unknown' Russian émigré Chebotarev, perhaps afraid that he would reveal his real identity and claim the Romanov jewels – and for a while Ireland was their refuge. They were finally married by an Orthodox priest sometime in 1946 and attempted to elope to the USA where Chebotarev was about to take up his UN posting. However, when she attempted to embark by ship for America, an agent of the British royal family brought Marina back forcibly to London.

The Windsors could not prevent Marina and Chebotarev from producing a child, however. This baby – a boy – was born sometime in late 1948 or early 1949. Marina's pregnancy had been kept secret by judicious couture and well-timed vacations. The child's parentage could never be acknowledged, since as the son of Tsarevich Alexei and Princess Marina – a woman of impeccable credentials for the strict rules governing the tsarist succession – this child was the legitimate heir to the Russian throne. The baby was farmed out to surrogate parents in Northern Ireland, to a respectable, but perfectly ordinary, lower-middle-class couple who had been found through contacts of Hilda Richardson. Mr and Mrs Gray did not go through a formal adoption process: the baby's papers were forged by the resourceful Nikolai Couriss.

Nikolai Chebotarev died in 1987 and was buried as Nicholas Tchebotareff, in Holt, Norfolk, where his niece Iya and her English husband John Hulbert lived (Iya was the daughter of Grand Duchess Marie who had also been rescued from Russia).

It was his unacknowledged son who discovered Chebotarev's true identity. The boy had been raised as plain Michael Gray in a stultifyingly quiet village in the 1950s in Northern Ireland. His true ancestry – so glamorous, so extraordinary, and so unlike the world of his surrogate parents – was concealed by a 'dense and suggestive web of personal connections' which Gray's resourcefulness and persistence finally unravelled. Unfortunately for him, uncovering these connections brought him to personal ruin. His career as a college principal in Northern Ireland ended ignominiously in late 1994 when he was dismissed, ostensibly for having failed to pay some telephone bills. A disciplinary hearing was called, which included a lot of questions about his 'Russian research'. Gray expected to receive a summons from the House of Windsor which would try to blackmail him into dropping the subject: 'I would be told that if I kept quiet I might be allowed to hang on to my job, where I would continue working all the hours that God sent and as a result my "research" would grind to a convenient halt.'[36] His determination to discover his true parents also led to personal ruin, when his 'surrogate father' – the man who had brought him up – tried to persuade Gray's wife to leave him and to take their two children with her. In 1995, the father died, cutting his 'adoptive son' out of his will.

This is the story that Michael Gray revealed in his book about his 'real' ancestry, *Blood Relative*. To make his case, Gray produces a mass of circumstantial evidence and a complex knot of connections – both real and speculative – between its characters, making his book read at times like Burke's *Peerage*. 'Michael Gray', however, is also a pseudonym, masking the real identity of the author: William Lloyd Lavery of Lisburn, County Antrim, retired principal of Lurgan College. Lloyd Lavery's family was not pleased to hear that William believed he was the Tsar's grandson, and cousin Noel Lyle insisted that one of the photographs in the book, which allegedly showed the author as a baby with the Russian aristocrats who had been intermediaries in placing him with his lower-middle-class surrogate Irish parents, was in fact a photograph of William with Aunt Henrietta and a family friend.[37]

If 'Michael Gray' was really the son of Nikolai Chebotarev and Princess Marina of Greece – both of them real figures – his identity as a Romanov still depends on Chebotarev's being the Tsarevich. Chebotarev never claimed that that is who he was. Gray has had his nuclear DNA tested against that of the skeletons of Nicholas and Alexandra. There was a close correlation, but not an exact match, certainly not enough to prove a grandparental relationship. Rather than accept this, however, Gray ingeniously explains the discrepancies by suggesting that the Tsar's bones are decoys. Perhaps the bones of the Tsar in the Ekaterinburg grave are actually those of his brother, Grand Duke Michael Alexandrovich, who was assassinated by the Bolsheviks in 1918 and whose body was never found?[38]

What were Lloyd Lavery's motives for embarking on such a wild claim? In an appendix to his book, Gray delicately touches upon the subject of the Tsar's fortune, suggesting that 5,500 kg of gold (worth £92 million) remained in Baring's Bank until the bank crashed in 1995. There may also have been other deposits. But who are their legal owners? The case of Lloyd Lavery-Gray also seems to be a classic example of 'family romance'. He writes, rather plaintively, that he wanted a resolution to the 'inchoate feeling of not belonging, of being different' that had tormented him from early childhood. What could be more glamorous, more romantic, and yet more certain than that he was the son of Tsarevich Alexei and Princess Marina? 'In the end,' he wrote,

> the quest which has taken me so far and led to my meeting so many people has brought me right back to myself. . . . Both as a detective story and as a human tragedy, it is a compelling tale. If I am not their son, then who on earth am I?[39]

The Polish spy[40]

Alexei did not die in Ekaterinburg. On the night of 16 July 1918 the whole family was smuggled out of the Ipatiev House in disguise. Alexei, still recovering from malaria, was drugged with a sleeping draught and hidden in a trunk. Nicholas, Alexandra, Marie and Alexei made up one party, escorted by Yurovsky in a convoy of trucks; the other three daughters left separately the same night. Having travelled by different routes to evade capture, the family was finally reunited many months later in Warsaw.

Alexei set up home with his parents and Maria in the city, and the other girls settled elsewhere in Poland; in 1922 Anastasia emigrated to the USA.

The Romanovs had escaped execution through the intervention of the Japanese Emperor Yoshihito who wanted to make amends for the disgrace brought on his country during his father's reign in 1891, when a fanatic had attacked the then Tsarevich Nicholas during his state visit to Japan, wounding him on the forehead. Using Yurovsky as an intermediary, the Japanese offered Lenin and Trotsky a huge bribe to secure the Imperial Family's release, on the condition that they should construct new lives and never reveal their true identity. So the former Tsarevich Alexei grew up in Poland with the name of Michal Goleniewski. He enlisted in the Polish army in 1945, and by 1955 had become a lieutenant colonel in Polish intelligence. His father, ex-Tsar Nicholas, who had also adopted the name Michal Goleniewski, died in 1952, adamant until the last that his real identity should remain unknown. Just ten months after this, Stalin died and the former Tsarevich saw his chance. He realized that he would need the support of the Americans if he were ever to retrieve his birthright, and he prepared to defect to the USA.

With his army rank, Goleniewski had access to secret information from the Eastern Bloc's intelligence agencies, and from April 1958 he began to supply information to the Americans in the form of microfilmed documents and under the code-name 'Heckenschiitze'. In December 1960 he defected, requesting asylum for himself and his East German fiancée Irmgard in West Berlin. In January 1961, in Washington DC, Goleniewski began a debriefing that lasted for three years. His information helped the CIA uncover more than a dozen of its agents who were also working for the KGB in Europe. He also 'gave up MI6 spy George Blake, Harry Houghton, and West German BND spies Hans Felfe and Hans Clemens'. In fact, he had been 'the most productive agent in the entire history of the CIA, revealing more than a dozen Soviet moles'.[41] Throughout his debriefing, Goleniewski said nothing about being the Tsarevich. Only when his supply of intelligence information began to dry up did he reveal the most remarkable secret of all: his true identity.

The CIA thereafter cut contact with Goleniewski, unable to be seen to endorse a spy who was making the bizarre claim to be the son and heir of Russia's last Tsar. Rebuffed by the CIA, Goleniewski went public in March 1964 with an interview on the Barry Farber radio show, after which the CIA let it be known that their former informer had gone insane. His case received additional publicity from the energetic New York newspaperman Guy Richards, who had uncovered Goleniewski's story and come to believe it, despite the CIA's spoiling operation. In 1966, Richards produced a book, *Imperial Agent*, a breathless account of his sleuthing to uncover Goleniewski's mysterious past. Providing the obligatory scientific proof (in days before DNA analysis) was a former CIA man Herman E. Kimsey, who claimed in 1965 to have identified Goleniewski as Alexei

100 False Alexeis

from medical records, blood tests, handwriting analysis and other evidence. Goleniewski soon became a New York celebrity, as Romanov fever gripped the town and 'New York City took Goleniewski to its heart as only New York can'.[42] He gave media interviews and produced a newspaper column for the *New York Daily Mirror* entitled 'Reminiscences of Observations' under the byline 'His Imperial Highness Aleksei Nicholaevich Romanoff, Tsarevich and Grand Duke of Russia'.

Goleniewski also persuaded a clergyman from the Russian Orthodox Church Outside Russia, Father Georgii, to endorse his imperial identity by marrying him and Irmgard according to the rites of the Russian Orthodox Church and to name the groom on the marriage certificate as Alexei Romanov, born 12 August 1904, son of Nicholas Romanov and Alexandra Romanova (née von Hesse). The ceremony itself, on 30 September 1964, was conducted with little decorum, however, as the bride was heavily pregnant. She was rushed to hospital from the church, where she gave birth to a girl, Tatiana Alexeevna Romanova. Soon after this, Fr Georgii came to regret his eagerness. He refused to baptize the baby girl, and claimed to have agreed to name the bridegroom as 'Romanov' only because 'in Russia there are as many Romanovs as in the United States there are Smiths'.[43]

Shortly before his marriage, Goleniewski had held an emotional reunion with his 'sister' Anastasia. On this occasion, too, the confirmation of his true identity had proven evanescent. 'Anastasia' had been living in Chicago as Mrs Eugenia Smith, and in November 1963 had published her 'memoirs'.[44] On 18 October, her story was on the cover of *Life* magazine as 'A New Case of a New Anastasia'. At Goleniewski's request, Eugenia Smith's New York-based publisher, Robert Speller, arranged a reunion between brother and sister on New Year's Eve in 1963. It was an emotional scene, conducted mainly in Russian, and tape-recorded by the publisher. Many tears were shed by 'Anastasia' when she recognized 'my brother, Alexei. My darling.' But although both became habitués of New York society, they did not become as close as siblings might have been expected: perhaps their stories did not tally.[45]

Richards's involvement in the Goleniewski case set him searching for other evidence of a Romanov rescue, and made him credulous in the extreme. It was Richards who swallowed the hoax diaries, published in 1920 by James P. Smythe as *Rescuing the Czar: Two authentic diaries arranged and translated*. On the basis of these 'authentic diaries', Richards in 1971 produced his *Hunt for the Czar*, and in 1975 his even more absurd *The Rescue of the Romanovs*. In fact, Goleniewski's real father turned out to be not Tsar Nicholas II but Michal Goleniewski, an alcohol distiller, born in Russia in September 1883 and buried (as Goleniewski said the Tsar had been) in the village of Wolsztyn, south-west of Poznan, in May 1952. His real mother was Janina Goleniewska, née Turynska. Their son, also called Michal, was born in 1922.[46] As the Tsarevich had been born in 1904, this near twenty-year discrepancy had been something of a complication for Goleniewski in his impersonation of Alexei. The middle-aged Pole – as even Guy Richards admitted – 'seemed slightly younger than the 60 years he would have to be if he were, indeed, the Grand Duke [Tsarevich] himself. But then lots of people *do* look younger than they are.' Goleniewski's own explanation was lame: 'For most of a decade I was an invalid and never grew at all.'[47]

What were Michal Goleniewski's motives for impersonating the Tsarevich? Guy Richards found him 'brilliant, exasperating, imperious, waspish, sarcastic, tactless, blunt and articulate'. Richards was also convinced 'beyond doubt' that he was 'not only sane but very bright'[48] – qualities essential for successfully perpetrating a deception that brought him real benefits. Goleniewski certainly hoped to put in a claim for the millions of tsarist dollars allegedly deposited abroad, but the 'exclusive knowledge' about the tsarist gold, which he claimed had been passed on to him by his late father, transpired to be 'the result of an intelligent sifting of the leading newspapers'. On the other hand, a British intelligence officer sent to evaluate his claim reported: 'In my view . . . I did not feel that he was trying to provide himself with extra income. He actually believed in his Romanoff connection.'[49] In New York society, he found an environment eager to believe in him as the long-lost Tsarevich. His moment of fame was brief, however, and in the end Goleniewski, having squandered his genuine value as a spy, became a fictional creation, although not his fantasy of the Tsarevich. A US official who interviewed him over a citizenship application described him as 'a creature who probably doesn't exist at all – a dashing, highly literate British cavalry officer'.[50]

The Royal Oak[51]

Alexei was not shot along with his family. But, to make it appear as though he had been murdered, the Romanovs' executioner Yakov Yurovsky carried out an elaborate scheme, which had been devised some months – or even years – earlier between the remnants of the Imperial Dynasty and the Bolsheviks. For Lenin had decided that, even if the rest of the family was to be executed, he needed to keep the Tsarevich alive as a bargaining chip in case the Revolution should fail, and by the summer of 1918 this appeared to be a real possibility. The Bolshevik leader had, in any case, been forced to spare Alexei under the terms of a secret codicil to the Brest Litovsk Treaty, which had concluded Russia's involvement in World War I in January 1918. The German government had demanded the Bolsheviks surrender some members of the Russian Imperial Family as part of the peace deal. After all, Tsar Nicholas and Kaiser Wilhelm were cousins.

So when the time came to kill the Romanovs, Yurovsky stage-managed the execution to keep Alexei and one of the Grand Duchesses alive. He carefully selected a specific victim for each member of the firing squad and preloaded some of the guns with blanks so that the two children could escape death. But Yurovsky's Bolshevik masters needed the world to believe that Alexei had died along with the others, so when the boy was evidently still alive after the shooting had stopped, Yurovsky fired his gun – loaded with blanks – straight at Alexei's right ear. The boy lost consciousness, and permanently lost hearing in that ear, but he survived the massacre.

Two of the Romanov victims left the cellar alive. Now there was the problem of ensuring that they remained so. In the Koptiaki forest the truck carrying the bodies became mired in the path. As the burial party struggled to free it, a local farmer called Johann Veerman arrived with his cart. Yurovsky ordered him to lift two of the bodies off the truck to lighten its load, and to take them to a mine shaft nearby. Three days later Alexei woke up in Veerman's farmhouse.

The apparently fortuitous meeting between Veerman and Yurovsky's truck was all part of a master plan. The choice of the farmer to implement the second part of the scheme to keep Alexei alive in secret had been dictated by two factors. First, Johann Veerman's wife had been born Paula von-Benckendorff-Känna, a distant relative of Count Paul Benckendorff, the Grand Marshal of the Imperial Court of Nicholas II. Second, the Veerman's son Ernst, who had been born in 1905, just one year after the Tsarevich, had died of typhoid in 1917. Alexei could begin his new life with this adopted family by assuming the identity (and the all-important documents) of their dead son. As Ernst Veerman, the former Tsarevich spent three years living on a farm near Koptiaki, close to the secret grave of his birth family, waiting and hoping for the time when the Bolsheviks would be driven out and he could resume his rightful place.

It was not to be. In 1921 the Veermans left Russia. They moved to Estonia during that former province's short period of independence, and settled in the capital, Tallinn. For the time being, the former Tsarevich gave up hope of ever ruling Russia. 'Ernst Veerman' served in the Estonian army, and then went into journalism. He soon became editor-in-chief of seven Estonian newspapers, and adopted the pen-name of Heino Tammet, or 'Henry Oak' in English. The pseudonym was a clue to Ernst Veerman's desire one day to regain his rightful place as Russia's tsar, for Henry signifies 'royal ruler' and 'Oak' hinted at the possibility of restoration by recalling the story of how the future Charles II of England had once been a fugitive and had escaped capture by hiding in an oak tree.

In 1944 Heino Tammet fled Nazi-controlled Estonia by arranging a marriage of convenience with a Finnish woman. He then moved to Sweden where he was divorced and contracted a second, genuine marriage. He and his new wife had two sons together, and in 1952 they emigrated to Canada. Heino had still not revealed his true identity, even to his wife, and their marriage ended a few years later under the strain of this concealment. By now the former Tsarevich was making a living as the manager of a dance studio south of Vancouver. In 1956 he met his third wife, the 16-year-old

Sandra Brown, and in July 1960, when Sandra was 20, they were married in a Russian Orthodox ceremony.

Finally, 'Alexei' was able to reveal who he really was to the sympathetic figures of his new young wife and her parents, Gill and Dorothy Brown. Gill had perceived early on that his daughter's suitor was probably someone of noble birth. Dazzled by Heino Tammet's old-fashioned courtesy and refined manners, his European accent and the occasional remark such as 'as a youngster I lived in many houses', the teenage Sandra and her parents swallowed his story. Tammet also possessed a diamond-studded decoration, an eight-pointed silver star, resembling the Prussian Order of the Black Eagle which had belonged to the Tsar. He used to wear it on his dinner-jacket, and had himself photographed in 1967 wearing evening dress and a monocle and with the Order pinned to his left jacket pocket. He never told Sandra the secret of how the jewel had come to be his, but it must be assumed that the decoration had been passed on to Alexei when he was given into the Veermans' care, and was intended to be a sign of his true identity when the time came to reveal it.

Alexei went public about his identity for the first time in 1971. His hand had been forced by the furore around the impostor, Polish intelligence agent Michal Goleniewski, who was also claiming to be the Russian Tsarevich. He wrote to the British Prime Minister Edward Heath, expressing his concern that the British government was about to recognize Goleniewski's fraudulent claims. The following year, as 'Alexei Romanov', he sent a telegram to Queen Elizabeth II offering condolences on the death of her uncle the Duke of Windsor (Edward VIII), who was Alexei's second cousin. While the British establishment was reluctant to concede that Alexei had survived, the Russian Orthodox Church Outside Russia was more accommodating. Sandra, who had converted to Russian Orthodoxy after their marriage in 1960, was given the name Alexandra Romanova by Father Andrei Somow, and shortly afterwards was presented to Metropolitan Theodosius of the ROCOR as Alexandra Romanova.[52] However, Alexei's two sons from his second marriage were unwilling to accept that they were the grandsons of the last Tsar of Russia, and rejected their father's claims.

On 26 June 1977 Alexei died after a long battle with the rare disease of chronic myelomonocytic leukaemia. This blood disorder causes easy bruising and bleeding, accompanied by high temperatures, but the attacks are short-lived and followed by sudden remission. The symptoms match exactly those manifested by the young Tsarevich.[53] He was buried in June 1977 in Burnaby, British Columbia, under the name of Alexei Heino Tammet-Romanov. Sandra Romanov completed her late husband's autobiography, but refused to release it for publication without guarantees that it would not be altered. However, she found a staunch supporter for Alexei's true identity in John Kendrick, an 'investigative reporter' based in Vancouver, who has worked diligently on his research of the Tammet-Romanov case since the first DNA tests were performed on the 'Ekaterinburg remains' in 1993. In 1997 Kendrick submitted his story of Alexei to numerous newspapers, but none bar the *St Petersburg Times* would publish it.[54] He was also rebuffed by the geneticists who were testing the Koptiaki bones when he asked for comparison tests with Tammet-Romanov. Undaunted, Kendrick set up several very professional websites through which he continues to campaign for Heino Tammet to be recognized as the Tsarevich Alexei.

Reviewing Oleg Filatov's story about his father 'Tsarevich Alexei', Orlando Figes asks in exasperation: 'What makes myths more saleable than history? Why do we persist in believing fantasies in the face of all the facts? It is simply inconceivable that anyone survived that brutal execution.' Figes is much exercised by the money to be made from writing such 'myths'. Filatov 'may not win the Romanov fortune,' he complains, 'but if the publicity his publisher has lavished on this book is anything to go by, he will make a fortune from book clubs.'[55] Figes's palpable irritation misses the point, and besides he surely need not fear that Filatov's book will outsell his own massive histories of the Revolution and of Russian culture. Money has certainly been a motive for impersonating Alexei, even when the impostor has coyly denied an interest in the Romanov fortune; but celebrity status and the psychological need for 'family romance' are also powerful impulses. To reinvent oneself as a direct descendant of Nicholas II may be extreme, and is almost always unconvincing, but the urge to tell and retell our histories, re-creating an identity to suit the circumstances of the moment, is a common human characteristic.

The fact remains, however, that not a single one of these 'false Alexeis' withstands close scrutiny. Figes again, brutal, but correct: 'None of the claimants has not turned out to be a crank. All their stories have broken on hard facts.' Why, then, do people persist in believing the claimants, at least to the extent of buying their books? The answer is, in the end, because we want to believe. We want the story to continue, not to stop dead in the basement room of the Ipatiev House. The stories about the survival of Tsarevich Alexei tempt our desire for narrative completion: the young hero is deposed from his rightful position, he must conceal his true identity and overcome hardship and trials, the cathartic resolution sees him restored to his true self. This is a classic pattern of fairytale and legend. Ultimately, however, the Alexei stories fail to satisfy because their execution is lamentably weak. No claimant has ever produced evidence for being the Tsarevich that can withstand even cursory scrutiny; and without this, the narratives drown in a wash of speculative maybes and conspiracy theories.

Perhaps, if we want narrative completion, we should give up reading these attempts at 'history' and turn to novels where the author has more licence to manipulate character and plot and can make a better job of telling the story. There have been numerous examples, of varying success. One of the most recent, Robert Alexander's *The Kitchen Boy*, uses some historical detail about the Romanovs' execution to make the escape of Alexei and his sister seem plausible but, crucially, subtitles his book 'A novel of the Last Tsar'.[56] Alexander imagines an ending that did not happen, but that might have happened, and tells it in an engaging way. The survival narratives of Kendrick, Richards, Gray, Filatov *et al.* also imagine an ending, but dress it up as fact (although they cannot compensate for the total absence of any hard proof of identity). Worse still, the authors of these narratives are so desperate to prove their claims that they let the 'facts' get in the way of telling their stories.

6   Tsar Martyr

[I]n every case I have also been concerned about the patient's soul. This vindicates my last decision, too, when I unhesitatingly orphaned my own children in order to carry out my physician's duty to the end, as Abraham did not hesitate at God's demand to sacrifice his only son.
(Letter from Dr Eugene Botkin, physician to Nicholas II, begun 3 July 1918, Ipatiev House, Ekaterinburg)

The Emperor [in Constantinople] accompanied the Russes to the church, and placed them in a wide space, calling their attention to the beauty of the edifice, the chanting, and the offices of the archpriest and the ministry of the deacons, while he explained to them the worship of his God. The Russes were astonished and in their wonder praised the Greek ceremonial. . . . 'We knew not whether we were in heaven or on earth. For on earth there is no such splendor or such beauty, and we are at a loss how to describe it.'
(The story of the Christianization of Rus', from the Primary Chronicle (AD 978–980)

In the summer of 1995, a Moscow priest narrowly escaped spending several nights in the police cells, thanks only to the miraculous intervention of Nicholas II. This is his story:

> In the middle of August 1995, when I was serving as a deacon in one of the churches near Moscow, I was returning one day from my dacha to the city. At the intersection of two busy metro stations – Lenin Library and Borovitskaya – where there's a particularly brisk trade in dirty magazines, I got into an argument with the newspaper sellers and tore up several copies of the *AIDS-Info* paper. I was arrested by the police and, when I refused to compensate the stall holders for the damage, I was put in the KPZ* at Komsomolskaya station.

---

* Kamera predvaritel'nogo zakliucheniia: preliminary detention cell in a police station.

The senior officer shut me in a cell, threatening among other things to 'stick me in the loony bin', and saying that he would come back for me on Monday (this was Thursday).

Saturday being the Feast of the Transfiguration, the next evening, Friday, there would be a night vigil and I would not be there. . . . In deepest gloom, I started to recall the holy music that I knew by heart. I remembered the anthem to the Tsarist Martyrs: 'Deprived of Your earthly kingdom . . .' and sang it several times, seeing before my eyes a kind of icon, on which was depicted the whole family of the last Russian Tsar wearing traditional Russian dress.

Not more than half-an-hour went by. The cell door opened, and I was escorted to the head of the department. His tone now betrayed a kind of comprehension for the motives of my 'crime'. He had my statement in his hands and asked me to explain it. It was clear that, on the whole, he agreed with me, but wasn't allowed to admit it. Questioning me sympathetically about my wife, children, and work, as if trying to understand me better, he brought out my confiscated possessions, one by one. After this, he gave me some kind of form to sign and released me. It was completely unexpected: half-an-hour earlier he had been screaming at me, whilst the other police chief (from Borovitskaya station) was making excuses along the lines of 'he would have let me go but the wheels were already turning', and now a complete change of tone, even a kind of respect. It felt like a miracle.

Father Aleksei Kagirin, Moscow oblast.[1]

The politics of canonization

In the 1990s Russia's religious media was full of stories like Father Aleksei's in which the dead Tsar miraculously intervened in ordinary people's lives. They were broadcast on the conservative religious radio station Radio Radonezh, they were published as cheap booklets sold at church kiosks, and they were assiduously collected and disseminated – electronically and in print – by those who supported the canonization of Nicholas II. This campaign eventually forced the Church hierarchy into action. The massive ceremony in August 2000, which canonized Nicholas, Alexandra and their children, along with over 1,000 other 'new martyrs' of the twentieth century, represented the formal acknowledgement of the Tsar's saintly standing. Yet numerous parishes and monasteries in Russia had already accorded him this status without waiting for the go-ahead from the Holy Synod.

The question whether Nicholas II should officially be canonized had been under discussion in the Moscow Patriarchate (the Russian Orthodox Church establishment in Russia) since 1990 at least. The Patriarchate had already begun to be more daring in its choice of candidates for canonization, as it sought to re-evaluate the Church's relationship with the state. During the Soviet period this relationship had been one of mutual dependence, but by creating 'new martyrs' out of the priests and believers who had perished in the Gulag, the Patriarchate could recast the Church purely as a victim of the Soviet state. The Bishops' Council of October 1989 decided to canonize Patriarch Tikhon, who had led the Church during the very early Soviet period and who symbolized the ROC's resistance to Soviet policies on religion. Tikhon's canonization took place during the *glasnost'* and *perestroika* era, when a reassessment of the Soviet past, sanctioned by Communist Party General Secretary Mikhail Gorbachev, allowed the injustices of Soviet policy towards the ROC to be publicly acknowledged.

By creating new saints the ROC could also reconfigure its role within post-Soviet society and proclaim its new political values. Of course, making saints for political reasons was nothing new for the ROC, and Nicholas II, ironically enough, had been responsible for the most politicized set of canonizations prior to the post-Soviet explosion of new saints. In the two decades between 1897 and 1917 the Church had performed six canonizations, compared with a total of four during the previous two centuries: a rash of new saints brought about largely at the insistence of Nicholas II in a failed 'naïve attempt to "resacralize" the religious foundation of autocracy'. The canonizations were actually a dismal failure: not only did they alienate non-Orthodox minorities and the powerful secular elites, but they also failed to speak to the religious sensibilities of the masses.[2] In the post-Soviet era, the ROC had to choose saints according to which political values it wished to promote. It faced the dilemma of whether these should be based upon the comparatively liberal and ecumenical stance of priests such as Aleksandr Men' – a popular advocate of scholarly Orthodoxy, who was murdered in 1990 – or upon the Orthodox fundamentalism whose spokesman was Metropolitan Ioann of St Petersburg, notorious for his anti-Semitic diatribes.[3] Depending upon which route it took, the Church would find its new saints predominantly either in the anti-Soviet 'new martyrs' or in the 'Black Hundred' priests of the late Imperial period.[4]

Nicholas II, were he to be canonized, would be a more polysemantic figure than either of these, and posed intractable problems of historical interpretation for the Moscow Patriarchate. For all that he had undoubtedly been a victim of Bolshevism, the last Tsar had also been an arch traditionalist. As late as 1998, Father Vsevolod Chaplin, the Director of Public Relations in the Moscow Patriarchate's Department for External Church Relations, was still saying that canonizing the last Tsar would be a dangerous move because it could be construed as indicating Church sanction for the principles of autocracy.[5] Moreover, for the ROC the Imperial era represented a largely negative period of state control over its freedom of action, starting with the abolition in 1725 by Peter the Great of the Church's semi-autonomous government – the Patriarchate – and its replacement by the Holy Synod, an institution subordinate to the state. Indeed, Nicholas II, for all his vaunted religiosity, had done as much as any of his ancestors to curtail the Church's autonomy. In 1907 he quashed the Church's attempts to modernize itself and prohibited the priests and hierarchs who were seeking Church 'renewal' (*obnovlenie* – a thoroughgoing institutional and theological reform to meet the demands of a modernizing society) from convening the Local Council (*Pomestny Sobor*) that they had been planning – with the permission of Nicholas II – since 1905. The Sobor was the Church's highest governing council, comprising both lay and ordained members, but it had not been summoned since the mid-seventeenth century. Ironically, had Nicholas allowed its convocation in 1907, it might have revived the Church's moribund institutions and given it greater strength to resist the anti-religious policies of Russia's new Bolshevik rulers.[6]

For the ROC in the 1990s, then, Nicholas II ought to have been a deeply ambivalent figure, but post-Soviet Russia's near-universal sentimentality about the last Tsar and his family blurred the historical record. The pressure for canonization proved irresistible. The campaign was co-ordinated by the Church's vocal fundamentalist wing which was concentrated predominantly in St Petersburg. Here, in the early 1990s, a group of conservative and anti-Semitic publicists had coalesced around Metropolitan Ioann. Their leading figure was Konstantin Dushenov, head of Ioann's 'press service', who ghost-wrote the flood of books and articles published under Ioann's name and also wrote for secular conservative nationalist politicians, including the Communist Party chairman Gennady Zyuganov and former Russian vice-president Aleksandr Rutskoi. The press service put out a newspaper, *Rus' pravoslavnaia* [*Orthodox Rus*], which contained virulent denunciations of Church reformers, secularists and Jews. Dushenov called his newspaper 'a mechanism of Orthodox propaganda to awaken the Church'.[7] During 2000, *Rus' pravoslavnaia* campaigned furiously for the Tsar's canonization as a way of returning Russia to the path of spirituality and autocracy. It argued that the Church ought to endorse an authentically Russian form of government. Metropolitan Mefody of Voronezh and Lipetsk, for example, wrote that the Tsar's canonization would represent 'the *return* of our Fatherland to that historical path of development which was halted by the bloody madness of "militant materialism"'.[8]

Rus' pravoslavnaia also used the campaign for the Tsar's canonization to undermine the moderates in the Moscow Patriarchate. The paper accused 'a small but extremely active group of people who detest Nicholas II' of opposing the canonization 'ever more desperately as the popular veneration of the Holy Tsarist Martyrs gains in strength'.[9] Naming names, *Rus' pravoslavnaia* whipped up hostility against some of the ROC's leading moderates for 'procrastinating' over the canonization issue. The paper pointed specifically to three powerful figures in the Moscow Patriarchate: Metropolitan Vladimir (Kotliarov), successor to the late Metropolitan Ioann in the St Petersburg diocese who had angered the fundamentalists by reversing Ioann's position on numerous issues; Metropolitan Yuvenaly of Krutitsy and Kolomna, chairman of the Synodal Commission for the Canonization of Saints; and Metropolitan Kirill of Smolensk and Kaliningrad, head of the Church's Department of External Relations. Metropolitans Vladimir, Yuvenaly and Kirill – wrote *Rus' pravoslavnaia* – constituted 'a narrow circle which has practically usurped the government of the Church ... They are desperately trying to support the heresy of ecumenism and are organising the persecution of supporters of Orthodox purity.'[10]

'Ecumenism' had been a major target for the Orthodox fundamentalists from *Rus' pravoslavnaia* since at least the mid-1990s. For them, the concept meant undermining Russia's unique global mission, and subordinating the Church to non-Russian leadership. In fact, suspicion about ecumenism – the idea of Christian unity – was widespread even among the moderates in the Church. The basic conservatism of its hierarchy led the ROC to shun the Protestant-dominated World Council of Churches in the late 1990s, because the 'preoccupations' of this body with interfaith communion, feminist language, women priests and gay rights held nothing of relevance to Russian Orthodoxy.[11]

Thus, by the end of the 1990s the Moscow Patriarchate was facing increasingly well-organized opposition to any further delay in turning the Tsar and his family into saints. There was another argument in favour of the Tsar's canonization that the Patriarchate had to consider: Nicholas II and his family had already been made saints by the Russian Orthodox Church Outside Russia (ROCOR) in 1981. This church had been founded in 1921 – initially with the blessing of Patriarch Tikhon – by members of the White emigration, but it had broken with the ROC in Russia after the latter had reached an uneasy accommodation with the Soviet government in 1927 under Tikhon's successor Metropolitan Sergi [Stragorodsky].[12] With the demise of the Soviet Union, the ROCOR had stepped up activity in Russia, and ROCOR publications, which were fairly widely available, contributed to the popular pressure for Nicholas's canonization by the Moscow Patriarchate. Many believed that the Tsar's canonization would bring the two wings of the Church closer together, and perhaps even facilitate their merger.[13] On the negative side, it was becoming clear by 2000 that continued procrastination could lead some of the ROC (Moscow Patriarchate) parishes within Russia to defect to ROCOR.

The ROC's Jubilee Bishops' Council of August 2000 endorsed a lengthy report by the chairman of the Synodal Commission for the Canonization of Saints, Metropolitan Yuvenaly, who explained why the Moscow Patriarchate now believed that the Tsar and his family should be canonized. Yuvenaly's key arguments focused on the popular support for canonizing Nicholas. 'The work of the Commission was absolutely free from any political pressure from any side,' he stated at a press conference marking the conclusion of the Council. 'At the same time,' he went on, 'the Commission did not consider it possible to ignore the opinion of dozens of thousands of citizens and organisations who supported in their appeals the idea of the glorification of the last Russian Emperor and his family among the holy passion-bearers.' The Commission insisted, however, that this was not an endorsement of autocracy: Nicholas was to be canonized not for his status as tsar, but for the manner of his death. For although the Commission recognized Nicholas II's personal piety – indeed, the piety of his whole family – it was more equivocal about his record as Tsar: while laudable, this 'did not contain sufficient grounds for his canonization'. It was, rather, the way in which the former Tsar and his family had conducted themselves in captivity that had prompted the Commission to regard them as saints: their patient suffering during their imprisonment of 'all the trials sent from above', their 'genuine striving to embody in their lives the commandments of the Gospel', and their 'amazing nobility and purity of spirit'.[14]

The Commission decided, however, that the Tsar and his family would be canonized 'as holy passion-bearers' [*strastoterptsy*] rather than as saints [*sviatye*]. This hair-splitting distinction was meant to circumvent the crucial theological objection that the Tsar's family had not died as martyrs for their faith and therefore did not deserve canonization. No one could ignore their political role and argue that they were killed only because they were Christians. By making them 'passion-bearers', the Commission skirted this problem and placed the Tsar firmly within a specific tradition of Russian sanctity that pertained particularly to the ruler. Metropolitan Yuvenaly explained: 'In the liturgical literature and saints' lives of the Russian Orthodox Church, the words "passion-bearer" have come to be applied to those Russian saints who, imitating Christ, patiently bore physical and moral suffering and death from the hands of their political opponents.'

The concept of 'passion-bearer' began with the first national Russian saints, Princes Boris and Gleb, who died in 1015 at the hands of their brother Sviatopolk in an internecine dynastic conflict, and were canonized in 1072. The medieval hagiographies (saints' lives) of Boris and Gleb highlight both their refusal to resist violence and their joyful acceptance of suffering in imitation of Christ. For the first time in hagiographical literature, these qualities were considered sufficient to merit the subject's canonization.[15]

The Moscow Patriarchate's contortions to justify canonizing Nicholas and his family naturally involved a selective reading of the evidence. (The diaries of Nicholas and Alexandra alone show that the Romanovs did not bear their captivity without complaint.) However, the theological arguments for canonizing the Tsar were of little interest to the vast majority of the ROC's adherents. Even those not convinced by the flood of 'miracles' attributed to the dead Romanovs were sufficiently swayed by the general sentimentality about the last Tsar and his family to support their canonization without worrying about the shaky theology and the historical falsification.

The predominant view of Nicholas was that he was a 'good man'. In the hagiographical literature about the last Tsar that appeared around the time of his canonization, the dominant theme was the contrast between Nicholas's elevated position as Tsar and his humble and family-oriented lifestyle. Of course, hagiography is a genre in which the subject is presented in conformity with an established pattern, and Nicholas's hagiographies conceptualized him as a saintly medieval Russian prince – a 'passion-sufferer' like Boris and Gleb – both in his life and the manner of his death. They say nothing about Nicholas's youthful indiscretions with ballet dancers, and his uproarious conduct as a junior army officer. They focus exclusively on the Tsar as a family man – dutiful son, uxorious husband and doting father – and as a devout Orthodox Christian. They also emphasize Nicholas's personal modesty and generosity, and his patriotism and love of Russian culture. The hagiographies emphasize his qualities as a peacemaker and defender of Russia's traditional form of government – autocracy and *sobornost'* (personally managed collective government). Nowhere is there a hint that Nicholas II ruled Russia during a period of massive social upheaval, or that his actions as the last representative of an outmoded form of autocratic government accelerated the process of disintegration.

A pamphlet published in Moscow in 2001 in both Russian and English epitomizes this vision of Nicholas. Entitled 'The Life of the Holy Royal Martyrs of Russia', it was compiled by Yury Balovlenkov from unnamed sources (actually, the propaganda of Nicholas's reign).[16] 'From his youth,' begins the pamphlet, 'Nicholas was exceptionally pious. . . . He began and ended each day with prayer. He knew the order of the church services well.' Nicholas was also an impressive scholar, who 'amazed his teachers with his extraordinary memory and outstanding capabilities. . . . He was deeply knowledgeable of Russian history and literature, and as a profound expert in the Russian language, he shunned the use of foreign words.' He was generous and charitable: 'He alleviated the plight of the imprisoned and cancelled many debts, while providing substantial assistance to scientists, writers, and students. . . . The Tsar was not mercenary. He gave generous help from his own resources to all in need, irrespective of the amount requested.' Meanwhile, he himself lived very simply. 'His clothes were often mended,' recalls a servant of the Tsar. 'His suit went back to the time when he was still a cadet.' He was a model father: 'The Tsar and Tsarina reared their children in devotion to the Russian people, and carefully prepared them for future labour and struggle. . . . The imperial family led a withdrawn life. They did not like formal ceremonies and speeches, and etiquette was a burden to them.' He was also a model ruler, guided by religious principles: 'The Sovereign realized the necessity for the rebirth of a Russia based upon the spiritual foundations of Holy Russia'; and a wise military strategist: 'the Sovereign, as commander in chief, possessed valuable qualities: great self-control, and a rare talent for making decisions both quickly and soberly under any circumstances.' In the manner of his death, the Tsar imitated Christ, and sacrificed himself for his people: 'The Tsar and his family set out on the way of the cross to Golgotha. . . . The Sovereign hath taken upon himself the guilt of the Russian people. The Russian people are forgiven.'

This presentation of Nicholas is found not only in overtly religious literature, but even in secular biographies of the last Tsar. For to conceptualize Nicholas as an exculpatory sacrifice for his people confers upon him a nobility which eradicates the shortcomings of his over-privileged life. The conclusion of a recent Russian study of Nicholas II by conservative historian Aleksandr Bokhanov shows to what extent the image of the Tsar-as-saint has infected academic histories.

> His [the Tsar's] murder was a profoundly political act. Alexandra Feodorovna was quite right when she said that Nicholas 'embodies Russia'. He remained a national symbol, a sign of Russian tradition, a living example of the great empire. Convinced internationalists destroyed Russia's link with its past. ... Nicholas II and the tsarist family drank the bitter cup of their fate to the last drop. They experienced every imaginable and unimaginable unhappiness and disappointment on earth, and even their fiercest enemies could have added nothing to it. By the tragedy of his life and death, the emperor redeemed his witting and unwitting, real and imagined mistakes and errors.[17]

This vision of Nicholas II was so ubiquitous that critiques of the Tsar's canonization barely figured in the Russian media. One of the few that did appear came from émigré historian Dmitry Pospielovsky. He was not bound by the obligation of unanimity that gagged those members of the Holy Synod who may also have felt uneasy about canonizing Nicholas, and he published articles in the Russian and émigré press arguing against Nicholas's canonization. Pospielovsky pointed out that the Holy Synod was being disingenuous in claiming that Nicholas was being canonized as a Christian and not as a Tsar. In fact, it was nationalistic pressure to glorify the 'monarchist myth' that had swayed the decision, and the Holy Synod was playing to a constituency of support composed of:

> people with little or no church experience, or if priests then either very unenlightened ones who live more by myths than thoughts, or very politicized nationalists of a red-brown [communist-fascist] hue who, for all their education, have forgotten that before the face of God 'there is neither Greek nor Jew'.[18]

Pandering to this constituency, warned Pospielovsky, was undermining the Russian Orthodox Church's chances of revival and reform. In any case, there were few enough grounds on which to canonize Nicholas for his Christian faith. The Tsar had not led a model Christian life. He drank and smoked excessively and – far worse – he had been largely indifferent to the sufferings of his people. In his diaries, Pospielovsky noted, Nicholas would write: 'Went out for a stroll with my rifle. Shot a little cat.' Imagine the icon of '"Saint" Nicholas,' wrote Pospielovsky, 'with a rifle, a dead cat, and a shot of vodka, not forgetting the cigarette dangling from his mouth.'[19] Moreover, the Synod was ignoring Nicholas's cavalier disobedience to the Church, a disobedience that had manifested itself in his decision to abdicate, which, strictly speaking, contravened his coronation oath, and also in his 'betrayal' of the Church by disallowing the convention of the 'renewal' (*obnovlenie*) Local Council in 1917.

The canonization of Nicholas was 'sainthood-lite',[†] grumbled Pospielovsky.[20] And the Holy Synod's decision to canonize only the Tsar and his family and not the servants who had been slaughtered with them was morally as well as theologically objectionable. The Synodal Commission on Canonization had argued that the servants had followed the Tsar into exile out of a sense of duty and therefore did not deserve to be made saints. Pospielovsky found this extraordinary: the Tsar – who had had no choice – was to be made a saint, whereas his servants – who had been free to leave, yet chose to accompany their master to imprisonment and death – were not to be glorified. 'How can we describe this decision other than as political-ideological and class elitist?' asked Pospielovsky.[21]

The bodies of the saints

Paying scant regard to the arguments of academics like Pospielovsky, the Jubilee Bishops' Council of 2000 went ahead and canonized the Tsar. Along with the Imperial Family, 1,154 people became saints in the ceremony of 14 August 2000, 1,090 of them classed as Russia's 'new martyrs' who had perished during the Soviet repressions. They did not include Dr Botkin, Anna Demidova, Trupp or Kharitonov: the four servants who had been shot together with the Romanovs in the Ipatiev House.

The ceremony in Moscow was a glittering performance, the kind of *son et lumière* spectacle at which the ROC excels, with the vast gilded arena of the Cathedral of Christ the Saviour as the backdrop. The hulking reappearance of this Cathedral – a replica of the nineteenth-century building dynamited by Stalin – on Moscow's skyline in the 1990s underlined the post-Soviet Russian state's determination to appropriate the cultural symbols of Imperial Russia. It made a forceful statement, too, about the new relationship between state and Church. This relationship went beyond symbolism: funds for the Cathedral's construction had come from state subventions, including a tax break for the ROC for – of all things – tobacco imports.[22]

The canonization ceremony for Nicholas and his family was the ROC's riposte to the interment of the 'Ekaterinburg remains' two years previously in St Petersburg. After the Russian government Commission had ruled that the bones were, indeed, those of the Tsar and his family and servants, a

---

† *oblegchennaia sviatost'*.

ceremony was organized to rebury the bones. But this occasion was not the grand church spectacle that the Russian state had expected. Neither the Patriarch nor any other senior member of the ROC attended the ceremony to reinter the bones in St Petersburg's Cathedral of Sts Peter and Paul in July 1998; indeed, the Holy Synod decided that the ceremony would be conducted by the Cathedral's lowly dean, Archpriest Boris [Glebov]. Meanwhile, Patriarch Aleksii II and the senior church hierarchy presided at a simultaneous service of commemoration for Nicholas II, held in Moscow.

The Patriarch's decision to boycott the reburial ceremony persuaded President Boris Yeltsin to do the same, and it seemed that the occasion would be an underwhelming affair, devoid of dignitaries from either Church or state. At the very last minute, however, on the advice of the doyen of Russian historians Dmitry Likhachev, Yeltsin changed his mind, prompting a mad rush by ministers and state functionaries to join in too. The behaviour of these officials during the ceremony contravened all the strict etiquette of church ritual – how to make the sign of the cross, how to light a candle, what to wear (women may not wear trousers and must cover their heads) – making the grand occasion something of a farce. *Moscow News* described the scene:

> Nearly all of Russia's VIPs were making the sign of the cross, not always sure about the sequence, and stealing glances at what their counterparts were doing. They were handing each other funeral tapers over the heads of the people standing next to them and lighting them as they would cigarettes from one another's light. On the first day of the burial ceremony, Culture Minister Natalia Dementeva wore a trouser-suit to the church, and on the day of the burial forgot to wear a black suit, or at least wear a black veil over her head.[23]

Although a great number of Romanov descendants attended the reburial – only the family's ostracized branch that claimed the non-existent throne for their Eurotrash teenager 'Grand Duke' Georgy was absent, gracing instead the Patriarch's service in Moscow – there was an air of improvisation about the ceremony's staging. It appeared to have been done on the cheap. The joke going around St Petersburg was that the Tsar's reburial would cost less than the party to mark Prime Minister Chernomyrdin's retirement. Even the coffins were paste and plyboard affairs with fake marbling, and had been made child-sized (1.2 metres long) to save money.[24] These gaffes were in sharp contrast to the meticulously staged ceremonies of canonization two years later in Moscow.

Even what lay inside those small coffins was still disputed. The Church did not agree with the government Commission that had decided once and for all that these were the bones of Nicholas II, his wife, three of his daughters, his doctor, and three servants. The Holy Synod therefore ruled that during the funeral service Archpriest Boris would not name the dead individually, but instead pray for them collectively as 'victims of the Civil War known only to God'. The reinterment ceremony was constructed around a vacuum because at no point did anyone declare openly that these were the last Tsar's bones. Even President Yeltsin acquiesced with the Church's stipulations by not naming names, making instead a platitudinous speech about national reconciliation. The ceremony that could have marked a step in post-Soviet Russia's evaluation and acceptance of the country's history turned out to be a divisive farce.

Other bodies

During the discussions about how and where the Tsar's bones should be reinterred, it was suggested that the remains of Nicholas II might be joined by the mummified corpse of Vladimir Lenin. According to Viktor Aksiuchits, an adviser to the government Commission on the Romanov remains, 'these questions [burying Nicholas and Lenin] are profoundly connected: at the end of the twentieth century, the martyred and the "martyrer" have come together again'.[25] The military hero Aleksandr Lebed, preparing his campaign for the 1996 presidential elections (in which he came third), envisaged a grand double burial, orchestrated by 'one of our inspired Russian – it must be a Russian – film-makers, like Nikita Mikhalkov'. Lebed's prescriptions for the double funeral attempted to achieve a patriotic melding of Russian and Soviet history. The ceremony, he wrote, should be a magnificent, emotive affair 'to the peal of bells throughout the country, to the lowering of standards, to the salute of artillery, to the sound of a thousand trumpets ... a great symbol of universal reconciliation and purification'.[26]

That Lenin and Nicholas II could be linked like this showed that the dead body was a powerful artefact, and also that post-Soviet Russia lived with a confused amalgamation of cultural symbols. While the ROC was doing its best to deny the soon-to-be canonized Tsar any physical remains, Vladimir Lenin – who had been deeply implicated in Nicholas's death – continued to lie in the Mausoleum, his embalmed body recalling the supposedly incorruptible remains of Russian Orthodox saints.

The proposal to bury Lenin's mummified remains had already been canvassed at crucial moments during Russia's post-Soviet transition when President Yeltsin wanted to project himself as doing battle with the forces of Soviet reaction: specifically the attempted coup by Soviet anti-reformers in August 1991, the shelling by government forces of the Soviet-era legislature in October 1993, and Yeltsin's re-election in July 1996 over the Communist Party's candidate. Yet a decade later the Mausoleum on Red Square still preserved this relic of Soviet communism, defiant among Moscow's renamed streets and shiny new buildings. While the Russian state tried to lay history to rest with the reinterment of the bones of Nicholas II, another dead body – Lenin's mummified corpse – represented that history, perpetually revived.

Meanwhile, in April 1997, Nicholas lost the only 'dead body' that the ROC could allow him to have, when an eleven-metre-high statue of the Tsar, erected a year earlier in Taininskoe outside Moscow, was blown up. The irony was that the statue – a potential substitute for Nicholas's absent corpse – was destroyed by a neo-communist group protesting against plans to bury – not the Tsar, but – Lenin. The explosion, read the statement put out by the 'Workers' and Peasants' Red Army and USSR NKVD', was 'an act of retribution against those who wish to commit outrage against a national shrine, the V.I. Lenin Mausoleum memorial complex'.[27]

When the Russian Orthodox Church turned Nicholas II into a saint, it ignored his body. In theological terms, the absence of a body was not important: there was no obstacle to canonizing someone without knowing where his physical remains lay.[28] For the Church was not only wary of the authenticity of the bones; it was also hesitant about fixing Nicholas II as an historical personage with an actual body, whose bones' reburial would symbolize the closure of an historical era.

Yet the ROC still needed some kind of facsimile for the physical presence of the Tsar, in order to make his image more immediate, and to draw attention away from the coffins and their disputed contents lying in St Petersburg. In order to achieve this, the Church deployed its most powerful aesthetic weapons (evidently the lesson of how the Byzantine church had persuaded the leaders of ancient Rus' to adopt Christianity in 988 was not lost on the Moscow Patriarchate). As well as the glittering canonization ceremony of August 2000, new church buildings were constructed to commemorate the Romanovs. These buildings stood as a substitute for the physical bodies of Nicholas and his family.

A huge cathedral was erected on the plot formerly occupied by the Ipatiev House in Ekaterinburg and was consecrated in July 2003, the eighty-fifth anniversary of the killings. The new cathedral was called the Church of the Saviour on the Spilled Blood, the name recalling the neo-Muscovite church in St Petersburg that marks the site where Populist revolutionaries had assassinated Nicholas's grandfather, Tsar Alexander II, in 1881. The altar of the new Ekaterinburg Cathedral supposedly lay above the site of the basement room where the Romanovs and their servants had been killed. Built with remarkable speed in just three years, it also demonstrated the Ekaterinburg authorities' determination to promote their city.

A second architectural complex was constructed – also with record speed – in the Koptiaki forest at the site of the Four Brothers' Mine. This place – according to the Church, which still revered the conclusions of the White investigation – was where the bodies of the Tsar and his entourage had been – as the tourist literature about the new monastery stated – 'chopped up and with the help of acid and petrol burned on two bonfires, to conceal from the world the evil that had been committed'.[29] A tabloid newspaper reported breathlessly that its photographer had seen the Patriarch appear 'in a column of green light' when laying the foundations for the new complex.[30] The complex at Four Brothers consisted of seven charming wooden churches – one for each new saint – built in traditional Russian style with overlapping wooden tiles on their onion domes. Together they formed the Monastery of the Holy Tsarist Passion-Bearers. In fact, only the Romanovs' clothing had been burned on this site. But since the Church refused to acknowledge the 'Ekaterinburg remains' as those of the Imperial Family, the actual burial site, where the Romanovs' bodies had been concealed for seventy years, was marked only by a cross.

Icons, miracles and images

The clearest substitutes for the physical remains of Nicholas and his family, however, were neither churches nor statues, but icons. Russian Orthodoxy retains a special role for icons. More than glorious pieces of art, icons are intrinsically holy objects, windows through which the worshipper connects with the person of the saint depicted.[31] For this reason an icon will be revered equally whether it be the priceless original or a flimsy paper copy worth just a few kopeks. For this reason, too, the icon painter must prepare himself spiritually for his work, for a sinner cannot paint a true icon.

The iconography of Nicholas II and his family is a visual language that describes the different aspects of their sainthood. In some icons the family group wears the flowing white robes of the righteous. These predominantly white icons may show very traditional, stylized drapery, with gold trim to the robes. Alternatively, they may have a more modern feel, such as the 1998 icon 'Heavenly Glory' in which the women's robes are more akin to Edwardian fashions and the Tsar and Tsarevich wear military uniform.

Other icons depict the Tsar alone. These are recognizable portraits of Nicholas II, with his rather large eyes, luxuriant moustaches and neat beard; but they depict him in the traditional Muscovite court dress of a wide, richly coloured kaftan, wearing the cap of Monomakh, the traditional Muscovite crown. These icons of the Tsar create a visual link between Nicholas and his role model, Tsar Alexei Mikhailovich (1645–1676), the second Romanov ruler after whom Nicholas named his own long-awaited heir. They also recall a photograph of Nicholas II which was widely disseminated during his reign. In the photograph, Nicholas was dressed as Alexei Mikhailovich for the costume balls of February 1903, at which he and his guests attired themselves in seventeenth-century garb. Reproductions of this famous photograph were sold at church stalls as an icon, 'the Tsar-Martyr'.

For Nicholas, the pre-Petrine monarchy evoked the ideals of the sacred bond between Tsar and people, Tsar and country, that shaped his understanding of his role as autocrat, and this in the face of all the evidence that Russia, at the beginning of the twentieth century, was moving towards modernity. 'Nicholas II clearly regarded seventeenth-century robes as something more than a costume,' writes Richard Wortman. 'They were a challenge to the norms of the Western imperial court. They set the Tsar and tsaritsa in a . . . cultural and aesthetic universe distant from Petersburg society.'[32] In broad terms these concepts of autocracy and the direct link between Tsar and people challenge the ideas of liberal democracy, but they are the political ideals of the post-Soviet national patriotic movement.

Icons of the Tsar and his family did not just provide a substitute for their physical remains. Some of them performed miracles that were important propaganda during the campaign to have Nicholas canonized. Two icons in particular became well known for their miraculous properties. One of these, which depicted the Tsar alone, had begun to flow with myrrh and emit a sweet smell; the other, which showed the whole family, had been seen to glow with bright colours and to weep blood from the faces and hands of the figures. The narratives about these miraculous icons were published in pamphlets and books and recounted in videos, all disseminated through the ROC's various publishing networks. The icons allegedly revealed their powers most vividly on days particularly associated with the life and death of the tsarist saints, although if all the name-days and anniversaries connected with the Romanovs are taken into account very few days of the year are left miracle-free.

The icon of Nicholas II that started to flow with 'fragrant myrrh' was a colour photocopy of a lithograph made from the original, which had been painted in the USA in 1996 by a Russian émigré, Pavel Tikhomirov. The icon depicts the Tsar in Muscovite coronation robes, with small portraits of St Nikolai (his patron saint) and [St] Job (on whose feast day he was born) in the upper left and right corners. In March 1998 at the St Nicholas Alms House in Ryazan, a colour photocopy of the lithograph of this icon was presented in a wooden icon case to a certain Dr Oleg Belchenko from Moscow. The story goes that in September 1998 Belchenko took the icon, wrapped in a clear plastic bag, to a service at the ancient Sretensky Monastery Cathedral in Moscow. One of the other worshippers began to question him. 'Doctor, what is that fragrance around you?' 'Probably incense,' Belchenko replied, 'but I can't smell anything; I have a cold.' When the man persisted, Belchenko opened the plastic bag and the whole church suddenly filled with a fragrant smell. The amazed congregation ripped the bag to pieces so that everyone could take home a part of the miracle.

Belchenko's icon soon acquired national renown. Even the ITAR-TASS news agency covered the miracle of the myrrh on two occasions in 1999, both times reporting it entirely unmediated and without comment. As the sweet-smelling myrrh continued to trickle over the glass, the icon made the rounds of Moscow's churches in a Volkswagen van; it was flown over the city of St Petersburg by helicopter; and it was taken on an aerial pilgrimage around Russia's borders.[33]

The other reputedly miraculous icon depicted the whole Romanov family. This, too, was a colour photocopy framed in a wooden icon case with a glass cover, again from the St Nicholas Alms House in Ryazan. It was

Figure 6.1 'Heavenly Glory'. Icon (painted 1998) of Nicholas, Alexandra and their children.

Figure 6.2 'The Tsarist Martyr Nicholas II'. Photograph of Nicholas in seventeenth-century court dress for a costume ball in 1903. Sold as postcard icon, Moscow, 2002.

122 *Tsar Martyr*

presented to Georgy Balovlenkov, a friend of Doctor Belchenko, at the same time as the doctor received his miraculous icon. (Balovlenkov, an economist also from Moscow, later compiled the hagiography of the Tsar quoted on p. 112.) This icon of the 'Holy Tsarist Martyrs' first demonstrated its miraculous properties on 17 July 1998, the eightieth anniversary of the Imperial Family's death. During a church procession to mark the occasion, in which the icon was being carried, the faces and hands of the figures

Figure 6.3 Myrrh-streaming icon of Nicholas II (painted 1996).

began to 'weep blood'. Over subsequent days, the colours and details of the icon were said to have became more distinct and to glow more brightly. One of the faithful who testified to this miracle emphasized that her experience as a professional art historian enabled her to recognize a genuine alteration in the picture.[34]

Given that both icons were cheap reproductions which had been photocopied and framed in the same place, one might ask what the St Nicholas Alms House was using to make its icons. For the believer, however, the icons' spiritual power would remain undimmed even if the miracles could be explained by the chemical properties of the wood in the icon cases or the qualities of the St Nicholas Alms House photocopier.

The same is true of scientific or psychological explanations for the miracles that occurred after intercession to the Tsar and his family, like Father Aleksei's liberation from the police cells. The dissemination of these miracle stories was carefully organized to give vital momentum to the canonization campaign. The stories were collected and published in five separate booklets between 1995 and 2000. Each publication generated further miracles. 'Suddenly I remembered that I had the book *New Miracles of the Imperial Martyrs*' [the second volume], writes one correspondent quoted in the third collection. 'I began to read it, and that night I placed this holy pamphlet under my pillow and begged the Imperial martyrs to help me get well. And a miracle occurred: in the morning, my leg hurt much less, and it was easier to walk.'[35]

In some of the miracle narratives, the inspiration to pray to the 'Imperial martyrs' comes from an icon or pamphlet published by ROCOR, the Church outside Russia, piling further pressure on the Moscow Patriarchate to canonize the Tsar. Archpriest Aleksandr Shargunov, who collated the stories, argued in a 1999 pamphlet that 'The glorification of Tsar Nicholas Alexandrovich is perhaps of greater significance than the glorification of any other Russian saint of the 20th century'. Revealing his allegiance with the national patriots, Shargunov demanded: 'Why has he [the Tsar] not yet been canonized by our Church? Why is his canonization so opposed by atheists, democrats, and neo-renovationists?'[36] And once the Tsar had been canonized, Shargunov's booklets were republished as a handsome two-volume hardback called *Miracles of the Imperial Martyrs*, with high-quality colour reproductions of icons of the Tsar.[37]

Reading the miracles recounted in these collections, one is struck by the very ordinariness of the Tsar's intervention in people's daily lives. The miracles relate to everyday problems: housing, health, financial and family matters. A man quarrels with his wife in a crowded market, and she walks off; feeling remorseful he prays for help from the 'Imperial Martyrs', and a mere two hours later finds her in the bustling market and they mend their quarrel.[38] A woman passes her entrance exams to train as an archivist while working full time, and all because she had 'prayed to the Tsar-Martyr, promising to pay for a service to him if I passed the exam'.[39] A woman has ended her unhappy marriage, but her estranged ex-husband will not leave their apartment. She prays 'in tears, to the holy Sovereign and Empress as the very model of married life for all Russia' for help 'to get out of this impossible situation'. The next spring her ex-husband leaves to marry another woman.[40] A doctor, a 29-year-old single mother with a young daughter, falls ill with 'flu, and has no one to help her. Praying to the 'Tsarist Martyrs', she wakes the next day, 'weak but without fever and with no pain. So, even though it was hard, I managed to look after myself and my daughter.'[41]

Simple in style to the point of naivety, these narratives are interesting for what they show about religious belief in Russia today. Even though all the 'miracles' can be explained through coincidence rather than divine intervention, for those who experience them as 'miracles' they make bearable the unfairness of the world. This is what religion does: as a symbolic system it renders explicable the 'enigmatic unaccountability of gross iniquity'.[42] Yet, at the same time, the way in which these miracle narratives concentrate on material problems suggests that belief has also largely become a matter of consumerism in contemporary Russia.

The narratives reveal repeatedly that the most pressing material problem for ordinary Russians remains, as in Soviet times, the housing issue. By way of example, here is a complete narrative in which a woman recounts how she was able to exchange her communal flat for more suitable accommodation after praying to the 'Imperial Martyrs'. In the communal flat, neighbours share kitchen and toilet facilities. To move house, the woman had to persuade her neighbour to move out as well so that the entire space could be liberated for the new tenants (it is through the exchange of apartments – rather than their sale and purchase – that the housing 'market' works for many in Russia).

> When my second child was born, I had to move out of the communal flat where I was living and exchange it for something more suitable. In 1992, it wasn't so easy to swap a run-down flat in the city centre, but I did find something. And so did my rather difficult neighbours, who would also move out to leave if the exchange were to go ahead: he was an alcoholic, parties all hours of the day and night, and so was his former wife who had moved to Moscow a few years before.
>
> Everything was going fine . . . until my neighbour suddenly refused to swap, saying that it suited him fine right there and he wouldn't take money or different accommodation to move out. Everything went to pieces; six months' work in vain, and worst of all, it's almost impossible to live with neighbours like that when you have two little children.
>
> Then a priest I knew gave me a prayer to the Tsarist martyrs which was used in the Church Abroad.
>
> I already used to venerate Tsar Nicholas and read lots about him and his family. So I went home and said the prayer three times before

the icons, where I had also pinned up a photograph of the Tsar's family.

I didn't really ask for anything; I just said the prayer, and I felt much calmer.

And the next day, my Dad called to say that the 'difficult' neighbour had found himself a room, and everything turned out just fine.
Elena Diuzheva, Moscow.[43]

This kind of 'everyday Orthodoxy', in which the mundane is altered by the miraculous, features widely in post-Soviet religious practice. It is more specific than the 'banal Orthodoxy' that permeates contemporary Russian culture through constant reminders of its presence: space is delimited by the architecture of church buildings, both old and new; time is punctuated by Orthodox festivals, some of them now national holidays.[44] The religious belief manifested in the miracle narratives, however, is rather different. Turning to the miraculous to meet everyday needs constitutes not the passive absorption implicit in 'banal Orthodoxy', but rather the deliberate use – even the consumption – of religion. Orthodoxy has become a consumer item. Icons, pamphlets, calendars, videos, holy oil, blessed water can all be purchased to assist in the trials of daily life. It is widely accepted that material needs such as accommodation or healing, which demand a great deal of money in contemporary Russia – a distinct shift from Soviet practice, where such needs were satisfied through the exchange of favours, the infamous *blat* – can be met through prayer. The miracle narratives relate numerous satisfied requests to the Holy Imperial Martyrs for material blessings. Here is one example:

> In February 1995 I was in a terrible way, almost desperate. Then I remembered the brochure I'd bought about six months before. It was called *Liturgy for the Holy Imperial Martyrs* and was published by the Orthodox Church Abroad. I sat down to read it to myself (this was at night), and then I prayed with my own words, asking the Sovereign Martyr and his holy family to help me.
>
> I thought that if the dreams when I'd seen the Sovereign had been from God, then he would surely pray for me, a sinner, before the Almighty.
>
> The next day I got a money order, from a complete stranger, which was enough for me and my family to live off for a whole month.
> Sergei Arseniev, St Petersburg.[45]

The ability to supply material needs through miraculous means is a common attribute of saints in Orthodox hagiography. So as well as being a 'passion-bearer', Nicholas-as-saint also follows the hagiographical tradition that relates the saint's power to satisfy material indigence. In one of the earliest Russian hagiographies, the Life of Feodosy of the Caves Monastery, a recurrent theme is Feodosy's miraculous provision of food and drink whenever the Monastery's supplies run out.[46] The miracle narratives of Nicholas II are firmly within one tradition of Russian Orthodox literature. However, the people who report these miracles are usually not devout Orthodox, obedient to all the Church's strictures and well versed in religious literature. The impact of these miracle stories rests precisely on their narration by ordinary people whose mundane lives have been touched by the intervention of the 'Holy Martyr Tsar'. The simple, conversational style of the narratives highlights their authenticity and gives them a greater affective power.

The miracle narratives include numerous stories in which the Tsar appears to the narrator in a dream. The dreamers always describe him as kind, open and unaffected: 'I dreamed about Tsar Martyr Nicholas II, and we chatted like equals, we talked about my life.'[47] (Some secular Russian biographies of Nicholas II, and some Western biographies, repeat these clichés about the Tsar's openness and simplicity, which perhaps had their roots in his deeply held populism, his belief in the devotion of the peasantry.[48]) It may be that the prevalence of physical representations of the Tsar in popular Russian culture today – in icons, photographs or films – predisposes people to see him in their dreams. It is also true that the clichés about his character combine with a formulaic description of his physical appearance, so that whether he appears as a living icon, in a dream or in a vision, Nicholas's 'kind eyes' are the main impression left upon the narrator. In the introduction to one of the collections of miracle narratives, Archpriest Aleksandr Shargunov writes political and religious significance into the Tsar's face.

> The Russian Tsar is different from European monarchs, and the Russian people is suited to this form of government. The Russian people is simple-souled, and needed a Tsar who was wise and simple-souled. In the last Tsar all this was combined. ... In the Tsar's face is the grace of God's peace. Looking at his photograph, one becomes calm. ... If one shows the Tsar's face to a child, it has a good influence upon his soul. ... The Tsar's face has something in common with the face of Christ. It has an expression of trust towards God and people. And this is a Tsar whose relations with the people were genuinely unique.[49]

Sometimes, but rarely, the Imperial Martyrs manifest themselves not through icons, miracles or dreams, but by their actual physical presence. One particular narrative – really a rather charming ghost story – has appeared at least three times in collections of miracle stories, including a children's book about the Tsar.[50] A woman called Nina Kartashova, who was ill with pneumonia, tells of how she saw a young nurse, aged about 17, in her bedroom. The nurse said her name was 'Maria' and spoke with a St Petersburg accent. She tended to the woman, covering her with 'Papa's officer's greatcoat. "You'll be quite well today," she said, "Papa told me. Today it's his birthday."' When Nina Kartashova woke the next morning a branch of fresh lilac was in the vase, and the rosary that had belonged to her late grandmother and had been buried with her was found hanging on the icon of Christ in the bedroom.

This story is unusual in that it focuses on one of the Tsar's daughters (Nicholas himself, 'Papa', is an absent, but benevolently powerful, figure) and also in the saint's physical presence. Maria is clearly described: 'a round face with big grey eyes, something dignified and gentle in her expression. She wore a simple pale grey dress.' She explained to Nina Kartashova that she was 'neither a dream nor an apparition. . . . It's just that sometimes, in extremis, people can see another world.'

Conclusions

The clearest impetus behind making saints out of the Romanovs came from a well-organized campaign by the fundamentalists in the Russian Orthodox Church, who pushed the hierarchy into canonizing Nicholas and his family. But the family also became saints because popular culture readily accepted Nicholas, Alexandra and their children as holy figures. It was not necessarily that they represented the virtues of sainthood as these are usually understood: poverty, chastity or martyrdom, for example. The Romanovs-as-saints spoke instead to a large constituency in Russia that, even if not particularly religious, had adopted Russian Orthodoxy or a kind of consumerist version of the faith. When Nicholas was made a saint, he became part of this popular consumption of religion.

The popularity of the Romanov saints also overlapped with the pervasive sentimentalism about the Romanovs as a family, a sentimentalism which was intensified by the manner of their deaths and the seductiveness of their glamorous lifestyle, as the next chapter explores. This attitude towards them recalls the 'canonization' of Diana, Princess of Wales, whose accidental death in 1997 was immediately transformed in the British media into martyrdom and whose life-story was suddenly rewritten as a selfless path to a kind of holiness. The Romanovs, however, were formally canonized by the Russian Orthodox Church which, given the privileged position of the Church in Russia, bestowed upon them the unwritten status of Russia's official saints. Many believers derived solace from their devotion to the last Tsar of Russia (often in the expectation of material blessings). This was a matter of personal faith. The problem, however, was that worshipping Nicholas as a saint militated against understanding the reasons for his death. So the martyred Tsar – a redemptive sacrifice for Russia – became simply a victim of his enemies and the enemies of Russia. And when this narrative of Nicholas as a martyred prince overlapped with Gothic horror stories about Jewish ritual murder, the result could be noxious and potent.[51]

7 Family portraits

At 2.15 went to the younger Levitsky's to be photographed, because the old man is ill. The photographs were taken in a variety of poses: the two of us together with our daughter, and each of us alone. Hope that an hour-and-a-half's suffering will produce some results.
(Nicholas II, diary entry for 3 May 1896)

What is called collective memory is not a remembering but a stipulating: that *this* is important, and this is the story about how it happened, with the pictures that lock the story in our minds. Ideologies create substantiating archives of images, representative images, which encapsulate common ideas of significance and trigger predictable thoughts, feelings.
(Susan Sontag, *Regarding the Pain of Others*, 2002)

Propaganda portraits

Most of us have a picture of the Romanovs stored somewhere in our mind's image bank. Probably a sepia photograph of an Edwardian family, posed in chocolate-box prettiness. At the centre sits the father dressed in military uniform; his son – a boy about 9 years old, wearing a cadet sailor suit – sits at his feet. The mother is middle-aged, her eyes deep-set and mournful; and four girls, identically dressed in white summer frocks, are draped around the central trio. This is the photograph that picture editors select to illustrate newspaper articles about the Romanovs, and which it is mandatory to include in every Romanov book, usually on the front cover.[1]

Our response to this photograph has been conditioned by hindsight. We cannot escape the knowledge that the perfect family group in the picture ended up as a pile of bloody corpses in a dim cellar, and so the photograph automatically has the texture of tragedy, of lives cut short. Some authors have found the contrast between the photograph and the imagined picture of what was to follow so strong that they have invented another photograph – of the Romanovs' deaths – to set against the image of the perfect family. Edvard Radzinsky, with the eye of a dramatist, even suggests that Yurovsky may have asked the Romanovs to pose docilely for their execution on the pretext of needing to take their photograph in order to show the world that they were still alive. And why would Commandant Yurovsky not then have photographed the Imperial Family's corpses as proof of their deaths? After all, he had once been a professional photographer, and had even confiscated the Romanovs' cameras when they arrived in the Ipatiev House.[2] Radzinsky is unperturbed by the lack of evidence for this hypothesis: it is just too tempting to abandon. But no photograph of the dead Romanovs has ever been found. There is just a rather badly executed painting showing the heap of mangled corpses. The dishevelled bare-breasted girl in the foreground, lying with her head towards the viewer almost as though she were upside down, and the central figure of a girl, with her skirts raised above her legs still encased in black stockings and lace-up boots, suggest sexual violation of the women. The unknown artist also appears to hint at the decapitation of the Tsar, whose head is off-centre from his shoulders, although perhaps this betrays the artist's lack of technical skill.

The more horribly we imagine the scene of the dead Romanovs, the more poignant becomes the iconic sepia photograph of the perfect family. 'Sentiment is more likely to crystallise around a photograph than around a verbal slogan', argues Susan Sontag.[3] And so, because of the 'sentiment crystallise[d] around [this] photograph' of the Romanovs, we have a ready-made visual narrative about Nicholas and his family, a narrative whose sentimentalized romanticism elbows aside the niggling doubts of history. For like all the narratives about Nicholas II, this superficially uncomplicated image conceals many layers of deception. In the case of the iconic picture of the Romanov family, the deception starts with the photograph itself.

First, there is more than one version in circulation, so that what we think is a unique photograph is actually one of a generic series of images; second, the photograph was staged for a specific propagandistic purpose. This is a given. Most family portraits are essentially propaganda: we present our best smiles to the wedding photographer, we hang the framed graduation portrait on the wall. The Romanovs, however, had rather more at stake with their family photographs. This particular image (or series of images) of the family was created in 1913 to mark the tercentenary of the Romanov dynasty's rule over Russia. The magnificent celebrations to mark this high point in Nicholas's reign began in St Petersburg in February with sumptuous official receptions and a ball in traditional Russian dress. In May, Nicholas, Alexandra and their children made a two-week pilgrimage through Russia's oldest cities, following the route travelled by the first Romanov Tsar, Mikhail Feodorovich, after his election to the throne in 1613. By carriage, river steamer and train they visited Vladimir, Suzdal and Nizhny Novgorod, Kostroma on the Volga, Yaroslavl, Rostov, Pereyaslavl and Sergiev Posad, and finally on to Moscow where more balls, receptions and church services awaited them.[4]

Nicholas exploited the tercentenary celebrations to the full in order to reinforce the 'scenario of power' which he performed as Tsar. The concept of a 'scenario of power' belongs to Richard Wortman, who argues that each nineteenth-century tsar gave expression to the political ideals which underpinned his reign through a panoply of culture, imagery and artefacts. The ceremonies that punctuated a tsar's reign were episodes in such 'scenarios'. Typically, these began with his coronation, but might include military parades, religious celebrations, or progresses through the empire. Each tsar changed the scenario of his predecessor in more or less subtle ways to reflect his own concept of power and the shifts in Russia's public culture. The scenario created by Nicholas II reflected his belief that the rule of the Muscovite tsars – before the legalism and bureaucratism of Peter the Great's reforms had undermined the Tsar's personal charisma – was the only form of government possible for Russia. Nicholas's obdurate rejection of any constitutional restrictions upon the powers of the monarchy (until forced grudgingly to grant the convocation of a State Duma, a legislature with limited powers, in 1905) sprang from his confidence that no institution should mediate in the Tsar's close relationship with the *narod*, the Russian folk. This relationship, of course, was an invention of Nicholas (and Alexandra), and a fallacy that Rasputin exploited to gain influence over the royal couple. But it was the foundation of Nicholas's scenario. In a classic example of 'invented traditions', Nicholas's counsellors devised 'new ceremonies, informal meetings of the tsar with the common people and mass historical celebrations, [which] showed the tsar's bonds with the people and his claim as leader of the nation to the heritage of Russia's heroic past'.[5]

So in May 1913 the Imperial Family's progress in the steps of Mikhail Romanov was punctuated by ceremonies which reinforced Nicholas's scenario. The Tsar paraded before military, church and civil dignitaries, and presided at outdoor receptions for carefully selected local peasant elders where he tasted the food that was provided for them to enjoy. Romanov propaganda always emphasized Nicholas's preference for 'simple peasant food' and his custom of tasting soldiers' rations. Palace menus tell a different story. One wonders, for example, what the peasants whom Nicholas met during his progress in May 1913 would have made of the gala dinner just a few days later at the conclusion of his trip, in the Nobles' Assembly in Moscow. The menu proposed 'celery consommé with assorted pastries; crab mousse with burbot and Oxford sauce; chicken, grouse and quail; Romaine lettuce with oranges', and to finish, 'hazelnut parfait'.[6]

At the centre of Nicholas's scenario, closely entwined with his faith in a paternalistic relationship with the peasantry, was his family. The family encapsulated Nicholas's political priorities. Here, at least, he was the kind of ruler that he idealized: master of the land, intimately connected with his subjects, gentle but always obeyed. As Russia became increasingly ungovernable, Nicholas retreated from the dysfunctional mechanisms of state into the privacy of his family which – in his scenario at least – represented a perfect world. The imagery of his immediate family was

Family portraits   131

integral to Nicholas's self-constructed role as 'Master of the Russian Land' (*khoziain russkoi zemli*). In this scenario, Nicholas and Alexandra were father and mother not just to five beautiful children but to all of Russia. The domestic and the political were thus enmeshed at the deepest level.

Another piece of propaganda devised, like the now iconic photograph, for the tercentenary celebrations was permeated with the imagery of the Tsar's family life. This was an unprecedented biography of a living tsar, *The Reign of the Sovereign Emperor Nicholas Alexandrovich*. Published in book form in 1913, it also appeared in numerous Russian journals, and English and French translations came out the following year. The book was written by Major-General Andrei Elchaninov – a member of the Tsar's suite – and was, of course, sheer propaganda.[7] Seeking to present the Tsar as both superhuman and ordinary, Elchaninov's uncertain style combined a mass of trivial detail about Nicholas's daily life and routine with an insistence that this mundane superhero was better than anyone else at whatever he undertook (hunting, swimming, photography, playing billiards, even administering an empire).[8] Describing Nicholas's favourite recreation while holidaying, for example, Elchaninov gushes:

> The Tsar's energy on these occasions, especially when walking in hilly country, is extraordinary. It is not by any means all of his suite who can keep up with him. Many of his aides-de-camp go into special training for these walks before the departure for the Crimea.[9]

Three of the twelve chapters in the book (chapters 3, 4 and 5) were devoted to the Tsar's family life. As Romanov propaganda, most of the material in the chapters about the family focused on Alexei, the personification of the dynasty's future. The English edition, for example, contained forty-seven photographs of the Romanovs, of which two were formally posed pictures of the family, and eleven featured the Tsar with Alexei or Alexei alone. The touching mutual devotion between father and son, and the boy's remarkable abilities – symbolizing the expectations for his future reign – were crucial to the image of Nicholas as father to five children, and to Russia. Needless to say, the boy's haemophilia was not mentioned: Nicholas even censored one passage, which described his prayers for his son's health, in order not to draw attention to the issue.[10] Today, one of the first things anyone learns about the Romanov family is that the Tsarevich suffered from this potentially life-threatening inherited condition; but at the time it was a state secret so closely kept that even the imperial children's tutor of French, Pierre Gilliard, knew nothing about it until he began to conduct formal lessons with the 8-year-old Alexei. 'He was a prey to a disease which was only mentioned inferentially,' Gilliard reminisced, 'and the nature of which no one ever told me.'[11]

Returning to the iconic 1913 Romanov family photograph(s), I want to suggest a critical reading that reveals the message of this particular image within Nicholas's scenario of power. The pictures were produced by the Imperial Family's favourite photographers, Boissonas & Eggler of St Petersburg, who favoured soft-focus pictures in carefully composed surroundings.[12] The 1913 photograph eschews any suggestion of imperial might and consciously situates the family in an idealized domestic setting. The subjects' dress emphasizes domesticity and simplicity. Nicholas wears ordinary military uniform, modelled upon the traditional loose side-buttoned, high-necked shirt of the Russian peasantry, and only two medals. The virginal white dresses of the daughters are simple rather than showy. The fabulous jewellery of the Romanovs is pared down to a minimum, signalling royalty but not overwhelming riches. The Tsarina, for example, wears only the most modest of tiaras and her double-rope pearl necklace. The daughters also wear pearls: the younger two (whose hair is still worn loose) have simple, single-strand necklaces; the older two, who wear their hair pinned up to delimit their status as being of age, have the more elaborate necklaces given to them on their sixteenth birthdays. The Tsarevich wears a sailor suit and a military order. This propagandistic balancing act between modest domesticity and fabulous wealth was poised upon the fulcrum of a close family group and calibrated to produce a specific response in Nicholas's subjects. In this image, produced to celebrate the dynasty's 300th anniversary, the viewer was meant to see a perfect family: the father and son devoted to Russia's army and navy, the daughters destined for marriage, the mother regal yet modest.

This tercentenary photograph was sold as a postcard to raise money for charity and thus became another item in the formidable Romanov publicity machine. Nicholas II was the first Russian tsar to use the whole gamut of modern communications to build up popular support. Enabled by the explosive growth of industrialization at the turn of the century that made possible the mass production of cheap consumer goods, Nicholas allowed his image to be disseminated via mundane household articles. Particularly in the tercentenary year, Nicholas's scenario of power was destined for consumption by the whole country and not just the restricted court and aristocratic circles of his predecessors. Before 1913, for example, Russian tsars had not appeared on postage stamps. In the tercentenary year of the Romanov dynasty the first stamps were issued depicting the tsars, most frequently Nicholas himself whose portrait was printed on three denominations of stamps. Equally important was the production of a number of souvenir objects commemorating the tercentenary, which incorporated portraits of Nicholas and his family. Supposedly subject to approval by the Ministry of the Court, these souvenirs were so numerous that they exceeded officials' capacity to authorize them or to control their production. The dynamic of commercialization meant that the imperial visage became a form of decoration for everyday objects such as calendars, sweet boxes and trinkets.[13]

Figure 7.1 Romanov family portrait, from the series of pictures taken to celebrate the Romanov tercentenary in 1913. Sold as postcard, Moscow, 2002.

A similar process had unrolled earlier in Nicholas's reign for another anniversary, the centenary of the birth of Russia's greatest writer, Alexander Pushkin. In 1899 the Russian state organized a jubilee year of celebrations for the 'national poet'. Some seven-and-a-half million copies of Pushkin's selected works were printed in cheap editions for popular reading, although there was little scholarly control over the texts themselves. Rapidly going beyond the poetry, entrepreneurs produced innumerable 'Pushkin' products, including 'cigarettes, tobacco, rolling papers, matches, candy, steel pens, stationery, ink stands, liqueur, knives, watches, vases, cups, shoes, dresses, lamps, fans, perfume ("Bouquet Pouchkine"), a variety of portraits and postcards, plus a board game ("Pushkin's Duel", which was roundly criticized in the press as being in thoroughly bad taste)', for Pushkin had died in 1837 at the age of only 38, after sustaining a fatal wound in a duel. That his opponent had been a foreigner, the Frenchman Georges D'Anthès, had made Pushkin's death a national tragedy and disgrace.[14]

The problem with the commercialization of anniversaries, as the Pushkin's Duel board game had epitomized, was that the medium undermined the message. It was a fatal paradox in popularizing the images of mighty national figures – whether poet or tsar – that the very objects which disseminated those images undermined their gravitas. For example, the two cheaper postage stamps that depicted Nicholas II were those most commonly used for letters within Russia. And although this meant that letters carried the face of the Tsar to every village within Russia, the stamps had to be cancelled by a postmark, which defaced the image of the sovereign. There were reports of postmasters refusing to stamp the postmark upon the Tsar's features. Entrepreneurialism, moreover, made it virtually impossible to control the production of commemorative objects to ensure that they were sufficiently grand or serious to bear the image of the Tsar. When officialdom did intervene, it tied itself in knots trying to protect the dignity of the sovereign. A request to sell scarves bearing Nicholas's image was admitted, but with the proviso that 'these [scarves] are not of a size suitable for use as handkerchiefs'.[15]

Ultimately it was futile to try and stop the people from blowing their proletarian noses upon the sacred image of the Tsar. Imprinting pictures of Nicholas and his family upon everyday objects risked turning the Imperial Family from remote figures of unimpeachable authority and dignity into cheap celebrities. This would have political consequences, in that it undermined the mystique of monarchy. But the trend had already had consequences of a more tragic kind at Nicholas's coronation in May 1896 when 1,350 people (according to official figures: it was probably many more) were trampled to death at the traditional coronation fair on Khodynka Field in Moscow in the rush for free beer and souvenir coronation mugs. (Nicholas and Alexandra's decision to attend, as planned, the ball given that evening by the French ambassador was popularly interpreted as evidence of their callousness.)

Despite the risk of inadvertently undermining his dignity, it remained part of Nicholas's cultural strategy to put pictures of himself and his family into popular circulation. Technological advances assisted the dissemination of the Romanovs' image: in fact, Nicholas's reign ran parallel with the evolution of cinema in Russia. The first films were shown in 1896, and by 1908 the first Russian-made films were being screened; by 1912 there were 1,412 permanent cinemas in Russia – 134 of them in St Petersburg and sixty-seven in Moscow – and by 1914 movies were the most popular form of entertainment in terms of tickets sold.

Audiences had an insatiable appetite for the products of the film companies, which were predominantly 'drawing-room thrillers' with themes of 'temptation, seduction, adultery, betrayal, false accusation, fraud, and tawdry relations of every kind, all set in an affluent milieu'.[16] Nicholas took a high-minded view of the film studios' mass output, calling it 'an empty, totally useless, and even harmful form of entertainment', and adding (in his annotations to a police report about cinema): 'only an abnormal person could place this farcical business on a par with art. It is complete rubbish, and no importance whatsoever should be attached to such stupidities.'[17] However, despite his ostensible revulsion, Nicholas was actually fascinated and seduced by film. He had a private cinema installed in the palace at Tsarskoe Selo and employed a court cinematographer. He encouraged the filming of himself and his family at ceremonies, parades, religious services and receptions. In fact, some of the earliest Russian films ever shot were of the Tsar and his family. Although these were at first for the Tsar's personal use, by 1908 such films began to be screened in public, and by 1913 studios were competing to capture and screen footage of the Imperial Family.[18]

As with the souvenirs depicting the Tsar, there were restrictions upon how the Tsar was portrayed when these movies were shown in cinema newsreels in an attempt to dissociate him from unsuitable contexts. Again, the effort was futile. Thus, the cinema curtain had to be lowered before and after the projection of newsreels showing the Tsar and his family, and these sequences had to be screened without musical accompaniment and at a slow, hand-cranked speed.[19] Yet Nicholas's efforts to harness the power of cinema ultimately weakened his authority, just as when he allowed his face to be printed on everyday objects to disseminate his image. The screening of the Imperial Family in the same space as the sensationalist films favoured by cinema audiences of the day contributed to the undermining of the Romanovs' mystique. In addition, the endlessly repeated rituals of court life – visits to the provinces, military parades and inspections, vacations on the *Shtandart* – were fantastically distant from the audience's experience and concerns.[20] Just how distant is revealed by the way that a documentary film of 1927 entitled 'The Fall of the Romanov Dynasty' used only original footage of the Tsar and his family in order to highlight, for a post-revolutionary audience, the Romanovs' idle degeneracy. The editor, Esfir Shub, intercut the footage – much of it shot by Nicholas's own cameraman and screened as positive propaganda during his reign – with sardonic commentary titles, thus subverting the original intention of the images.[21]

If moving pictures were hard to regulate, the Tsar had more control over the numerous formal photographs of himself, Alexandra and their children that were taken on every conceivable anniversary occasion. Nicholas could not dictate the way in which such photographic portraits would be received, nor could he prevent their association with unsuitable consumer goods. Nevertheless, it was easier to determine the composition of these static images than that of the moving pictures. And although Nicholas grumbled in his diaries about having his portrait taken – admittedly a cumbersome process in 1896, although the term 'suffering' surely exaggerates his experiences that afternoon – he was shrewd enough to know that he could 'produce results' by projecting the right image as a loving husband and father in his photo-portraits.

Alexandra was complicit in this image creation. As Princess Alix of Hesse-Darmstadt, she had been influenced by her grandmother Queen

Figure 7.2 Formal photograph of Nicholas II. Sold as religious calendar for 2002, Moscow.

Victoria, who made a principled 'Victorian value' out of family. This was as much politics as morality. Victoria's public role in the latter decades of the nineteenth century was that of national matriarch, and thanks to the dynastic matches of her numerous offspring she had also become the 'grandmother of Europe'. Like the Victorian Court in British royal propaganda, the Romanov Court of Nicholas and Alexandra was presented to the Russian public as a kind of domestic novel, in which the perfect family lived untouched by the concerns of state, cocooned from the outside world.[22] The official Romanov family photographs of 'warm scenes with beautiful cherubic children, as exemplars of family happiness' were staged as though the viewer were catching glimpses through the windows of the family home. This set the Nicholas and Alexandra photographs in stark contrast to earlier Romanov family portraits, 'in which members strike stiff formal poses appropriate to royalty viewed through a proscenium'.[23] And with the birth of every child to Alexandra came a new, intimate photograph, in which yet another baby girl held in her mother's arms was surrounded by her adoring toddler sisters until, at last, in 1904, Alexandra produced a son, Alexei.

The Tsarevich, nicknamed 'Baby', 'Sunbeam', 'the Little One' by the family, was the star of the Romanov publicity machine, and with his birth the four daughters became a glamorous supporting cast. The portrayals of the royal children – both in photographs and in *The Tsar and His People* – reinforced Nicholas's role as paterfamilias, a key element of his scenario. The girls, who would sometimes sign notes collectively as 'OTMA' (the initial letters of their Christian names), found their collective identity reinforced by their secondary role to the heir. In Elchaninov's book, for example, they are an undifferentiated foursome.

Their official portraits underlined this. It also revealed their predetermined roles. As children the girls were always photographed wearing virtually identical outfits, either sailor suits or white summer dresses. Later, in adolescence, the distinction of approaching adulthood split the 'elder pair' (Olga and Tatyana) from the 'younger pair' (Maria and Anastasia), since coming-of-age at 16 dictated that hair should be pinned up rather than left loose and that girls wear long rather than three-quarter-length dresses. This distinction is clearly seen in the tercentenary photographs. By this stage, however, the portraits of the girls were also prefiguring their role as brides to entwine further the branches of Europe's royal family tree. An official series of pictures of the four girls, taken by Boissonas & Eggler in 1914, presented them as ethereal, virginal beings.[24] The girls are posed on gilt chairs or upholstered benches, holding flowers as props, as though they were sitting with their chaperones at a ball awaiting an invitation to dance that would never come. None looks directly into the camera; each girl's gaze is slightly averted, emphasizing her remoteness and purity.

In 1913 Elchaninov described the girls as junior versions of their virtuous mother: 'the Tsar's daughters have been brought up in the rules of the

138 Family portraits

Holy Orthodox church and trained to be good and careful housewives. They are always occupied with some kind of needlework.' In addition to their numerous accomplishments (sporting, linguistic, artistic and musical), they were endowed with sympathy and practical charity, 'helping the poor, especially poor children, their presents taking the form, not of money, but of useful objects which they have made or knitted themselves'.[25]

The son and heir, Tsarevich Alexei, however, was a different being. Elchaninov emphasized his intellectual and physical abilities, which mirrored those of his father.

> The Tsesarevich takes a lively interest in his lessons, asks continual questions, is very quick at understanding, and is particularly fond of being read to or told stories. . . . Naturally active and full of life, the Tsesarevich delights in gymnastic exercises, and has thoroughly mastered the elementary military exercises, which form the subject of instruction of 'poteshnye' [the regiment of playmate soldiers instituted by Peter I].[26]

The role of this future tsar Alexei was also prefigured in his official photographic portraits, which depicted him as a soldier or sailor in miniature. The famous sailor suit of the 1913 picture(s) was sometimes exchanged for the miniature uniform of a soldier in the Russian army, as in another Boissonas & Eggler portrait from 1910.[27] After 1915, however, when Alexei went away with his father to Army headquarters, the dressing-up was for real.

Photography, like cinema, was a relatively recent innovation which Nicholas and his family enthusiastically adopted as a hobby. Developments in optical technology meant that European societies in the late nineteenth century 'observed and recorded themselves with a precision and a fascination that no civilisation had displayed before'.[28] Between them, the members of Nicholas's family took hundreds of pictures of each other and their lives together, away from the formal receptions and state occasions. These photographs constituted the Romanovs' own private family record. At least sixteen Moroccan leather photograph albums went with them into the Ipatiev House, and the Russian archives today hold over a hundred photograph albums and numerous loose photographs of the Romanovs. Since the demise of the Soviet Union these photographs have flooded out in exhibitions and glossy picture books to feed a modern public brought up on a diet of revelations about the private lives of celebrities. The children in outdoor clothes, mud on their boots, resting after working in their kitchen garden while under house arrest at Tsarskoe Selo; Anastasia outside, smoking, with her sister Olga; Rasputin with Alexandra and all the children in their private quarters in Tsarskoe Selo in 1908; Alexei sick in bed, being nursed by his mother; the girls flirting with the sailors of the

Figure 7.3 Wartime photograph of Tsarevich Alexei. Sold as religious calendar for 2002, Moscow.

Figure 7.4 Nicholas II, with guards, under arrest (March to December 1917).

imperial yacht *Shtandart*: none of these photographs would have been suitable propaganda pictures during Nicholas's reign, yet today they are treasured as evidence of the Imperial Family's essential humanity.[29]

This is not to say that there was always a clear divide between the public and private photographs: the Romanovs themselves frequently blurred the distinction between the two genres. The Imperial Family would, for example, frequently autograph offprints of the posed formal photographs as personal gifts for their relatives' own albums.[30] These photographs, better focused and printed, were naturally preferable to the family snaps: professional photographers tend to produce more flattering portraits than do amateurs. On the other hand, successful amateur pictures were sometimes used for propaganda. Alexandra's 1916 photograph of Alexei wearing military uniform and standing, rather stiffly, beside his spaniel was published as a postcard and sold to raise money for the war charities that Alexandra patronized. The previous year she had written to Nicholas about a different photograph of their son, demanding that it be made into a postcard and that father and son be 'done' (that is, photographed) together, both for their private albums and 'for the public'. 'How charming Alexei's photos are,' wrote Alexandra, 'the one standing ought to be sold as a postcard – *both* might be really – please, be done with Baby, also for the public and then we can send them to the soldiers.'[31]

Subverting the scenario

Unfortunately for Nicholas, it took very little to destroy the Tsar's image as perfect paterfamilias, and hence father of the Russian land. The romanticized myth of Nicholas II and his family presented in Romanov propaganda collapsed rapidly after about 1915. There was already an intrinsic contradiction in the way in which the Tsar's elevated personage had been presented through mundane items such as postage stamps and handkerchiefs. With the growing tensions of his reign, Nicholas's scenario became unsustainable, for as Russia's fortunes in World War I declined and as social malaise increased, the Tsar began to be portrayed in popular culture as a cuckolded husband, who was being deceived by a nymphomaniac foreign wife with the priapic peasant Rasputin.[32] This was a carnivalesque inversion of his propaganda image, and it was enormously damaging.[33] Given that Nicholas's scenario of power rested upon his role as head both of his own small family and of the larger family of the Russian nation, undermining his sexual authority meant undermining his authority as ruler. (This mockery of Nicholas and Alexandra echoed the rumours that circulated in the 1780s about Louis XVI and Marie Antoinette – another royal husband cuckolded by a foreign consort – and which contributed to the desacralization and downfall of the French monarchy.[34])

It is highly improbable that Rasputin was ever Alexandra's lover, but she was dependent upon him for emotional support, particularly when

Figure 7.5 'The Russian Royal Household'. Cartoon of Nicholas and Alexandra, with Rasputin, 1916 (unknown artist).

Nicholas was away at army headquarters. The reasons for Alexandra's dependency – her belief that Rasputin was able to halt her haemophiliac son's haemorrhages – could never be explained to the public, however. The family was a prisoner of its own propaganda of Alexei as the healthy future of the Romanov Dynasty.

Alexandra's own mystical leanings also reinforced her sentimental regard for Rasputin's Russian folk 'wisdom' and 'spirituality'. Yet the outside world came to believe that Rasputin was Alexandra's lover and that Alexandra was a German spy, and these 'facts' were repeated over and over in semi-pornographic postcards, pamphlets, films and cabaret. The scandal was common currency, from the peasants and ordinary soldiers right up to government officials and the intelligentsia. One typical cabaret sketch from 1917 was called 'Rasputin's Night-time Orgies'. In the text, 'Grisha' Rasputin incites his 'Sasha' (the Empress) to destroy 'that wimpy Nicky of yours'. She replies that 'Wilhelm [the Kaiser] is strong and he and I are allies. . . . If I want, you, Grisha, will be the Russian tsar.' Then, as 'Sasha' becomes hysterical at the thought that 'Grisha' might leave her, Rasputin takes her off-stage to 'expel the demon' from her, while the two other characters present – Anna Vyrubova, the Empress's friend, and Interior Minister Protopopov – discuss Rasputin's 'huge talent'.[35]

This and other similar depictions of Alexandra as Rasputin's mistress punched holes in the image of Nicholas II. The perfect Romanov family in the official propaganda was being presented in popular culture as its complete inversion – a debauched ménage à trois. Nicholas was no longer the father-Tsar and respected paterfamilias: he was a weak, impotent husband, ruled by a German wife who was consorting with the enemy and satisfying her lust with Rasputin. The Tsar's image thus destroyed, by 1917 all monarchist sentiment had evaporated, and when Nicholas abdicated there was widespread rejoicing at the news: 'the festivities lasted three days', remembered one peasant. It was not surprising, therefore, that the official announcement of Nicholas's execution in July 1918 was of little public concern, prompting 'amazing indifference' among ordinary Muscovites, according to the British consul in Moscow, Bruce Lockhart.[36]

Websites, movies and celebrity culture

Almost a century later, however, the Romanovs have regained the mystique that they attempted to create in their own propaganda. This time around, though, it is the manner of their deaths which is the crucial element in their romanticization. The 'aura of violated domesticity'[37] that surrounds the narratives of their execution suggests that the perfect family of Romanov propaganda is actually a more iconic image today than it ever was in the early twentieth century, even before it shattered under the pressures of war and social unrest.

Of course, we consume Romanov images today in a context far removed from that of Nicholas's subjects a century ago. It is far easier to become sentimental about the Romanov family when not suffering wartime privations under tsarist autocracy. There are also fundamental differences in the media that convey these idealized images of the Romanovs. Nicholas's scenario of power could be disseminated to his subjects thanks to increased literacy and the mass production of consumer goods. In the late twentieth and early twenty-first centuries, however, we have the ramified communication of the internet, where a 'virtual community' of numerous Romanov websites has taken over from the publicity machine of Nicholas's reign. This 'virtual community' is self-creating and self-selecting: the medium of the internet encourages – even demands – that the reader become a writer. Paradoxically, this means that consumers of the Romanov image today tend to be less critical than they were in Nicholas's reign. Recipients of Romanov propaganda in the late nineteenth and early twentieth centuries were unable to modify the medium (print, photographs, consumer goods) through which the Imperial Family presented their myth. They could show their disagreement only by satirizing or inverting the myth. The 'virtual community' of Romanov fans today is a self-selecting group of largely uncritical adherents who can, through the internet, perpetuate the myths about the perfect Imperial Family.

To take a few outstanding examples: a website called 'atlantis-magazine.com' invites visitors to the site to 'join other interested, enthusaistic *Atlanteans* as we combine our distinctive interests and energies to form a truly creative community dedicated to a world which has vanished from experience but not from our hearts'.[38] The website is linked with a print publication dedicated to the Romanovs, *Atlantis Magazine: In the courts of memory*. The website attempts to re-create in as much detail as possible the 'vanished world' of the Romanovs. It is an obsessive collectors' paradise, an accumulation of material with no critical discrimination, for the internet's limitless pages allow authors to evade the constraints of publishing on paper.

Another website, which calls itself 'The Unofficial Nicholas & Alexandra Romanov Homepage', is more akin to a small celebrity fanzine. To the musical accompaniment of 'Lara's Theme' from *Dr Zhivago*, visitors to the site can learn some 'Russian Fun Facts' and find out about the 'Romanov Family Pets'.[39] The site comes with a health warning: visitors are urged to 'Explore Imperial Russia'; however, the site continues, 'we must warn you, once you learn about the family, you take a piece of them with you. Enjoy, remember, and learn from them.'

Rather different is the enormous and informative 'Alexander Palace' group of websites. The first of these, the 'Alexander Palace Time Machine', has been live since 1995 and claims to be in the top 3 per cent of most visited websites. The site started as a virtual tour of Nicholas and Alexandra's home in the Alexander Palace at Tsarskoe Selo, created by Bob Atchison, and has burgeoned into a virtual re-creation of their lives and a 'databank of information on the last years of Imperial Russia'. With input from its numerous visitors, the website contains detailed information about palace protocol, family members, servants, menus, interior décor, and other topics of palace life. The site also manages ramified discussion boards where Romanov enthusiasts share information, often in exhaustive detail.[40]

The Livadia dot org website, on the other hand, is a smaller operation, describing itself as 'Kali's and Anna's tribute to the Romanov children', which provides a forum for fantasy role-play about 'OTMAA' (the four sisters – OTMA – and their brother Alexei). The website's two creators are in the process of setting up web page scrap-books for each child, 'written in first person, as if the children had put their own journals, art, and photo albums up on the web'. Visitors can choose their favourite of the five children, download the 'OTMAA' photographs to their own computers, and post messages to the (dead) Romanov children on the 'dream-page' which has been created for each of them.[41]

Websites are a popular medium for the virtual community of Romanov fans partly because they are relatively inexpensive to establish and run. Feature films are a far more costly way to romanticize the Imperial Family. It is significant, therefore, that the most recent Romanov biopic is a Russian-made film, *The Romanovs: A Crowned Family*, which came out in 2000. The film took ten years to come to fruition, according to its director, Gleb Panfilov, during a period of heightened interest in Russia in the Romanovs and their fate.[42]

The film narrates the lives of the Imperial Family from Nicholas's abdication up until the execution. In its tone, it is close to the historical interpretation suggested in Radzinsky's 1993 bestseller, *The Last Tsar*. The film even includes Radzinsky's speculative scene leading up to the execution, in which Yurovsky poses his victims as though to take their photograph. But at this point, instead of framing the dead bodies as that tempting hypothetical photographic counterpart to the iconic family portrait of 1913, Panfilov cuts to actual footage of the 2000 canonization ceremony in Moscow. This editing suggests a visual echo of the concluding moments of Andrei Tarkovsky's 1966 masterpiece, *Andrei Rublev*. In the resolution of this heightened dream narrative, and having switched for the first time into colour, the camera slowly pans over the fragments of frescos painted by the eponymous fifteenth-century artist. In Panfilov's film, the emotional charge of the moment when the execution scene dissolves into the canonization ceremony implies that the Romanovs' canonization has resolved the misery and suffering of their imprisonment and death. The movie's title – in Russian, *Romanovy: Ventsenosnaia sem'ia*, with its distinct connotations of martyrs' crowns and Christ's crown of thorns – elides the distinction between secular and religious visions of the Romanovs. Similarly, and again following Radzinsky's interpretation, Panfilov portrays Nicholas offering absolution to his executioners at the moment of his death, with Christ's plea: 'Lord, forgive them, for they know not what they do.'

In essence, however, the film is less a religious tract than a romantic narrative of personal relationships. The dominant theme is family: Nicholas is portrayed as a Chekhovian hero – an Uncle Vanya – for whom family is the crux of his existence.[43] The Romanov family members are heavily romanticized: Nicholas and Alexandra are ideal parents to their delightful children. The four girls are charming and graceful: even in captivity they sing and play the piano, and dance with their little brother, as though imagining the balls they will never now attend.

Panfilov's film was positively received in Russia: it was released in the year that the Romanovs were canonized and rode the crest of Romanov mania. Nevertheless, as long as the idealized Romanov family remained the principal focus of the narrative, there was little intrinsic tension in the movie. Panfilov tried to inject some drama: Nicholas and Alexandra have a minor argument because she is jealous at Nicholas's implied continuing regard for his former lover Kseshinskaya; there is also a sub-plot implying a chaste romance between one of the girls and a young soldier of the Tobolsk house guards. Yet Panfilov's film ultimately remained tedious, and could be little else: the family is idealized, the Romanovs' lives are routine, and the audience already knows the outcome. As a general rule, Romanov films only become interesting when Rasputin takes centre stage. His character can enliven the dullest Romanov epic, even if most do not go as far as the 1965 Hammer Horror film *Rasputin – the Mad Monk*, in which the title role was played by (Count Dracula) Christopher Lee and the audience was given fake Rasputin beards to wear at the opening night.[44] But for a film like Panfilov's, Rasputin is a problematic figure who does not fit well with the idealistic romanticized vision of the family.

Away from the movies and the websites, the Romanovs' innumerable family photographs also contribute to the aura of romance around the Imperial Family today. The iconic pictures of the perfect family from the Tsar's official propaganda still have resonance, as continued awareness of the 1913 family photograph(s) shows. But there is greater curiosity about the private Romanov photographs that were destined only for the family album and until very recently remained locked in the Soviet archives. The question remains: Why are these images of the Romanov family so enthralling? What makes us buy, in our thousands, books showing interminable photographs of a closed circle of uncles, aunts and cousins – indistinguishable from one another after a while – enjoying the mundane distractions of the aristocracy at the turn of the nineteenth century?[45]

One hypothesis for the proliferation of such books is a circular economic argument: public interest in Nicholas, Alexandra and their family has created a market for Romanov photographs, which in turn have become a lucrative source of funds for the perpetually cash-strapped Russian state archives.[46]

But at its most basic, the reason behind the popularity of the Romanovs' private photographs is our curiosity. For late capitalist societies (including Russia's), which are obsessed with the minutiae of celebrities' private lives, the Romanovs provide a wealth of material.

For some viewers, the romance of royalty is sufficient to make the Romanovs fascinating. The imperial children were undoubtedly attractive, but their status gives them the additional glamour of an escapist fantasy. 'The camera loved them,' writes one aficionado, Charlotte Zeepvat, because they possessed 'that peculiar combination of beauty, wealth and destiny that was theirs by accident of birth.'[47] Even in 1970s Russia, the Romanovs had the power to animate the Soviet archivist 'with the bloodless (archival) face' who showed the photographs to Edvard Radzinsky. 'Forgetting herself,' he recalls, 'she waxed enthusiastic and explained each one to me, as if boasting of this amazing vanished life. The dim pictures in those tsarist photographs were a window out of her destitute boring life.'[48] Yet at the same time as playing upon the romance of royalty, the collections of Romanov photographs also insist upon the family's ordinariness, which brings them closer to us, the viewer, the ordinary public. This is precisely what the Romanovs' own propaganda was aiming to achieve, and today's audience has apparently been seduced by the fantasy. Zeepvat, for example, claims that the Romanovs were 'ordinary human beings who happened to be trapped on one of history's most glittering stages'.[49]

This is corrosive and mendacious nonsense. The insistence upon the 'ordinariness' of the Romanovs, while gawping at the glamour and glitter of their lives, blinds us to the political realities of their actions and to the less-than-perfect nature of their family life. How 'ordinary' can it be to spend one's childhood reviewing horseguards; to be given, every birthday, a diamond and a pearl to be made into a necklace when one came of age at 16; to move between at least three palaces and a private yacht; to have one's personal nanny and maid, private tutors, but no friends or playmates outside one's immediate family? The imperial children may have slept on 'narrow camp-beds', but they expected clean sheets on them every day.[50] A moment's reflection suggests that 'ordinariness' is unattainable in the family life of royalty – despite all the attempts to manufacture it – and that the throne is more likely to be occupied by a member of a dysfunctional family than a happy one. Writing of the British monarchy, David Cannadine sums up the problem:

> Far from inhabiting some idealised form of middle-class suburbia, royal life is carried on in vast palaces, with scores of servants, which makes any sort of comfortable intimacy or confidential closeness virtually impossible, while allowing the quirks, oddities and indulgences of individual character to flourish and luxuriate like hot-house plants. Most monarchs and their consorts have been badly educated, have little if any historical understanding of themselves or their circumstances, are

not used to thinking or talking about their feelings, tend to bottle them up and bury them deep, and occasionally give way to explosions of towering rage, in which hairbrushes are thrown and crockery is broken.[51]

Entirely disregarding this truism, however, today's published collections of Romanov family photographs often appear to have borrowed their commentary from Elchaninov's panegyric of 1913. They uncritically reflect the myth of perfect family relationships between Nicholas, Alexandra and their children, which the Tsar's own propaganda created. Compare, for example, Elchaninov (1913): 'The Tsar's children set the greatest store on every moment spent with their father. They obey him unhesitatingly. When they are ill his mere presence is sufficient to soothe them and dry their tears' with this eulogy from Oustimenko and Tyutyunnik (1993): 'All the members of the family were united with sincere feelings of love, mutual respect and friendship. The relations between the parents and their children were cordial and simple, without a shade of estrangement and formality.'[52]

This myth is easily shattered. For example, the expressions of affection in the notes and letters exchanged daily between the members of the Imperial Family cannot possibly reflect the irritations that naturally arose as the children hit adolescence. But hints of discord occasionally break to the surface in complaints voiced by Alexandra in letters to her husband. 'The children', she wrote in 1916, 'still have quite other ideas and rarely understand my way of looking at things.' For the teenage daughters, meanwhile, there was the tedium of coping with a sick mother who was often absent or distant and who, even when present, disapproved of frivolity and adolescent high spirits. All the children suffered from their isolation from their peers imposed by the parents, perhaps to protect the secret of Alexei's illness, perhaps in imitation of Nicholas's own childhood. Few friends of their own age were allowed, and the girls developed with an emotional immaturity inconsonant with their calendar ages: 'even when the two eldest had grown into real young women, one might hear them talking like little girls of ten or twelve', wrote one courtier.[53]

Alexei, meanwhile, frequently behaved with wilful selfishness, which was hardly surprising given his peculiar status. For if Alexei, as the Tsar's only son, were to die without issue the throne would pass to Nicholas's brother Michael, who had been ostracized because he had contracted an unsuitable marriage. Michael's children (were he to have any) would not, therefore, be eligible to inherit the throne, which would pass to another branch of the family entirely, the Vladimirovichi, descendants of Nicholas's uncle Vladimir Alexandrovich. Alexei therefore had to be protected, and his haemophilia meant that he was over-protected, accompanied constantly by his sailor 'uncles' (Derevenko and Nagorny) who carried him, watched over him, and tried to stop him falling down. Unsurprisingly, Alexei became a spoilt brat. 'He liked,' recalled an aristocratic summer neighbour, 'to greet people who bowed to him with a bloody nose by hitting them in the face as they bowed. I remember one day his sailor-nanny taking him by the hand so that he couldn't greet people with a bloody nose, and so the Heir greeted us, in public, with very bad language.'[54]

The myth of the Tsar's perfect family has spread to the extended Romanov clan. Zeepvat gushes of them: 'They were, for the most part, a lively, intelligent, disparate group of people bound together by a genuine love of their country and by the knowledge that the Tsar's interest was their interest.' She gives no hint of the intrigues among Nicholas's uncles to replace the Tsar and his sickly son by a representative of another branch of the family; or of the stultifying upbringing of the children of the imperial house, for whom 'an intellectual mediocrity was both a refuge and a protection'; or of Nicholas's constant struggles with his dissolute uncles and cousins, and even his brother, who all habitually contracted liaisons beneath Romanov dignity.[55]

This disappointing news should not surprise us. The Romanovs were human beings, not ciphers, and they existed in a peculiarly isolated and dysfunctional family. The photographs which seem so romantic betray few of the tensions beneath the surface; but despite all the information available today about the Romanovs, coffee-table picture books continue to subscribe to the perfect family myth and fail to explore the artifice of the images.

Another myth that explains the attraction of the Romanovs today is that of their preference for a 'simple' way of life. Elchaninov again:

> The amusements of the Russian Tsar and his family are few, simple, and innocent. To many of his subjects the life of the Palace would seem dull and monotonous – and in saying this have we not the best evidence of the simplicity, frugality, and unpretentiousness which characterise it.[56]

In fact, the 'simplicity, frugality, and unpretentiousness' that Elchaninov praised was the ideal bourgeois domesticity of Alexandra's Victorian upbringing, which, ironically enough, excited the disdain of the Russian aristocracy. Even her devoted friend Baroness Buxhoeveden could comment of Alexandra's taste in interior design that 'her's [sic] was a sentimental rather than an aesthetic nature'.[57] In their principal family residence, the Alexander Palace at Tsarskoe Selo, Nicholas and Alexandra re-created 'a middle-class home meant to raise children in a setting accessible to, but separated from, the state and the court'.[58] The dominant theme was 'cosiness', 'cosy' being one of the highest terms of praise in the imperial couple's aesthetic vocabulary. Despite the classical elegance of the building, their private rooms were decorated in clashing styles and cluttered with ornaments and objects of sentimental value. Alexandra's famous 'mauve boudoir' was one of the worst offenders. A photograph of the Tsarina reclining in a corner of this room shows a jumble of books and photographs, many frilled cushions, embroidered rugs and ornaments.[59]

The would-be middle-class family life of the Romanovs, deliberately separated from the glittering rarefied world of the Court, seems to bring them closer to us, while the simultaneous context of fabulous wealth and royal charisma – far outside our experience – gives them the patina of glamour that we demand of celebrities. Moreover, this domesticity and 'cosiness' – *uiut* in Russian – are attainable ideals in post-Soviet Russia. They are, at last, something that the emergent middle class can now realize, rather than merely aspire to (as in Stalin's day).[60] This is, perhaps, another reason why the idealized image of the Romanovs and the attractive banalities of their cosy bourgeois domesticity now comfortably inhabits post-Soviet Russia, a society nostalgic for the myth of a kinder, gentler past.

Needless to say, the simple way of life that Elchaninov extolled in order to make Nicholas seem closer to his subjects was an enormous exaggeration, at least until the Tsar abdicated and was placed under house arrest. Perhaps it was only in captivity that the Romanovs began to lead anything remotely like an 'ordinary' life. The relative privations of house arrest and the sudden cancellation of all their official duties meant that the whole family at this point were forced into working for their existence, albeit initially in a somewhat make-believe fashion. In Tsarskoe Selo, the children and their father planted and tended a kitchen garden. Later, in Ekaterinburg, the Grand Duchesses learned to help their lone maid with the washing, since their insistence on having fresh bed linen daily had run up an excessive laundry bill at the Ipatiev House, to the irritation of the Urals Regional Soviet. In the Ipatiev House, also for the first time, they learned from their sole remaining cook how to bake bread.[61]

These new routines gave the captives' lives a semblance of 'ordinariness' that for the first time was genuinely something akin to the lives of their former subjects. Yakov Yurovsky, who became commandant of the Ipatiev House after the family had been living there for some ten weeks, certainly thought so. He wrote in his memoirs:

> They lived, as far as I could see, an ordinary bourgeois way of life. They would drink their tea in the morning, and once they had finished each of them would set to some kind of distraction: sewing, darning, embroidery. . . . If this had not been the tsarist family, which had drunk so much of the people's blood, one might have thought of them as ordinary people, not stuck up. . . . If one looks at this family without political consciousness, one might have said they were completely inoffensive.[62]

'Ordinariness' was something that the Romanovs actually brushed against only during their captivity; it was not the same as the faked modesty and simplicity of the staged propaganda photographs, or even the private family photographs from before their arrest. In the photographs taken during their captivity the Romanovs may be seen carrying out manual tasks, dressed in genuinely plain clothes, and wearing no jewels at all. Yet it is the mythical 'ordinariness' that the Romanovs supposedly manifested when they were still the Imperial Family that is given prominence in the romantic vision of Nicholas II.

The attraction of the dazzling, vanished Russian Court and a sentimentality towards the perfect, 'cosy' Imperial Family seduces both Western and Russian audiences today. But in Russia there is a political dimension to this romanticization of the Romanovs. Fascination with a lost world is all the more poignant when that world represents the path not taken in one's country's history. When it is shaped by a romantic vision of Nicholas II as a humane family man, revelling in simple bourgeois pleasures, it becomes virtually irresistible.[63]

It is not hard to turn Nicholas into a secular saint with the help of his photogenic family, but we sentimentalize at our peril. If we want to understand *why* the Romanovs were killed, the romantic vision provided by the family portraits cannot penetrate the story. It can only give an emotional charge to the simplistic interpretation of Nicholas as a good father and a good husband, tragically murdered together with his family by the evil Bolsheviks. An emotional undertow sweeps reason aside, a fatal combination of star-struck sentimentality about the glamorous-ordinary Romanovs and the historical hindsight of knowing where it will all end. We owe it to the Romanovs to do better than that.

Conclusion
Miscalculating history

> Recently, the intention was to put the former tsar on trial for all his crimes against the people; only current developments interfered with bringing this about.
>
> (*Pravda*, 19 July 1917)

On the evening of 18 July 1918 the Council of People's Commissars (the fledgling Soviet government) was discussing a draft law for the creation of a free popular health service. Comrade Semashko, the People's Commissar for Public Health, was in the midst of giving his report on the issue when the proceedings were interrupted. Sverdlov came in and sat down behind Lenin. He waited patiently until Semashko had finished speaking and then approached Lenin, bending down to whisper in his ear. Lenin showed no obvious reaction to the news, but then informed his colleagues that 'Comrade Sverdlov wishes to make a statement'.

Vladimir Milyutin, who was present at the meeting, recorded what happened next in his diary.

> 'I have to say,' Sverdlov began in his customary even tones, 'that we have had a communication that at Ekaterinburg, by a decision of the Regional Soviet, Nicholas has been shot. Nicholas wanted to escape. The Czecho-Slovaks were approaching. The Presidium of the All-Russian Central Executive Committee has resolved to approve.'
>
> Silence from everyone.
>
> 'Let us now go on to read the draft clause by clause,' suggested Ilich.* The reading clause by clause began.[1]

So, the dramatic news from the cellar of the Ipatiev House, namely the destruction of the Romanov Dynasty, was greeted with silence. Milyutin offers no explanation for Lenin's studied indifference to the ex-Tsar's execution, but seems a little disappointed that the announcement of such

---

* Lenin. Ilich was his patronymic, used affectionately by comrades to refer to him.

a remarkable event had prompted nothing more than a return to the mundane business at hand: the reading, clause by clause, of the draft public health legislation.

In part, the explanation is simple. Lenin, Sverdlov and the other members of the inner circle of government in the Presidium of the Central Executive Committee (CEC) of the Soviets already knew what had happened in Ekaterinburg. Sverdlov had announced to a gathering of the Presidium earlier that day that the Urals Regional Soviet had informed him that Nicholas Romanov had been shot. Sverdlov then composed a press release, which explained that the Urals Bolsheviks had been 'forced' into the decision to shoot the ex-Tsar by the imminent attack on Ekaterinburg by the Czechoslovak forces, and by the discovery of 'a new counter-revolutionary plot . . . that had as its goal tearing the crowned executioner from the hands of Soviet power'. The CEC Presidium had 'discussed all the circumstances' around the Urals Regional Soviet's decision, and recognized 'that the . . . decision was correct'. Sverdlov omitted to tell the public that the whole Romanov family had been shot too. 'Nicholas Romanov's wife and son have been sent to a secure place' was the lie that he peddled, although he – and possibly the other members of the CEC Presidium – knew from a coded telegram sent from the Urals on 17 July that 'the entire family suffered the same fate as its head'.[2]

The way in which the news of Nicholas's death was presented to the public on the pages of *Pravda* is perfectly understandable: Sverdlov spun the shooting of the former Tsar as a necessary decision, taken by the local Bolsheviks in Ekaterinburg under the force of circumstances and dictated by the actions of the counter-revolutionaries in attempting to rescue Nicholas. But Lenin's behaviour over the announcement of Nicholas's death to the Council of People's Commissars is more puzzling. The creation of the new Soviet health service was undoubtedly important, but why would he not have taken a few moments from the business in hand to say at least a few words to mark the historical significance of the ex-Tsar's execution?

The answer, of course, is that Lenin had not wanted Nicholas's death to happen in this manner. If the Tsar had to die in order for the Revolution to assume legitimacy as Russia's new government, then his death ought to have been a public execution, following a public trial which had found him guilty of the crimes he had committed as the personification of autocratic monarchy. This was how the French and the English Revolutions had dealt with their *anciens régimes*, by putting them on trial in the person of the monarch. These monarchs had then been publicly executed, not killed secretly in the dark. Thus, when the former Tsar's execution actually happened, in a gloomy cellar far from Moscow, Lenin ignored it. The provision of health care for the population was of greater importance than the death of a former monarch. If a public trial of the ex-Tsar could not be staged (because he could not be safely brought to Moscow), then Nicholas had no value. As an individual citizen, Nicholas Romanov was irrelevant.

154 Conclusion: Miscalculating history

For the Whites the ex-Tsar remained a potential figurehead, if only they could get their hands on him. Indeed, any member of the former Imperial Family might provide a rallying point for counter-revolution. Thus, with the Whites closing in on Ekaterinburg, those actually in possession of the royal prisoners – the Urals Bolsheviks – unflinchingly calculated that all must die. But if the summary execution of the ex-Tsar and his family was tactically inevitable, strategically it was a major blunder – albeit a forced one – and Lenin's behaviour at the session of the Council of People's Commissars suggests that he knew this. By shooting Nicholas in secret, without being able to put the monarchy on trial, the Bolsheviks lost a key opportunity to legitimize the new regime. Furthermore, by killing the entire family, concealing their bodies, and lying about the fate of the Tsarina and her children, the Bolsheviks planted the persistent seeds of rumour and mystery. In Russia there was no detailed report, no authenticated description of the execution, and no account of what had happened to the bodies. The ex-Tsar and his family had simply vanished. So, naturally, from the moment that Nicholas's death was announced, people began to imagine what had become of him. Killing the ex-Tsar should have finished with autocracy and the Romanovs for good. Yet the manner of his death had quite the opposite effect: it fuelled a stream of contradictory stories and gave Nicholas and his family a restless immortality.

Contrast this with the public executions of Louis XVI and Charles I. Not only had both been publicly tried as monarchs – thereby providing the opportunity to pass judgement on their regimes and bestow legitimacy upon the revolutionary governments that replaced them – but their judicial executions had been witnessed by thousands. Some of those who attended the beheadings of these kings were there out of monarchist sentiment: there are reports of hysterical former subjects dipping their handkerchiefs in the blood dripping from the scaffold in the belief that it had miraculous properties.[3] Nevertheless, the moment when the monarch's severed head was held aloft for all to see was crucial. It left no room for doubt that the king was dead and the old order destroyed. It marked a moment of literal severance with the *ancien régime* and, therefore, the birth of the new.

The secretive manner of the death of Nicholas and his family gave the act the overtones of a crime rather than an execution. This was compounded by the bungled concealment of the bodies, on the grounds that the Whites might have turned them into 'holy relics' (although this fear reveals more about the Bolsheviks' ideas of the Whites than about the reality of White ideology). There are no known photographs of the corpses. Perhaps it was reasoned that photographs of the Tsar's body, and those of his children in particular, would have been powerful anti-Bolshevik propaganda in the hands of the Whites. (In the absence of photographs the Whites had to imagine how the dead Romanovs might have looked with images such as that depicted on the front cover of this book.) Just as with Lenin's reaction to the news of the Tsar's death, for the Bolsheviks, Nicholas's body –

whether his actual physical remains or a photograph of his corpse – was of little value, again because there had been no trial. An extra-judicial execution offered no assistance in establishing the legitimacy of the new government. Had there been a trial, the very nature of absolutism could have been prosecuted with all of the incendiary brilliance of Trotsky's oratory. As it was, the squalid nature of Nicholas's death, rather than bolstering the legitimacy of the Revolution, instead seemed an embarrassment; a piece of ineptitude necessitating silence and lies.

The secrecy surrounding the fate of Nicholas's corpse extended even to the eyewitness statements, which ended up in classified archives. No one must learn of the chaotic secret burial. The Bolsheviks could not, of course, know that six decades later an inquisitive geologist would dig up the bones; still less did they suspect that eighty years after the shooting of the ex-Tsar and his family, science would penetrate the molecular structure of their bones, buried for almost a century, in order to establish with certainty that they were the authentic remains of the Romanovs.

By the time that the identity of the bones had been proven, the ex-Tsar's death had given birth to so many stories that some people refused to believe the scientific and historical evidence of what had happened to him. Other versions of Nicholas's fate made more sense to them than what the anthropological and DNA tests and the documentary record showed about his death, and even about his life. For many, Nicholas had become a saint; secular or religious, it made little difference. The stories about his death filled an emotional and political void for many in Russia and beyond who were looking for meaning in an uncertain world.

Russian émigrés, their lives destroyed by the Bolshevik Revolution, created myths about the Tsar's death that made some sense of the cataclysmic upheaval in their familiar environment. Lurid Gothic versions of Nicholas's murder circulated, in which his dead body was decapitated so that his head could become an unholy relic for the gloating Bolsheviks in Moscow. This story supplied the dispossessed with a way of interpreting the Revolution that satisfactorily demonized Bolshevism. In post-Soviet Russia, too, it was attractive to the extremist national patriots, people whose grasp on the world had become uncertain and who wanted to restore meaning to Russia's history, principally by interpreting it as the victim of 'Judaeo-Bolshevism'. The Gothic horror decapitation narrative, with its encrustations of stories about the Tsar's murder as a ritual act performed by the Jews, circulated all the more widely because the Russian Orthodox Church denied the authenticity of the Romanov bones. This was mainly a political decision, stemming from the ROC's desire to unite with the Russian Orthodox Church Outside Russia and its fear of schism by the extremist patriots in its parishes. Fundamentally, though, all these stories emerged from the clandestine manner in which Nicholas was killed.

Needless to say, a public execution would also have put a stop to Romanov pretenders. The mystery surrounding the death of the Tsar immediately led to a plethora of sightings of Nicholas and his family, apparently still alive after 17 July 1918. There were those who, from the start, wanted to believe that Nicholas had not died but had escaped, together with his family, and had continued to bring up his son Alexei in private, waiting for the day when he could reclaim the throne. It would surely not have been lost on Lenin that the next worst thing to the Whites making Nicholas and his family into figureheads would be the emergence of pretenders to the throne, if there were any mystery about the death of the Imperial Family. What Lenin could not know was that with the discovery in 1991 that Alexei's bones were missing from the mass grave, a whole new set of impostors would arise with claims to be the lost Tsar of Russia.

Without the context of a trial and a judicial execution, the ex-Tsar's death also became a focus for religious sentiment. Stories that he had died with words of absolution for his executioners were elaborated with tales of miracles, weeping icons and visions of the Tsar, in order to suggest that he had sacrificed himself for Russia's salvation in the Russian Orthodox tradition of martyr princes.

The biggest fund of stories about the Tsar, though, focused on him as husband and father in a perfect family. These, too, derived their power from the manner of his death. It is because we now know how Nicholas and his family were killed, in a cramped cellar, thick with cordite smoke, that we romanticize them. The death of the Tsar is the ideal tragic conclusion to myths about the perfect family of Nicholas, Alexandra and their beautiful offspring. The Romanovs' own propaganda established the foundations of the story, of course, with all those soft-focus photographs of the adorable children, but it is the hindsight of knowing that they were all to perish in such a sordid fashion which charges that material today with enormous tragic intensity.

The Bolsheviks committed a serious strategic error, not by executing the former Tsar, but in the manner of the act. His extra-judicial killing gave Nicholas greater mystique than would have been the case had he been put on trial. He became a martyr, his death demonized the Bolsheviks, impostors staked claim to his identity, and most of all it cast an unshakeable aura of romance over an otherwise unremarkable individual. This has made for some good stories, but it has militated against a historical understanding of Nicholas, either as the embodiment of a discredited form of government or simply as a middle-aged man with haemorrhoids and halitosis.

History-writing is always a process of groping towards an unattainable truth; the pursuit of a phantom which remains stubbornly beyond reach. Sometimes history hits hardest when written in the form of a story. The narratives included in this book show that history can be written as fiction and that myth can too often pass for history. But the distinction between them is fundamental and should be maintained. The 'many deaths' of Nicholas II show why.

Notes

1 Cruel necessity

1 This account re-creates what occurred during the killing and burial of Nicholas II and his entourage from the viewpoint of a member of the execution squad. The narrator is a composite figure, whose experience, related here, has been imagined from the evidence supplied in the eyewitness accounts left by some members of the execution squad, the forensic data turned up in the investigations of the physical remains in the 1920s and the 1990s, and the first Bolshevik narratives of the Romanovs' execution. Citing English translations where possible, these sources include the memoirs by Mikhail Medvedev (Kudrin) and G. I. Sukhorukov, and the radio interviews with Grigory Nikulin and Isai Rodzinsky, quoted in V.V. Alekseyev, *The Last Act of a Tragedy: New documents about the execution of the last Russian Emperor, Nicholas II*, Yekaterinburg: Urals Branch of Russian Academy of Sciences, 1996, pp. 142–64; Yurovsky's 1920 'note' and his 1934 speech, quoted in Mark D. Steinberg and Vladimir M. Khrustalëv, *The Fall of the Romanovs: Political dreams and personal struggles in a time of Revolution*, New Haven, CT: Yale University Press, 1995, pp. 351–56; Yurovsky's 1922 memoir, in *Istochnik*, 0 (1993), pp. 107–16; the memoir of A.D. Avdeev (the first Commandant of the Ipatiev House) in *Krasnaia nov'*, 5 (1928), pp. 185–209; and P.M. Bykov, *The Last Days of Tsardom* (translated with an historical preface by Andrew Rothstein), London: Martin Lawrence, 1934.

2 True crime

1 Narrative reconstructed from: Aleksandr Avdonin, 'Taina staroi Koptiakovskoi dorogi', *Istochnik*, 5 (1994), pp. 60–76; Geli Riabov [interview], 'Zemlia vydala tainu', *Moskovskie novosti*, 16, 16 April 1989, p. 16; Geli Riabov, *Kak eto bylo: Romanovy: sokrytie tel, poisk, posledstviia*, Moscow: Politburo, 1998; depositions by Avdonin (8 August 1991) and Riabov (14 September 1991) to Sverdlovsk Region Public Prosecutor V.I. Tuikov about their excavations in 1979 and 1980 in V.V. Alekseyev, *The Last Act of a Tragedy: New documents about the execution of the last Russian Emperor, Nicholas II*, Yekaterinburg: Urals Branch of Russian Academy of Sciences, 1996, pp. 275–90 (docs 108 and 109).
2 Narrative reconstructed from the sources in Note 1 and 'Protocol of the Place of Event [Scene of Crime] Examination' and 'Information from V.I. Tuikov, Prosecutor of the Sverdlovsk Region, for V.G. Stepankov, General Prosecutor of the Russian Federation about the conduct of the prosecutor's verification on the fact of the human remains discovery in a group grave on July 11–13, 1991' (dated 13 August 1992), in Alekseyev, *The Last Act of a Tragedy*, pp. 252–75

(docs 106, 107); Peter Kurth, 'The Mystery of the Romanov Bones', *Vanity Fair*, January 1993, http://www.peterkurth.com/ROMANOV%20BONES.htm (accessed 6 November 2003).
3 Of the literature on cultural shifts in post-Soviet Russia, see: Adele Marie Barker (ed.), *Consuming Russia: Popular Culture, Sex, and Society since Gorbachev*, Durham, NC, and London: Duke University Press, 1999; Svetlana Boym, *Common Places: Mythologies of Everyday Life in Russia*, Cambridge, MA, and London: Harvard University Press, 1994; Dmitri N. Shalin (ed.), *Russian Culture at the Crossroads: Paradoxes of Postcommunist Consciousness*, Oxford: Westview Press, 1996; Masha Gessen, *Dead Again: The Russian Intelligentsia After Communism*, London and New York: Verso, 1997; Nancy Ries, *Russian Talk: Culture and conversation during perestroika*, Ithaca, NY, and London: Cornell University Press, 1997.
4 Richard Stites, 'Crowded on the Edge of Vastness: Observations on Russian Space and Place', in *Beyond the Limits: The concept of space in Russian history and culture*, Jeremy Smith (ed.), Helsinki: SHS, 1999, pp. 259–69, is an amusing and innovative take on the reasons for this.
5 Information from Tuikov to Stepanov, in Alekseyev, *The Last Act of a Tragedy*, pp. 273–4.
6 'The Tsar of All the Russias' was a chapter in Maples's professional autobiography: William R. Maples and Michael Browning, *Dead Men Do Tell Tales: The strange and fascinating cases of a forensic anthropologist*, London: Souvenir Press, 1995; first published New York: Doubleday, 1994, pp. 238–68.
7 A good summary is in Robert K. Massie, *The Romanovs: The final chapter*, London: Jonathan Cape, 1995, pp. 162–251. On Anastasia see also Peter Kurth, *Anastasia: The life of Anna Anderson*, Glasgow: Fontana, 1985; James Blair Lovell, *Anastasia: The lost princess*, London: Robson Books, 1992; and the more balanced John Klier and Helen Mingay, *The Quest for Anastasia*, London: Smith Gryphon, 1995.
8 Peter Gill, Pavel L. Ivanov *et al.*, 'Identification of the Remains of the Romanov Family by DNA Analysis', *Nature Genetics*, 6 (1994), pp. 130–5.
9 W.R. Maples, Affidavit, Circuit Court for the city of Charlottesville, Case No. 8021, 12 November 1993. Cited as fn. 3 in Pavel L. Ivanov *et al.*, 'Mitochondrial DNA Sequence Heteroplasmy in the Grand Duke of Russia Georgij Romanov establishes the Authenticity of the Remains of Tsar Nicholas II', *Nature Genetics*, 12 (1996), pp. 417–20.
10 This, and many other unflattering descriptions of Ivanov and what Olga called the 'official' investigation, may be read in Ol'ga Nikolaevna Kulikovskaia-Romanova, *Nevravnyi poedinok*, Moscow: AO ZT Rodnik, 1995.
11 For the 'Ten Questions' see Iu. A. Buranov (ed.) *Pravda o ekaterinburgskoi tragedii*, Moscow: [no publisher], 1998, pp. 194–7, 199–201.
12 Vadim Viner [interviewed by Strana.Ru], 'Izuchenie "ekaterinburgskikh ostankov" budet prodolzheno', *Pravoslavnaia gazeta*, Ekaterinburg, 22 (2001), pp. 12–13.
13 Soloviev's letter to the Patriarch of 15 January 1998 answering the 'Ten Questions' is in Viktor Aksiuchits (ed.) *Pokaianie: Materialy pravitel'stvennoi Komissii po izucheniiu voprosov, sviazannykh s issledovaniem i perezakhoroneniem ostankov Rossiiskogo Imperatora NIKOLAIA II i chlenov ego sem'i: Izbrannye dokumenty*, Moscow: VYBOR, 1998, pp. 265–70. On Soloviev as Sokolov's successor, see L. Anninskii, 'Solov'ev, letiashchii vosled Sokolovu', *Rodina*, 7 (1998), p. 10; and Soloviev's interview in the same issue, pp. 11–14, '"Razstreliat' i skharonit' tak, chtoby nikto i nikagda ikh trupa ne nashol"'. On the serial number of the investigation see the exchange between Olga Kulikovskaia-Romanova and Soloviev in *Izvestiia*, 28 October 1994, p. 4, and 19 November 1994, p. 6.

14 Professor V. Popov; Prosecutor V. Solov'ev, 'Bor'ba za istinu ili igra v kosti?', *Izvestiia*, 15 January 1998, p. 4. Soloviev named Popov's books as *Identifikatsiia ostankov Tsarskio Sem'i Romanovykh*, and *Gde Vy, Vashe Velichestvo*.
15 Personal communication to the author.
16 Aksiuchits (ed.) *Pokaianie*.
17 See Holy Synod resolutions of 26 February and 9 June 1998, in Buranov (ed.) *Pravda*, p. 239.
18 Robert B. Pickering and David C. Bachman, *The Uses of Forensic Anthropology*, Boca Raton, FL: CRC Press, 1997, pp. 69–96.
19 For an explanation of mtDNA see Bryan Sykes, *The Seven Daughters of Eve: The science that reveals our genetic ancestry*, London: Bantam Press, 2001; on the DNA testing of the Tsar's bones see pp. 63–78.
20 The details of the tests were published in Gill *et al.*, 'Identification of the Remains'. The Duke of Fife was officially named as the source of the comparison sample of mtDNA in Ivanov, 'Mitrochondrial DNA', p. 418.
21 Ivanov, 'Mitrochondrial DNA', p. 419.
22 King's research remained unpublished, but was cited in Ivanov, 'Mitrochondrial DNA', p. 418, and on p. 340 in the same issue of *Nature Genetics*.
23 Olga Nikolaievna Kulikovskaia-Romanova, interview, 'The Bones of Contention', *Road To Emmaus: A journal of Orthodox faith and culture*, 12 (winter 2003).
24 *Nature*, 392, 118, 12 March 1998. Rogaev reported his experiments in *Pokaianie*, pp. 171–82.
25 Nagai's papers were 'No Heteroplasmy at Base Position 16169 of Tsar Nikolai II's Mitochondrial DNA' presented at the Nineteenth International Congress of the International Society for Forensic Genetics in Muenster, Germany, in August 2001; and 'Mitochondrial DNA Sequence of Romanoff Family' at the Seventh Indo-Pacific Congress on Legal Medicine and Forensic Sciences in Melbourne, Australia, in September 2001. For interview, see *Izvestiia*, 23 July 2001.
26 Viktor Belimov, 'Reaktsiia rossiiskikh uchenykh na issledovaniia Tatsuo Nagai', stranaRu, 24.09.01; http://www.strana.ru/print/63087.html (accessed 27 May 2004). See also Viner interview, *Pravoslavnaia gazeta*.
27 Lev Zhivotovskii [interview], 'Oshibki bluzhdaiushchikh atomov', *Literaturnaia gazeta*, 2002, on http://www.romanov-center.ural.org/news/com_o%20nagai.htm (accessed 27 May 2004). For Ivanov's rebuttal of Nagai's results, see Pavel Ivanov, 'Zakhoronenie tsaria – do sikh por goriachaia tema', *Izvestiia-nauka*, 27 July 2001, http://www.romanov-center.ural.org/news/otvet_ivanov_to%20japan.htm (accessed 27 May 2004).
28 L.A. Zhivotovsky, 'Recognition of the Remains of Tsar Nicholas II and his Family: A Case of Premature Identification?', *Annals of Human Biology*, 26 (1999), pp. 569–77; A. Knight, L.A. Zhivotovsky *et al.*, 'Molecular, Forensic and Haplotypic Inconsistencies Regarding the Identity of the Ekaterinburg Remains', *Annals of Human Biology*, 31 (2004), pp. 129–38; Richard Stone, 'Buried, Recovered, Lost Again? The Romanovs May Never Rest', *Science*, 303 (2004), p. 753.
29 Lev Zhivotovskii, in Buranov, *Pravda*, pp. 100–3; see also Zhivotovsky, 'Recognition'.
30 This is the figure calculated in Ivanov, 'Mitrochondrial DNA', p. 420.
31 *Pokaianie*, pp. 71, 139, 160.
32 On the Tsar's teeth see *Pokaianie*, p. 122; Maples, *Dead Men*, pp. 258–9; and Vyacheslav Popov, *Izvestiia*, 15 January 1998, p. 4.
33 Maples, *Dead Men*, p. 258.
34 *Pokaianie*, p. 88.
35 *Pokaianie*, pp. 59, 63. The reconstructions were cited as yet more proof that Maria, and not Anastasia, was the missing girl.

160 *Notes*

36 Pickering and Bachman, *The Uses of Forensic Anthropology*, p. xx.
37 Robert Massie interviews with Abramov and Maples in *The Romanovs*, pp. 42–8, 66–7, 74–8.
38 *Pokaianie*, pp. 41, 43–4.
39 *Pokaianie*, pp. 73–5, 90–1.
40 For conclusions on burning see *Pokaianie*, p. 90; for decay theory see Maples, *Dead Men*, pp. 262–3.
41 Edvard Radzinsky, *The Last Tsar: The life and death of Nicholas II*, New York: Anchor Books, 1993, pp. 414–18.

3 The many deaths of Nicholas II

1 Aleksandr Avdonin, 'Taina staroi Koptiakovskoi dorogi: Ob istorii poiskov ostankov imperatorskoi sem'i', *Istochnik*, 5 (1994), pp. 60–76; p. 62. The story is also told in Edvard Radzinsky, *The Last Tsar: The life and death of Nicholas II*, New York: Anchor Books, 1993, p. 396. Radzinsky's source was allegedly Mikhail Medvedev, son of Medvedev-Kudrin (a member of the execution party).
2 Marc Ferro, *Nicholas II: The last of the tsars*, trans. Brian Pearce, London: Viking, 1991, p. 285.
3 The leitmotiv of Mikhail Bulgakov's *The Master and Margarita*, 1967, in which the Master's burned novel is miraculously restored thanks to the intervention of the Devil and the love of Margarita.
4 Nicolas Sokoloff, *Enquête judiciare sur l'Assassinat de la Famille Impériale Russe*, Paris: Payot, 1924.
5 N.A. Sokolov, *Ubiistvo tsarskoi sem'i*, Moscow, St Petersburg, 1990, first published Berlin: Slovo, 1925; M.K. Diterikhs, *Ubiistvo tsarskoi sem'i i chlenov doma romanovykh na Urale*, Moscow: Skify, 1991, first published Vladivostok, 1922; Robert Vil'ton, *Poslednie dni Romanovykh*, Moscow: Pamiat', 1998, first published Robert Wilton, *The Last Days of the Romanovs, from 15th March 1917. Part I: The narrative; Part II: The depositions of eye-witnesses*, London: Thornton Butterworth, 1920; O.A. Platonov, *Ternovyi venets Rossii: zagovor tsareubiits*, Moscow: Rodnik, 1996; journal *Tsar kolokol*, Moscow, 1990– .
6 David Remnick, 'Letter from St Petersburg: The Next Tsar', *The New Yorker*, 6 July 1998, pp. 40–53, p. 49.
7 For the most recent absurd escape narrative see Shay McNeal, *The Plots to Rescue the Tsar: The truth behind the disappearance of the Romanovs*, London: Century, 2001.
8 For romanticized Russian biographies of Nicholas II see the works of Aleksandr Bokhanov. Among recent English-language publications on the Romanovs see Rosemary Crawford and Donald Crawford, *Michael and Natasha: The life and love of Michael II, the last of the Romanov tsars*, New York: Scribner, 1997; Patricia Phoenix, *Olga Romanov: Russia's last Grand Duchess*, Toronto: Viking, 1999; Charlotte Zeepvat, *Romanov Autumn: Stories from the last century of Imperial Russia*, Stroud: Sutton Publishing, 2000.
9 Julian Barnes, *A History of the World in 10½ Chapters*, London: Jonathan Cape, 1989, p. 245.
10 Hayden White, *The Content of the Form: Narrative discourse and historical representation*, Baltimore, MD: Johns Hopkins University Press, 1987. For a discussion of history as the product of historians' writing, see Alun Munslow, *Deconstructing History*, London and New York: Routledge, 1997.
11 Simon Schama, *Dead Certainties (Unwarranted Speculations)*, London: Granta and Penguin, 1991.
12 Schama, *Dead Certainties*, p. 320.

13 E.H. Carr, *The Bolshevik Revolution, 1917–1923*, 3 vols, London: Macmillan, 1950, vol. 1, p. 166.
14 Acts of abdication of Nicholas II and Mikhail Aleksandrovich Romanov, Docs 26 and 29 in Mark D. Steinberg and Vladimir M. Khrustalëv, *The Fall of the Romanovs: Political dreams and personal struggles in a time of Revolution*, New Haven, CT: Yale University Press, 1995, pp. 100–2; p. 105.
15 Richard Pipes, *The Russian Revolution, 1899–1919*, London: Vintage, 1991, p. 788.
16 Oleg Platonov, *Ubiistvo tsarskoi sem'i*, Moscow: Sovetskaia Rossiia, 1991, p. 3.
17 Orlando Figes, *A People's Tragedy: The Russian Revolution, 1891–1924*, London: Jonathan Cape, 1996, p. 639.
18 Histories of the revolutionary period written from this cultural perspective include Christopher Read, *From Tsar to Soviets: The Russian people and their revolution, 1917–21*, London: UCL Press, 1996; Martin A. Miller (ed.) *The Russian Revolution: The essential readings*, Oxford: Blackwell, 2001; S.A. Smith, *The Russian Revolution: A very short introduction*, Oxford: Oxford University Press, 2002.
19 See Doc. 152 and facsimile [coded telegram] in Steinberg and Khrustalëv, pp. 337–8.
20 Lev Trotskii, 'Ssylka, vysylka, skitaniia, smert'', *Znamia*, 8 (1990), pp. 165–98; pp. 179–80.
21 Ibid.
22 Ibid.
23 The details of this incident are much disputed. For an exhaustive discussion see Greg King and Penny Wilson, *The Fate of the Romanovs*, Hoboken, NJ: John Wiley & Sons, 2003, pp. 71–102.
24 Peter Kenez, 'The Ideology of the White Movement', *Soviet Studies*, 32 (1980), pp. 58–83.
25 Pipes, *The Russian Revolution*, p. 788.
26 Dominic Lieven, *Nicholas II Emperor of all the Russias*, London: John Murray, 1993, pp. 248–9.
27 George Leggett, *The Cheka: Lenin's political police*, Oxford: Clarendon Press, 1986.
28 Docs 155 and 156 in Steinberg and Khrustalëv, pp. 341–5.
29 Doc. 157 in Steinberg and Khrustalëv, p. 345.
30 Chicherin's remarks reported in *The Times*, 25 April 1922; Ferro, *Nicholas II*, p. 242. On the sightings see Anthony Summers and Tom Mangold, *The File on the Tsar*, London: Orion Books, 2002 [1st edn London, Victor Gollancz, 1976], pp. 186–7.
31 P.M. Bykov, *The Last Days of Tsardom*, translated with an historical preface by Andrew Rothstein, London: Martin Lawrence, 1934 [translation of *Poslednie dni Romanovykh*, Sverdlovsk, 1926]. Bykov's original sketch was 'Poslednie dni poslednego tsaria', in *Rabochaia revoliutsiia na Urale*, Sverdlovsk, 1921, republished in Taras Stepanchuk and Zinaida Stepanchuka (eds), *Dom Romanovykh: k 300-letnemu iubileiu tsarstvovaniia 1613–1913; Poslednie dni poslednego tsaria (unichtozhenie dinastii Romanovykh)*, Moscow: TsEK Zhivaia voda, 1991.
32 A.D. Avdeev, 'Nikolai Romanov v Tobol'ske i v Ekaterinburge: (Iz vospominanii komendanta)', *Krasnaia nov'*, 5 (1928), pp. 185–209; p. 209.
33 Richard Halliburton, *Seven League Boots*, London: Geoffrey Bles, 1936, pp. 95–121.
34 For text of Yurovsky's 1920 'note' and his 1934 speech see Docs 159 and 160 in Steinberg and Khrustalëv, pp. 351–6. Yurovsky's 1922 memoir was published

in *Istochnik*, 0 (1993), pp. 107–16. It is not, therefore, the case that King and Wilson in *The Fate of the Romanovs* use a document that 'has never before been published' (p. 20), as they claim of Yurovsky's 1922 memoir.
35 Correspondence, including facsimiles, Docs 137–42 in Steinberg and Khrustalëv, pp. 310–20.
36 Intourist, *A Pocket Guide to the Soviet Union*, Moscow and Leningrad, Vneshtorgisdat, 1932, p. 416; The Right Hon. Wedgwood Benn and Margaret Benn, *Beckoning Horizon: The story of a journey around the world*, London: Cassell, 1935, p. 321; Margaret Stansgate, *My Exit Visa*, London: Hutchinson, 1992, pp. 178–9.
37 On the vogue for Russian nationalism in the 1970s see Yitzhak M. Brudny, *Reinventing Russia: Russian nationalism and the Soviet state, 1953–1991*, Cambridge, MA: Harvard University Press, 1998; Peter J.S. Duncan, *Russian Messianism. Third Rome, Revolution, Communism and After*, London: Routledge, 2000.
38 Lengthy extracts from Medvedev-Kudrin's memoir, and transcripts of the radio interviews with Nikulin and Isai Rodzinsky, Docs 42–4 in V.V. Alekseyev, *The Last Act of a Tragedy: New documents about the execution of the last Russian Emperor, Nicholas II*, Yekaterinburg: Urals Branch of Russian Academy of Sciences, 1996, pp. 144–64.
39 M.K. Kasvinov, *Dvadtsat' tri stupeni vniz*, Moscow, 1978, first published *Zvezda*, 1972; on *Agoniya* see Anna Lawton, *Kinoglasnost: Soviet cinema in our time*, Cambridge: Cambridge University Press, 1992, p. 29; for an example of academic history, see G.Z. Ioffe, *Krakh rossiiskoi monarkhicheskoi kontrrevoliutsii*, Moscow, 1977.
40 Boris Yeltsin, *Against the Grain: An autobiography*, trans. Michael Glenny, London: Jonathan Cape, 1990, pp. 64–6.
41 Katherine Verdery, *The Political Lives of Dead Bodies: Reburial and postsocialist change*, New York: Columbia University Press, 1999, p. 18.
42 Edvard Radzinskii, quoted in R.W. Davies, *Soviet History in the Yeltsin Era*, London: Macmillan, 1997, p. 51.
43 Orlando Figes, 'Burying the Bones', *Granta: Russia: The Wild East*, 64, winter 1998, pp. 95–111; p. 106. This attitude is the subject of Chapter 7. There were just a few articles that questioned the funeral's romanticization of the Romanovs (e.g. Aleksandr Bovin, 'Primirenie i pokaianie', *Izvestiia*, 11 July 1998, p. 4, called the burial 'a theatre of the absurd').
44 On monarchism, see Aleksei Mukhin, *Pravoslavnye monarkhisty v Rossii 1988–1996 gody: Istoriia, ob"edineniia, biografii*, Moscow: SPIK-Tsentr, 1997; Prince Nikolai Romanovich Romanov, 'Da khraniat nas Bog i Rossiia!', *Rossiiskie vesti*, 6 June 2001.
45 *Time*, 2 March 1998, Online. Available at: <http://www.time.com/time/magazine/1998/int/980302/europe.r.i.p.at_long_las8.html> (accessed 30 June 2005). Maria and her family are promoted in Il'ia Tkachev, *Dinastiia Romanovykh*, Moscow: Izdatel'skii Dom GELEOS, 1998; The Russian-language website of Maria and her family is online at <http://www.imperialhouse.ru> (accessed 8 September 2005).
46 For an assessment of the strength of nationalist tendencies within the ROC see Thomas Parland, 'Christian Orthodoxy and Contemporary Russian Nationalism' in David Westerlund (ed.), *Questioning the Secular State: The worldwide resurgence of religion in politics*, London: Hurst, 1996, pp. 117–39; Stephen D. Shenfield, *Russian Fascism: Traditions, tendencies, movements*, Armonk and London: M.E. Sharpe, 2001, pp. 60–72; Aleksandr Verkhovsky, 'The Role of the Russian Orthodox Church in Nationalist, Xenophobic and Antiwestern Tendencies in Russia Today: Not Nationalism, but Fundamentalism,' *Religion, State and Society*, 30 (2002), pp. 333–45.

47 Dmitry Pospielovsky, 'The Russian Orthodox Church in the Postcommunist CIS' in Michael Bourdeaux (ed.), *The Politics of Religion in Russia and the New States of Eurasia*, Armonk and London: M.E. Sharpe, 1995, pp. 41–74.
48 On fundamentalism and anti-modernism see Carl F. Hallencreutz and David Westerlund, 'Anti-Secularist Policies of Religion' in Westerlund (ed.), *Questioning the Secular State: The worldwide resurgence of religion in politics*, London: Hurst, 1996, pp. 1–23; Mark Juergensmeyer, *The New Cold War? Religious nationalism confronts the secular state*, Berkeley: University of California Press, 1993.
49 Author's interview with Father Vitalii Borovoi, Daniilevskii Monastery, Moscow, 25 April 1996; Hilarion Alfeev, 'Reviving the Russian Orthodox Church: A Task Both Theological and Secular' in Heyward Isham (ed.) with Natan M. Shklyar, *Russia's Fate through Russian Eyes: Voices of the new generation*, Boulder, CO: Westview Press, 2001, pp. 235–49; author's discussions with Bettina Weichert, London, 2002 to 2003.

4 Gothic horror

1 Nikolai Nikolayevich Breshko-Breshkovsky had been a prolific writer of sensationalist romantic novels for the boulevard press, and emigrated to Warsaw in 1921. On the mood of his émigré readership see Marc Raeff, *Russia Abroad: A cultural history of the Russian emigration, 1919–1939*, New York and Oxford: Oxford University Press, 1990, p. 8.
2 N.N. Breshko-Breshkovskii, *Tsarskie brillianty*, Paris: Presse Franco-Russe, 1921, pp. 10–13.
3 Oleg Platonov; Sviatoslav Rybas; Vladimir Soloukhin, 'Zhizn' i tragediia Imperatora Nikolaia II po arkhivnym materialam i pisatel'skim issledovaniiam', *Literaturnaia Rossiia*, 32, 9 August 1991, pp. 16–22, p. 19, allegedly translated from *Hannoverscher Anzeiger*, 7 December 1928, no. 288. O.A. Platonov, *Ternovyi venets Rossii: Istoriia tsareubiistva*, Moscow: Entsiklopediia russkoi tsivilizatsii, 2001, pp. 321–4.
4 Evgenii Gol'tsev, 'Revoliutsioner sprava: Istoriia Ieromonakha Iliodora', *Nedelia*, 25 June to 1 July 1990, p. 10.
5 Tom Reiss, *The Orientalist: Solving the mystery of a strange and dangerous life*, New York: Random House, 2005.
6 Mohammed Essad-Bey, *Nicholas II: Prisoner of the purple*, trans. Paul Maerker Branden and Elsa Branden, London: Hutchinson, 1936, pp. 280–1; first published in German as *Nikolaus II. Glanz und Untergang des letzten Zaren*, Berlin, 1935.
7 For Bulygin's reminiscences see Captain Paul Bulygin, *The Murder of the Romanovs*, London: Hutchinson, 1935.
8 Sergei Melgunov, *Sud'ba Imperatora Nikolaia II posle otrecheniia: Istoriko-kriticheskie ocherki*, Paris: Editions "La Renaissance", 1951, p. 411.
9 S. Fomin, 'Vokrug Ekaterinburgskoi Golgofy', intro. to Gen. M.K. Diterikhs, 'Ubiistvo tsarskoi sem'i', *Nash sovremennik*, 7 (1991), pp. 151–2.
10 The programme was broadcast on NTV in February 1996. For references to it see Oleg Platonov, *Ternovyi venets Rossii: Istoriia tsareubiistva*, pp. 321–2; L.E. Bolotin, 'Sredstva massovoi informatsii o tsareubiistva' in Iu.A. Buranov (ed.), *Pravda o ekaterinburgskoi tragedii*, Moscow: [no publisher], 1998, pp. 151–62; p. 154.
11 V. Rodikov, '"Grob, torzhestvenno vnesennyi ..." Pravda i lozh' o rasprave nad tsarskoi sem'ei', *Inzhenernaia gazeta*, 7 (1990).
12 M.K. Diterikhs, *Ubiistvo Tsarskoi Sem'i i chlenov Doma Romanovykh na Urale*, Part I, Moscow: Skify, 1991 [Vladivostok: 1922], p. 3.
13 Diterikhs, *Ubiistvo Tsarskoi Sem'i*, pp. 245–6, 248–50, 256–8.

14 Robert Wilton, *The Last Days of the Romanovs, from 15th March 1917. Part I: The narrative; Part II: The depositions of eye-witnesses*, London: Thornton Butterworth, 1920, Part I, pp. 79, 81.
15 Gisela C. Lebzelter, *Political Anti-Semitism in England, 1918–1939*, London: Macmillan, 1978.
16 Wilton, *The Last Days of the Romanovs*, Part I, p. 148.
17 Ibid., p. 104.
18 Platonov, *Istoriia tsareubiistva*, p. 311, cites Wilton's 1920 French version in support of the 'bearded Jew' (there is no reference to him in Wilton's 1920 English version); Platonov, *Zagovor*, 1996, p. 426, cites Wilton and Diterikhs with reference to the black-garmented 'rabbi'; the phrase also appears in V. Ushkuinik, *Pamiatka russkomu cheloveku: paradoksy istorii*, Moscow: PT "Kap"', 1993, pp. 22–3 [New York: Politicheskoe vospitanie, 1982, p. 25].
19 Enel, *Sacrifice*, Brussels: J. Schicks, n.d., 2nd edn, p. 19.
20 Platonov, *Ternovyi venets Rossii*, p. 314.
21 King and Wilson, *The Fate of the Romanovs*, devote a lengthy and informative footnote to the question (pp. 582–3), but are too glib in asserting that 'the issue of Yakov Yurovsky's ethnic background is of little historical interest'.
22 Platonov, *Ternovyi venets Rossii*, pp. 296, 310–11, 320.
23 Simon Schama, *Citizens: A chronicle of the French Revolution*, London: Viking, 1989, p. 673. See also Daniel Arasse, *The Guillotine and the Terror*, trans. Christopher Miller, London: Allen Lane, 1989, first published Paris: Flammarion, 1987.
24 Mark S. Simpson, *The Russian Gothic Novel and its British Antecedents*, Columbus, OH: Slavica Publishers, 1986, p. 10.
25 C.V. Wedgwood, *The Trial of Charles I*, London: Collins, 1964, p. 202.
26 Hans Rogger, 'The Beilis Case: Anti-Semitism and Politics in the Reign of Nicholas II', *Slavic Review*, 25 (1966), pp. 615–29.
27 Eric Naiman, *Sex in Public: The incarnation of early Soviet ideology*, Princeton, NJ: Princeton University Press, 1997, pp. 148–80.
28 I.M. Vasilevskii (Ne-Bukva), *Chto oni pishut? Memuary byvshikh liudei*, Leningrad: Gos. uchebno-prakt. shkola-tip. im. tov. Alekseeva, 1925, p. 26.
29 Vasilevskii, *Chto oni pishut?*, p. 32.
30 Naiman, *Sex in Public*, p. 151, quoting Dale Peterson, 'Russian Gothic: The Deathless Paradoxes of Bunin's *Dry Valley*', *Slavic and Eastern European Journal*, 31 (1987), pp. 36–49.
31 Naiman, *Sex in Public*, p. 289.
32 Bruce A. Beatie and Phyllis W. Powell, 'Story and Symbol: Notes Towards a Structural Analysis of Bulgakov's *The Master and Margarita*', *Russian Literature Triquarterly*, 15 (1978), pp. 219–51. For recent esoteric interpretations see e.g. A. Korablev, *Master. Astral'nyi roman*, Donetsk, 1996; G.V. Makarova and A.A. Abrashkin, *Tainopis' v romane* Master i Margarita, Nizhnii Novgorod, 1997.

5 False Alexeis

1 On Ioann of Kronstadt see Nadieszda Kizenko, *A Saint's Two Bodies: John of Kronstadt and the Russian People*, University Park, PA: Pennsylvania State University Press, 2000.
2 Viatkin's report, together with depositions from Shitov and the nun Natalia Feodorovna, and the protocol of sentencing drawn up by the OGPU, are published in Mariia Malysheva and Vladimir Poznanskii, '"Prishlos' uslyshat' o svoem tsarskom proiskhozhdenii"', *Istochnik*, 6, (1995), pp. 41–9.
3 Malysheva and Poznanskii, '"Prishlos' uslyshat"', pp. 43–4.

4 On the central importance of this substitution see Christopher Read, 'Values, Substitutes, and Institutions: The Cultural Dimension of the Bolshevik Dictatorship' in Vladimir Brovkin (ed.), *The Bolsheviks in Russian Society: The revolution and the civil wars*, New Haven, CT, and London: Yale University Press, 1997, pp. 298–318.
5 Vladimir Brovkin, *Russia After Lenin: Politics, culture and society, 1921–1929*, London and New York: Routledge, 1998, pp. 110–12.
6 Edward E. Roslof, *Red Priests: Renovationism, Russian Orthodoxy, and Revolution, 1905–1946*, Bloomington: Indiana University Press, 2002.
7 William B. Husband, *"Godless Communists": Atheism and society in Soviet Russia, 1917–1932*, DeKalb, IL: Northern Illinois University Press, 2000, p. 118.
8 Stephen Kotkin, *Magnetic Mountain: Stalinism as a civilisation*, Berkeley: University of California Press, 1995, esp. pp. 198–237. The diary of a young worker in the 1930s reveals his struggles to reshape his consciousness: Jochen Hellbeck, 'The Diary of Stepan Podlubnyi, 1931–1939' in Sheila Fitzpatrick (ed.), *Stalinism: New Directions*, London: Routledge, 2000, pp. 77–116.
9 Sheila Fitzpatrick, 'Making a Self for the Times: Impersonation and Imposture in 20th Century Russia', *Kritika: Explorations in Russian and Eurasian History* 2 (2001), pp. 469–87; p. 482.
10 Fitzpatrick, 'Making a Self for the Times', p. 481. Lunacharskii was Commissar for Enlightenment; Prince Kropotkin a famous anarchist.
11 Anthony Summers and Tom Mangold, *The File on the Tsar*, London: Orion Books, 2002 [first published London: Victor Gollancz, 1976], pp. 185–7.
12 Robert Harris, *Selling Hitler*, London: Faber and Faber, 1986, p. 50.
13 For Radzinsky quote see David Remnick, 'Letter from St Petersburg: The Next Tsar', *The New Yorker*, 6 July 1998, pp. 40–53; p. 49; for Nicholas Romanov quote see http://media.dagospia.com/public_html/articolo_2272.html (accessed 4 July 2005).
14 John M.L. Kendrick, 'Alexei stories'. E-mails (4 July 2005; 4 February 2006).
15 William Clarke, *The Lost Fortune of the Tsars*, London: Weidenfeld & Nicolson, 1994, pp. 270, 276.
16 Pierre Gilliard, *Le Tragique Destin de Nicolas II et de sa Famille*, Paris: Payot, 1921, p. 237; cited in Summers and Mangold, *The File on the Tsar*, pp. 188–9.
17 Edvard Radzinsky, *The Last Tsar: The life and death of Nicholas II*, New York: Anchor Books, 1993, pp. 420–4, citing reports from Semyonov's doctors and a fellow-prisoner; David Remnick, 'Letter from St Petersburg', p. 49.
18 Sigmund Freud, 'Family Romances' in *The Standard Edition of the Complete Psychological Works of Sigmund Freud*, trans. and ed. James Strachey, London: The Hogarth Press, 1959, Vol. IX, pp. 235–41.
19 Gilliard, p. 237, quoted in Summers and Mangold, *The File on the Tsar*, p. 189.
20 PINKLADY, online posting on Alexander Palace Discussion Board, 16 June 2005 at <http://hydrogen.pallasweb.com/cgi-bin/yabb/YaBB.cgi?board=loonies; action=display;num=1097613572;start=75> (accessed 4 July 2005).
21 http://www.romanovfamily2000.com/default1.html (accessed 4 July 2005).
22 http://mywebpage.netscape.com/rmgibsonryan/The_Great_Romanov_ Deception.html (accessed 4 July 2005).
23 Robert Massie, *The Romanovs: The final chapter*, London: Jonathan Cape, 1995, pp. 148; 144–5.
24 Remnick, 'Letter from St Petersburg', p. 49.
25 G.B. Egorov, I.V. Lysenko and V.V. Petrov, *Spasenie Tsesarevicha Alekseia: Istoriko-kriminalisticheskaia rekonstruktsiia rasstrela Tsarskoi Sem'i*, St Petersburg: Russko-Baltiiskii informatsionnyi tsentr BLITs, 1998, p. 87.
26 O.V. Filatov, *Istoriia dushi, ili portret epokhy: Sud'ba Tsesarevicha Alekseia, syna Imperatora Rossii Nikolaia II*, St Petersburg: Fond 'Derzhavnye traditsii', 2000, p. 36.

27 Filatov, *Istoriia dushi*, p. 45.
28 Remnick, 'Letter from St Petersburg', p. 40; Filatov, *Istoriia dushi*, p. 17.
29 The Russian version is Egorov *et al.*, *Spasenie Tsesarevicha Alekseia*; the English version is Vadim Petrov, Igor Lysenko and Georgy Egorov, with personal reminiscences by the family of Vasily Filatov, *The Escape of Alexei, Son of Tsar Nicholas II: What happened the night the Romanov family was executed*, trans. Marian Schwartz and Antonina W. Bouis, New York: Harry N. Abrams, 1998.
30 Filatov, *Istoriia dushi*, p. 54.
31 Orlando Figes, 'Czar Vasily? Another Account of a Romanov Survivor', *New York Times Book Review*, 22 November 1998, p. 46; Remnick, 'Letter from St Petersburg', p. 53; Abrams quote from *Publishers' Weekly*, 20 July 1998.
32 http://www.ceo.spb.ru/eng/literature/filatov.o.v/index.shtml (accessed 27 September 2005).
33 Remnick, 'Letter from St Petersburg', pp. 44, 53.
34 Michael Gray, *Blood Relative*, London: Victor Gollancz, 1998.
35 The diary entry is quoted in full in Summers and Mangold, *The File on the Tsar*, pp. 365–6.
36 Gray, *Blood Relative*, p. 244.
37 *The News Letter*, 25 September 1998; *Birmingham Post*, 25 September 1998; *Mirror*, 16 October 1998. All online at <http://www.highbeam.com (accessed 5 and 6 July 2005).
38 Gray, *Blood Relative*, pp. 74–80.
39 Ibid., pp. 6, 254.
40 Guy Richards, *Imperial Agent: The Goleniewski–Romanov Case*, New York: The Devin-Adair Company, 1966.
41 Frederick L. Wettering, 'Counterintelligence: The Broken Triad', *International Journal of Intelligence and CounterIntelligence*, 13, 3 (2000), pp. 265–300; Edward Jay Epstein, 'The Spy Wars', *New York Times Magazine*, 28 September 1980. Available online at: http://www.edwardjayepstein.com/archived/spywars_print.htm (accessed 27 September 2005).
42 Summers and Mangold, *The File on the Tsar*, pp. 189–90.
43 *Novoe russkoe slovo*, New York, 8 December 1964; cited in Richards, *Imperial Agent*, p. 251.
44 *Anastasia: The autobiography of HIH the Grand Duchess Anastasia Nicholaevna of Russia*, New York: Spellman, 1963.
45 Richards, *Imperial Agent*, pp. 252–6.
46 William Clarke, *The Lost Fortune of the Tsars* (rev. edn), London: Orion Books, 1996, pp. 176–82.
47 Richards, *Imperial Agent*, p. 43.
48 Ibid., pp. 106, 39.
49 Clarke, *The Lost Fortune* (rev. edn), pp. 176, 186.
50 Richards, *Imperial Agent*, p. 19.
51 John M.L. Kendrick, 'Tsarevich Alexei: Lenin's greatest secret'. Available online at <http://www.npsnet.com/tsarevich_alexei/> (accessed 23 January 2004); 'The Spala Crisis of 1912: Rasputin Explained and Alexei Found'. Available online at: <http://www.npsnet.com/alexei_found/> (accessed 27 January 2004).
52 John M.L. Kendrick, 'Alexei Tammet-Romanov'. E-mail (27 January 2004).
53 John M.L. Kendrick, 'Russia's Imperial Blood: Was Rasputin not the Healer of Legend?', *American Journal of Hematology*, 77, 1 (2004), pp. 92–102.
54 John Kendrick, 'Russia's Last Tsar: Why are Alexei's Bones Absent?', *St Petersburg Times*, 2001. Available online at: <http://www.sptimesrussia.com/special/tsar/why.htm> (accessed 27 January 2004).
55 Figes, 'Czar Vasily?'

56 Robert Alexander, *The Kitchen Boy: A novel of the last Tsar*, New York: Viking, 2003. A survey of fiction about the Romanovs is Janet Ashton, 'Locked Windows, Locked Minds: The Fictional Portrayal of the Romanovs', *Atlantis*, 5, 1, pp. 166–88.

6 Tsar martyr

1 Aleksandr Shargunov, *Novye chudesa Tsartsvennykh muchenikov*, Moscow: Novaia kniga, 1996, pp. 62–4.
2 G.L. Freeze, 'Subversive Piety: Religion and the Political Crisis in Late Imperial Russia', *Journal of Modern History*, 68 (1996), pp. 308–50.
3 On Men' see Michael A. Meerson, 'The Life and Work of Father Aleksandr Men' in Stephen K. Batalden (ed.), *Seeking God: The recovery of religious identity in Orthodox Russia, Ukraine, and Georgia*, DeKalb, IL: Northern Illinois University Press, 1993, pp. 13–26. On Ioann (who died in 1995) see Wendy Slater, 'A Modern-day Saint? Metropolitan Ioann and the Postsoviet Russian Orthodox Church', *Religion, State and Society*, 28 (2000), pp. 313–25.
4 This is well discussed by Boris Orlov and Sophia Kotzer, 'The Russian Orthodox Church in a Changing Society' in Nurit Schleifman (ed.), *Russia at a Crossroads: History, Memory and Political Practice*, London: Frank Cass, 1998, pp. 147–71.
5 Author's interview with Fr Vsevolod Chaplin, Daniilevskii Monastery, Moscow, 27 October 1998.
6 James Cunningham, *A Vanquished Hope: The movement for church renewal in Russia, 1905–1906*, Crestwood, NY: St Vladimir's Press, 1981; G.L. Freeze, 'Handmaiden of the State? The Church in Imperial Russia Reconsidered', *Journal of Ecclesiastical History*, 36 (1985), pp. 82–102; Gerhard Simon, 'Church, State and Society' in George Katkov *et al.*, *Russia Enters the Twentieth Century, 1894–1917*, London: Temple Smith, 1971, pp. 199–235; Simon Dixon, *Church, State and Society in Late Imperial Russia: The Diocese of St Petersburg 1880–1914*, Ph.D. thesis, London: SSEES, 1993.
7 Author's interview with Konstantin Dushenov, St Petersburg, 19 April 1996.
8 Mefodii, Metropolitan of Voronezh and Lipetsk, 'Znemenie Edinstva: O proslavlenii Tsarstvennykh Muchenikov', *Rus' pravoslavnaia*, 3–4 (2000), pp. 4–5.
9 'Proslavlenie Tsaria-Muchenika', *Rus pravoslavnaia*, 3–4 (2000), p. 1.
10 Sergei Grigor'ev, 'Izmena, trusost' i obman ...', *Rus pravoslavnaia*, 2 (2000), pp. 1–2.
11 Metropolitan Kirill, 'Kredit nashego doveriia k Vsemirnomu sovetu tserkvei ischerpan', *Tserkov' i vremia*, 2 (1998), pp. 24–9; author's interview with Artem Chirikin, secretary to Fr Hilarion Alfeev, secretary for Inter-Christian Affairs, Daniilevskii Monastery, Moscow, 27 October 1998.
12 On Sergii see William Fletcher, *A Study in Survival: The church in Russia, 1927–1943*, London: SPCK, 1965; Arto Luukkanen, *The Party of Unbelief: The religious policy of the Bolshevik Party, 1917–1929*, Helsinki: Societas Historica Finlandiae, 1994.
13 The argument was made explicit in Mefodii, 'Znamenie Edinstva'. By 2005, preparations to reunite the two wings of the Church were quietly and steadily proceeding.
14 Press Conference on the results of the Jubilee Bishops' Council, 17 August 2000. Communications Service of the Department of External Church Relations, Moscow Patriarchate. Available online at http://www.russian-orthodox-church.org.ru/s2000e36.htm (accessed 1 July 2004); and 'Doklad Mitropolita Krutitskogo i Kolomenskogo Iuvenaliia, predsedatelia Sinodal'noi komissii po kaninizatsii sviatykh, na Arkhiereiskom iubileinom sobore', Moscow, 13–16 August 2000,

Communications Service of the Department of External Church Relations, Moscow Patriarchate, http://www.russian-orthodox-church.org.ru/s2000r05.htm (accessed 1 July 2004).
15 John Fennel and Antony Stokes, *Early Russian Literature*, London: Faber and Faber, 1974, pp. 11–32; Wendy Slater, 'Boris and Gleb in Hagiography and Iconography, 11th to 14th centuries', unpublished MA dissertation, Cambridge: University of Cambridge, 1991.
16 Georgy (Yury) Balovlenkov (compiler), *The Life of the Holy Royal Martyrs of Russia*, trans. Hieromonk Ephraim (Krassovsky) and Professor Gerald Ephraim Nectarios Thompson, Moscow: [no publisher], 2001.
17 Aleksandr Bokhanov, *Imperator Nikolai II*, Moscow: Russkoe slovo, 1998, pp. 531, 536.
18 Dmitrii Pospelovskii, 'Ne pora li vspomnit' o khristianstve?', *Nezavisimaia gazeta*, 24 November 1999.
19 Pospelovskii, 'Ne pora li'.
20 Ibid.
21 D.V. Pospelovskii, 'Vopros o kanonizatsii Nikolaia II i Aleksandry Fedorovny', *Vestnik russkogo khristianskogo dvizheniia*, 176 (1997), pp. 243–55.
22 Andrew Gentes, 'The Life, Death and Resurrection of the Cathedral of Christ the Saviour, Moscow', *History Workshop Journal*, 46 (1998), pp. 63–95; Kathleen E. Smith, 'An Old Cathedral for a New Russia: The Symbolic Politics of the Reconstituted Church of Christ the Saviour', *Religion, State and Society*, 25 (1997), pp. 163–75.
23 Viktoria Voloshina, 'Burial Ceremony: A Great Success', *Moscow News*, 23–29 July 1998, p. 10.
24 See articles in *Ogonek*, 28 (1999), pp. 15–23.
25 Viktor Aksiuchits [interview] in Aksiuchits (ed.), *Pokaianie: Materialy pravitel'stvennoi Komissii po isucheniiu voprosov, sviazannykh s issledovaniem i perezakhoroneniem ostankov Rossiiskogo Imperatora NIKOLAIA II i chlenov ego sem'i: Izbrannye dokumenty*, Moscow: VYBOR, 1998, p. 17.
26 Aleksandr Lebed, *Za derzhavu obidno*, Moscow: Moskovskaia pravda, 1995, pp. 440–1.
27 *Kommersant-Daily*, 4 April 1997, in *Current Digest of the Soviet Press*, XLIX, 13 (1997). A new statue to Nicholas was unveiled in the same village on 20 August 2000. On the role of statues as substitute corpses see Katherine Verdery, *The Political Lives of Dead Bodies; Reburial and postsocialist change*, New York: Columbia University Press, 1999, p. 33.
28 Vsevolod Chaplin, 'Tserkov' ne speshit kanonizirovat' Romanovykh', *Kommersant-Daily*, 28 Feburary 1998.
29 '*Monastyr' v chest' sviatykh tsartsvennykh strastoterptsev*', pamphlet, Ekaterinburg: Ganina Yama, 2002.
30 Anna Salymskaia, 'Chudo na meste zakhoroneniia ostankov Tsarskoi Sem'i', *Zhizn'*, 27 November 2000, p. 8.
31 Leonid Ouspensky and Vladimir Lossky, *The Meaning of Icons*, Crestwood, NY: St Vladimir's Seminary Press, 1983.
32 Richard S. Wortman, *Scenarios of Power: Myth and ceremony in Russian monarchy. Volume Two: From Alexander II to the Abdication of Nicholas II*, Princeton, NJ: Princeton University Press, 2000, p. 378.
33 ITAR-TASS, 30 January 1999 and 2 April 1999. For ROC publications about the icon see: Hegumen German (Podmoshenskii) (ed.), *Blagodatnyi Tsar' nad Rossiei*, Moscow: 1999, 2000; N. Sedova, *Blagodatnyi dar Gosudaria: Ikona Tsaria-Muchenika ot mirotocheniia do skhozhdeniia blagodatnogo ognia*, Moscow: Novaia kniga, Kovcheg, 2000; and the video films *Gosudar' Imperator Nikolai II: vozvrashchenie* (1999), author Elena Kozenkova, director Andrei

Plakhov. See also Richard (Thomas) Betts, 'From America to Russia: The myrrh-streaming icon of Tsar Nicholas II', *Road to Emmaus*, 1, 1 (spring 2000), pp. 39–54.
34 Liudmila Kniazeva in *Bog proslavliaite svoikh sviatikh*, Moscow: n.p., 1999, pp. 8–13.
35 Aleksandr Shargunov (ed.), *Chudesa Tsarstvennykh Muchenikov* (2 vols), Moscow: Khronos-Press, 2001, p. 284.
36 Aleksandr Shargunov, *O znachenii kanonizatsii tsarstvennykh muchenikov*, Moscow: Novaia kniga, 1999, p. 3.
37 Shargunov (ed.), *Chudesa*.
38 23 April 1997, Evgenii Pozdniakov, Shchelkovo, Moscow oblast, from Aleksandr Shargunov, *Bogom proslavlennyi Tsar*. Available online at http://www.tzar.orthodoxy.ru/n2/chud/4htm (accessed 23 August 2004).
39 A.V. Vorontsova, Moscow, Shargunov, *Bogom*.
40 Larisa Polianskaia, Moscow, 1997, Shargunov, *Bogom*.
41 Servant of God, Anna, Moscow, Shargunov, *Bogom*.
42 Clifford Geertz, *The Interpretation of Culture: Selected essays*, London: Hutchinson, 1975, p. 107.
43 Shargunov (ed.), *Novye chudesa*, pp. 101–2.
44 Michael Billig, *Banal Nationalism*, London, and Thousand Oaks, CA: Sage, 1995. Bettina Weichert has developed this idea into the concept of 'banal Orthodoxy'.
45 Shargunov (ed.), *Chudesa*, part I, p. 98.
46 Fennell and Stokes, pp. 32–40.
47 Shargunov (ed.), *Novye chudesa*, p. 85.
48 Dominic Lieven, *Nicholas II: Emperor of All the Russias*, London: John Murray, 1993, pp. 164–8.
49 Shargunov (ed.), *Chudesa*, part I, pp. 173; pp. 178–9.
50 Nina Kartashova, in *Detiam o Tsare*, St Petersburg: Tsarskoe delo, 2000, pp. 13–15; Oleg Slavin, *Kovcheg spaseniia*, Moscow: Russkii dom, 2001, pp. 147–8; Shargunov, *Chudesa*, part I, pp. 228–30.
51 As expounded, for example, in O.A. Platonov, *Ternovyi venets Rossii: istoriia tsareubiistva*, Moscow: Entsiklopediia russkoi tsivilizatsii, 2001.

7 Family portraits

1 For example, Ferro's *Nicholas II*; Massie's *The Romanovs*; inset on Kurth's *Tsar*; back cover of Bokhanov's *Imperator Nikolai II*.
2 Edvard Radzinsky, *The Last Tsar: The life and death of Nicholas II*, New York: Anchor Books, 1993, p. 386.
3 Susan Sontag, *Regarding the Pain of Others*, New York: Farrar, Straus & Giroux, 2002, pp. 85–6. Sontag is referring principally to the images of horror that have permeated the twentieth century, specifically photographs of the Holocaust.
4 On the tercentenary see Orlando Figes, *A People's Tragedy: The Russian Revolution, 1891–1924*, London: Jonathan Cape, 1996, pp. 3–24; photographs in Bokhanov et al., *The Romanovs: Love, power and tragedy*, UK: Leppi Publications, 1993, pp. 242–61.
5 Richard S. Wortman, *Scenarios of Power: Myth and ceremony in Russian Monarchy. Volume Two: From Alexander II to the Abdication of Nicholas II*, Princeton, NJ: Princeton University Press, 2000, p. 9; Eric Hobsbawm and Terence Ranger (eds), *The Invention of Tradition*, Cambridge: Cambridge University Press, 1983.
6 Facsimile in E.M. Iukhumenko and M.V. Falaleeva, *Russkii paradny obed: meniu iz kollektsii Gosudarstvennogo istoricheskogo muzeia*, Moscow: Interbuk-Bines, 2003, p. 79.

7 A. Elchaninov, *Tsarstvovanie Gosudaria Imperatora Nikolaia Aleksandrovicha*, Moscow: Knigoizdatel'stvo Selskago Vestnika, 1913. There were two English editions, a hardback: Major-General A. Elchaninov, *Tsar Nicholas II*, translated from the Russian by A.P.W., London: Hugh Rees, 1913; and a paperback, costing 2 shillings, by Major-General E. [*sic*] Elchaninov, *The Tsar and His People*, translated from the Russian by A.P.W., London: Hodder & Stoughton (Hugh Rees), 1914. On Elchaninov see Wortman, *Scenarios*, pp. 489–502.
8 Elchaninov, *The Tsar and His People*, pp. 49, 33, 41, 52, 10–58.
9 Ibid., pp. 36–7.
10 Wortman, *Scenarios*, p. 490.
11 Pierre Gilliard, *Thirteen Years at the Russian Court*, New York: Doran, 1921, ch. 2. Available online at <http://www.alexanderpalace.org/gilliard/II.html> (accessed 20 February 2006).
12 The pictures were taken by A.A. Pasetti, who had won the patronage of many of the extended Romanov family, and whose studio had been bought out by Boissonas & Eggler. Charlotte Zeepvat, *The Camera and the Tsars: A Romanov family album*, Stroud: Sutton Publishing, 2004, p. x.
13 Wortman, *Scenarios*, pp. 481–4.
14 Marcus C. Levitt, 'Pushkin in 1899' in Boris Gasparov, Robert P. Hughes and Irina Paperno (eds), *Cultural Mythologies of Russian Modernism*, Berkeley: University of California Press, 1992, pp. 183–203, pp. 192–3. On D'Anthès and Pushkin, see Serena Vitale's wonderful *Pushkin's Button*, New York: Farrar, Straus & Giroux, 1999.
15 Wortman, *Scenarios*, pp. 483–4.
16 Richard Stites, *Russian Popular Culture: Entertainment and society since 1900*, Cambridge: Cambridge University Press, 1992, pp. 30, 32.
17 Nicholas II, quoted by Denise J. Youngblood, *Movies for the Masses: Popular cinema and Soviet society in the 1920s*, Cambridge: Cambridge University Press, 1992, p. 37.
18 Victor Belyakov, 'Russia's Last Star: Nicholas II and Cinema', trans. Denise J. Youngblood, *Historical Journal of Film, Radio and Television*, October 1995.
19 Wortman, *Scenarios*, p. 486.
20 Belyakov, 'Russia's Last Star'.
21 *Padenie dynastii Romanovykh*, director Esfir Shub, 1927; Belyakov, 'Russia's Last Star'.
22 Thomas Richards, *The Commodity Culture of Victorian England: Advertising and spectacle, 1851–1914*, Stanford, CA: Stanford University Press, 1990, pp. 102–3.
23 Wortman, *Scenarios*, p. 336.
24 The series is reproduced in Zeepvat, *The Camera*, p. 19.
25 Elchaninov, *The Tsar and his People*, pp. 58, 59–60.
26 Ibid., pp. 56–7.
27 Zeepvat, *The Camera*, p. 83.
28 David Cannadine, *History in Our Time*, New Haven, CT, and London: Yale University Press, 1998, p. 132.
29 Bokhanov *et al.*, *The Romanovs*, pp. 299, 303, 241, 223, 184.
30 For example, the postcards reproduced in Bokhanov *et al.*, *The Romanovs*, pp. 200–1, 203, 205.
31 Zeepvat, *The Camera*, p. 199, quoting *A Lifelong Passion*, p. 442.
32 Orlando Figes and Boris Kolonitskii, *Interpreting the Russian Revolution: The language and symbols of 1917*, New Haven, CT and London: Yale University Press, 1999, esp. pp. 9–29.
33 The concept of carnival as the inversion of the hierarchical world belongs to Mikhail Bakhtin in e.g. *Problems of Dostoevskii's Poetics*, trans. R.W. Rotsel,

Ann Arbor, MI: Ardis, 1973. The inversion of the official propaganda image of the Tsar was seen in the popular *skazki* (pseudo-folk-tales) that proliferated in the revolutionary era: Elizabeth Jones Hemenway, 'Nicholas in Hell: Rewriting the Tsarist Narrative in the Revolutionary *Skazki* of 1917', *The Russian Review*, 60 (2001), pp. 185–204.
34 Simon Schama, *Citizens: A chronicle of the French Revolution*, London: Viking, 1989, pp. 203–27; Lynn Hunt, *The Family Romance of the French Revolution*, London: Routledge, 1992, pp. 17–51.
35 V.V. Ramazanov, 'Rasputin's Night-time Orgies (the Tsarist Miracle-worker): A Tale in One Act' (1917) in James von Geldern and Louise McReynolds (eds), *Entertaining Tsarist Russia: Tales, songs, plays, movies, jokes, ads and images from Russian urban life, 1779–1917*, Bloomington and Indianapolis: Indiana University Press, 1998, pp. 385–92. A more academic version of the scandal is the 1918 publication by 'A Russian', *The Fall of the Romanoffs: How the ex-Empress and Rasputine caused the Russian Revolution*, 1918, intro. Alan Wood, Cambridge: Ian Faulkner, 1992.
36 Peasant quoted by Figes and Kolonitskii, *Interpreting the Russian Revolution*, p. 138; R.H. Bruce Lockhart, *Memoirs of a British Agent*, London: Macmillan, 1985, first published 1932, p. 304. For announcement see Docs 155, 156 in Mark D. Steinberg and Vladimir M. Khrustalëv, *The Fall of the Romanovs: Political dreams and personal struggles in a time of Revolution*, New Haven, CT: Yale University Press, 1995, pp. 340–5.
37 Jeffrey Richards 'Review of Barrell, *Imagining the King's Death*', *History*, 2, October 2000. Richards points out that this 'aura of violated domesticity' also shapes narratives of the executions of Charles I and Louis XVI.
38 *Atlantis Magazine. In the Courts of Memory*. Available online at <http://www.atlantis-magazine.com/intro> (accessed 15 September 2005).
39 *The Unofficial Nicholas and Alexandra Romanov Homepage*. Available online at <http://www.geocities.com/Vienna/9463> (accessed 15 September 2005).
40 *Alexander Palace Time Machine*. Available online at <http://www.alexanderpalace.org/palace/mainpage.html> (accessed 20 February 2006).
41 *Livadia dot org*. Available online at <http://www.livadia.org/scrapbooks.html> (accessed 15 September 2005).
42 Gleb Panfilov, 'Chelovecheskaia tragikomediia', *Izvestiia*, 17 July 1998, p. 6.
43 Panfilov, 'Chelovecheskaia tragikomediia'.
44 John Tebbut, 'Video Vulture', *FFWD Weekly*, 12 March 1997. Available online at http://www.ffwdweekly.com/Issues/1998/0312/vid1.html (accessed 16 September 2005).
45 Among these are: Charlotte Zeepvat, *The Camera and the Tsars: A Romanov family album*, Stroud: Sutton Publishing, 2004; Alexander Bokhanov *et al.* (eds), *The Romanovs: Love, power and tragedy*, UK: Leppi Publications, 1993; Larissa Yermolova, *The Last Tsar*, Bournemouth: Parkstone Press/Planeta, 1996; Carol Townend, *Royal Russia: The private albums of the Russian Imperial Family, from the James Blair Lovell Archive*, London: Smith Gryphon, 1995; Prince Michael of Greece and Andrei Maylunas, *Nicholas and Alexandra: The family albums*, London: Tauris Parke Books, 1992.
46 Review article by Victoria S. Steinberg and John W. Steinberg, 'Romanov Redux', *The Russian Review*, 60 (2001), pp. 420–9.
47 Zeepvat, *The Camera*, p. 1.
48 Radzinsky, *The Last Tsar*, p. 9.
49 Zeepvat, *The Camera*, p. xiv; see also Zeepvat, *Romanov Autumn: Stories from the last century of Imperial Russia*, Stroud: Sutton Publishing, 2000.
50 Necklaces: see Radzinsky, *The Last Tsar*, p. 114; camp-beds: see Figes, *A People's Tragedy*, p. 25, and Massie, *The Romanovs*, p. 166; clean sheets: see Greg King

and Penny Wilson, *The Fate of the Romanovs*, Hoboken, NJ: John Wiley & Sons, 2003, p. 161.
51 David Cannadine, *History in our Time*, New Haven, CT, and London: Yale University Press, 1998, p. 4.
52 Elchaninov, *The Tsar and his People*, p. 31; Vladimir Oustimenko and Lyubov Tyutyunnik in Alexander Bokhanov *et al.* (eds), *The Romanovs: Love, power and tragedy*, p. 119.
53 Letter from Alexandra to Nicholas, 13 March 1916; Alexander Mossolov, *At the Court of the Last Tsar*, London: Methuen, 1935, p. 247, both quoted in King and Wilson, *The Fate*, pp. 45; 51.
54 Irina Fromenko (ed.), *Krymskii al'bom*, Sevastopol: Taurida, 1998, p. 31, quoted in King and Wilson, *The Fate*, pp. 53–4.
55 Zeepvat, *The Camera*, p. 21. The family intrigues are discussed in John Curtis Perry and Constantine Pleshakov, *The Flight of the Romanovs: A family saga*, New York: Basic Books, 1999, esp. part 1; 'intellectual mediocrity': Grand Duchess Marie of Russia, *Education of a Princess*, New York: Viking Press, 1931, p. 116, quoted in Perry and Pleshakov, p. 19; on unsuitable marriages see also Rosemary and Donald Crawford, *Michael and Natasha: The life and love of Michael II, the last of the Romanov tsars*, New York: Scribner, 1997.
56 Elchaninov, *The Tsar and his People*, p. 53.
57 Dominic Lieven, *Nicholas II: Emperor of all the Russias*, London: John Murray, 1993, pp. 57–9.
58 Wortman, *Scenarios*, pp. 336–9.
59 Photograph in Bokhanov *et al.*, p. 166.
60 New work on these ideas about Stalinist culture may be found in Sheila Fitzpatrick (ed.), *Stalinism: New directions*, London and New York: Routledge, 2000. The concept is not a new one, however: see Nicholas Timasheff, *The Great Retreat: The growth and decline of Communism in Russia*, New York: E.P. Dutton, 1946.
61 Laundry: King and Wilson, *The Fate*, p. 161; bread: Nicholas's diary entry from 5 June, in Radzinsky, *The Last Tsar*, p. 315.
62 Iakov Iurovskii, 'Slishkom vse bylo iasno dlia naroda', *Istochnik*, 0 (1993), pp. 107–16, pp. 110–11.
63 Orlando Figes, 'Burying the Bones', *Granta: Russia: The Wild East*, 64 (winter 1998), pp. 95–111.

Conclusion: miscalculating history

1 Quoted by P.M. Bykov, *The Last Days of Tsardom* (1926), trans. Andrew Rothstein, London: Martin Lawrence, 1934, p. 82 (source cited as V. Miliutin, *Pages from My Diary*, *Projektor*, 4 (1924)).
2 See docs 152–6 in Mark D. Steinberg and Vladimir M. Khrustalëv, *The Fall of the Romanovs: Political dreams and personal struggles in a time of Revolution*, New Haven, CT: Yale University Press, 1995, pp. 337–45.
3 Daniel Arasse, *The Guillotine and the Terror*, trans. Christopher Miller, London: Allen Lane, 1989; first published Paris: Flammarion, 1987, pp. 61–5.

Bibliography

Primary sources

A Russian, *The Fall of the Romanoffs: How the ex-Empress and Rasputine caused the Russian Revolution*, 1918, intro. Alan Wood, Cambridge: Ian Faulkner, 1992.
Aksiuchits, Viktor (ed.), *Pokaianie: Materialy pravitel'stvennoi Komissii po izucheniiu voprosov, sviazannykh s issledovaniem i perezakhoroneniem ostankov Rossiiskogo Imperatora NIKOLAIA II i chlenov ego sem'i: Izbrannye dokumenty*, Moscow: VYBOR, 1998.
Aleksandra Fedorovna, *The Last Diary of Tsaritsa Alexandra*, ed. Vladimir A. Kozlov and Vladimir Khrustalëv, intro. Robert K. Massie, New Haven, CT: Yale University Press, 1997.
Aleksandrov, Georgii, 'Drug vragov Khrista', *Rus' pravoslavnaia*, 2 (2000), p. 3.
Alekseev, V.V., *Gibel' tsarskoi sem'i: Mify i real'nost*, Ekaterinburg, 1993.
Alekseyev, V.V., *The Last Act of a Tragedy: New documents about the execution of the last Russian Emperor, Nicholas II*, Ekaterinburg: Urals Branch of Russian Academy of Sciences, 1996.
Alexander Palace Time Machine. Available online at <http://www.alexanderpalace.org/palace/mainpage.html> (accessed 20 February 2006).
Anastasia: The autobiography of HIH the Grand Duchess Anastasia Nicholaevna of Russia, New York: Spellman, 1963.
Anninskii, L., 'Solov'ev, letiashchii vosled Sokolovu', *Rodina*, 7 (1998), p. 10.
Anon., *Bog proslavliaet svoikh sviatykh*, Moscow, 1999.
Anon., *Russkii Tsar's Tsaritseiu na poklonenii moskovskim sviatyniam*, Moscow 2000.
Atlantis Magazine. *In the Courts of Memory*. Available online at <http://www.atlantis-magazine.com/intro> (accessed 15 September 2005).
Avdeev, A.D., 'Nikolai Romanov v Tobol'ske i v Ekaterinburge: (Iz vospominanii komendanta), *Krasnaia nov'*, 5 (1928), pp. 185–209.
Avdeev, Sergei, 'Vagonchik tronetsia, a tsar' ostanetsia?...', *Komsomol'skaia pravda*, 25 November 1997, p. 1.
Avdonin, Aleksandr, 'Taina staroi Koptiakovskoi dorogi: Ob istorii poiskov ostankov imperatorskoi sem'i', *Istochnik*, 5 (1994), pp. 60–76.
Avdonin, Aleksandr [interview], 'Shchelokov pomogal iskat' tsarskie ostanki', *Kommersant-Daily*, 6 February 1998, p. 1.
Balovlenkov, Georgy (Yuri) (compiler), *The Life of the Holy Royal Martyrs of Russia*, trans. Hieromonk Ephraim (Krassovsky) and Gerald Ephraim Nectarios Thompson, Moscow: [no publisher], 2001.

174 Bibliography

Belimov, Viktor, 'Reaktsiia rossiiskikh uchenykh na issledovaniia Tatsuo Nagai', stranaRu, 24.09.01. Available online at http://www.strana.ru/print/63087.html (accessed 27 May 2004).

Bolotin, Leonid (ed.), Notes to Viktor Kobylin, *Anatomiia izmeny* (St Petersburg, 1998); first published as *Imperator Nikolai II i general-ad'iutant M.V. Alekseev* (Vseslavianskoe izdatel'stvo, New York, 1970).

Bolotin, Leonid, 'Kuda vedet doroga "Velikogo kniazia?"', *Tsar' kolokol*, 1, (1990), pp. 11–42.

Bolotin, Leonid, *Tsarskoe delo: materialy k rassledovaniiu ubiistva tsarskoi sem'I*, Moscow, 1996.

Bovin, Aleksandr, 'Primirenie i pokaianie', *Izvestiia*, 11 July 1998, p. 4.

Breshko-Breshkovskii, N.N., *Tsarskie brillianty*, Paris: Presse Franco-Russe, 1921.

Bruce Lockhart, R. H., *Memoirs of a British Agent*, London: Macmillan, 1985; first published 1932.

Buida, Iurii, 'Moshchi i strasti', *Izvestiia*, 10 June 1998, p. 5.

Bulygin, Captain Paul, *The Murder of the Romanovs: The authentic account*, including *The Road to the Tragedy* by Aleksandr Kerensky, introduction by Sir Bernard Pares, trans Gleb Kerensky, London: Hutchinson, 1935.

Buranov, Iu. A. (ed.), *Pravda o ekaterinburgskoi tragedii*, Moscow: [no publisher], 1998, pp. 115–21.

Buranov, Iu. A. (ed.), *Pravda o ekaterinburgskoi tragedii*, Moscow: [no publisher], 1998.

Buranov, Iu. A. and Khrustalëv, V. M., *Ubiitsy tsaria. Unizhtozhenie dinastii*, Moscow: Terra, 1997.

Buranov, I.A. and Khrustalëv, V.M., *Romanovy: Gibel' dinastii*, Moscow: Olma-Press, 2000.

Butrin, Fr Aleksandr, 'Poslednii imperator', *Rus derzhavnaia*, 5 (2000), p. 3.

Bykov, P.M., *The Last Days of Tsardom*, trans. with an historical preface by Andrew Rothstein, London: Martin Lawrence, 1934 [translation of *Poslednie dni Romanovykh*, Sverdlovsk, 1926].

Bykov, P.M., 'Poslednie dni poslednego tsaria', in *Rabochaia revoliutsiia na Urale*, Sverdlovsk?: 1921; reprinted in Taras Stepanchuk and Zinaida Stepanchuka (eds), *Dom Romanovykh: k 300-letnemu iubileiu tsarstvovaniia 1613–1913; Poslednie dni poslednego tsaria (unichtozhenie dinastii Romanovykh)*, Moscow: TsEK Zhivaia voda, 1991, pp. 116–27.

Chaplin, Vsevolod, 'Tserkov' ne speshit kanonizirovat' Romanovykh', *Kommersant-Daily*, 28 Feburary 1998.

Chapnin, Sergei, 'Khotim li my uznat' pravdu?: Spekuliatsii vokrug "tsarskikh" ostankov prodolzhaiutsia', *Nezavisimaia gazeta*, 17 June 1998, p. 9.

Communications Service of the Department of External Church Relations, Moscow Patriarchate, Press Conference on the results of the Jubilee Bishops' Council, 17 August 2000. Available online at http://www.russian-orthodox-church.org.ru/s2000e36.htm (accessed 1 July 2004).

Communications Service of the Department of External Church Relations, Moscow Patriarchate, 'Doklad Mitropolita Krutitskogo i Kolomenskogo Iuvenaliia, predsedatelia Sinodal'noi komissii po kaninizatsii sviatykh, na Arkhiereiskom iubileinom sobore', Moscow, 13–16 August 2000. Available online at <http://www.russian-orthodox-church.org.ru/s2000r05.htm> (accessed 1 July 2004).

Demin, V., 'Podlog', *Tsar' kolokol*, 2 (1990), pp. 10–28.

Detiam o Tsare, St Petersburg: Tsarskoe delo, 2000.
Diterikhs, M.K., 'Ubiistvo tsarskoi sem'i', *Nash sovremennik*, 7 (1991), pp. 151–65; notes and introduction, 'Vokrug Ekaterinburgskoi Golgofy', S. Fomin.
Diterikhs, M.K., *Ubiistvo tsarskoi sem'i i chlenov doma romanovyikh nu Urale*, Moscow: Skify, 1991; first published Vladivostok, 1922.
Egorov, G.B., I. V. Lysenko and V.V. Petrov, *Spasenie Tsesarevicha Alekseia: Istoriko-kriminalisticheskaia rekonstruktsiia rasstrela Tsarskoi Sem'i*, St Petersburg: Russko-Baltiiskii informatsionnyi tentr BLITs, 1998.
Elchaninov, A., *Tsarstvovanie Gosudaria Imperatora Nikolaia Aleksandrovicha*, Moscow: Knigoizdatel'stvo Selskago Vestnika, 1913; trans. A.P.W., *Tsar Nicholas II*, London: Hugh Rees, 1913; and Major-General E. [*sic*] Elchaninov, *The Tsar and His People*, London: Hodder and Stoughton (Hugh Rees), 1914.
Enel (Mikhail Vladimirovich Skariatin), *Sacrifice* (2nd edn), Brussels: J.Schicks, n.d. [in French], 19pp.
Essad-Bey, Mohammed, *Nicholas II: Prisoner of the Purple*, trans. Paul Maerker Branden and Elsa Branden, London: Hutchinson, 1936.
Filatov, O.V., *Istoriia dushi, ili portret epokhy: Sud'ba Tsesarevicha Alekseia, syna Imperatora Rossii Nikolaia II*, St Petersburg: Fond 'Derzhavye traditsii', 2000.
German, Hegumen (Podmoshenskii) (ed.), *Blagodatnyi Tsar' nad Rossiei*, Moscow, 1999, 2000.
Gill, Peter, Pavel L. Ivanov *et al.*, 'Identification of the Remains of the Romanov Family by DNA Analysis', *Nature Genetics*, 6, February 1994, pp. 130–5.
Gilliard, Pierre, *Thirteen Years at the Russian Court*, New York: Doran, 1921. Available online at <http://www.alexanderpalace.org/gilliard> (accessed 20 February 2006).
Gol'tsev, Evgenii, 'Revoliutsioner sprava: Istoriia Ieromonakha Iliodora', *Nedelia*, 26, 25 June–1 July 1990, p. 10.
Gosudar' imperator Nikolai II: Vozvrashchenie.
Gray, Michael, *Blood Relative*, London: Victor Gollancz, 1998.
Grigor'ev, Sergei, 'Izmena, trusost', i obman . . .', *Rus' pravoslavnaia*, 2, (2000), pp. 1–2.
Gubanov, Vladimir (ed.), *Nikolai II: Venets zemnoi i nebesnyi*, Moscow: Lestvitsa, 1999.
Gubanov, Vladimir (ed.), *Pravoslavnye chudesa v XX veke: Svidetel'stva ochevidtsev*, vol. 3, Moscow: Izd. otdela Vladimirskoi eparkhii, 2001.
Halliburton, Richard, *Seven League Boots*, London: Geoffrey Bles, 1936, pp. 95–121.
Intourist, *A Pocket Guide to the Soviet Union*, ed. L.A. Block, Moscow and Leningrad: Vneshtorgisdat, 1932.
Ioann, *Odolenie smuty: slovo k russkomu narodu*, St Petersburg: Tsarskoe delo, 1995.
Ioffe, G.Z., *Krakh rossiiskoi monarkhicheskoi kontrrevoliutsii*, Moscow, 1977.
Iukhumenko, E.M. and M.V. Falaleeva, *Russkii paradny obed: meniu iz kollektsii Gosudarstvennogo istoricheskogo muzeia*, Moscow: Interbuk-Bines, 2003.
Iurovskii, Iakov, 'Slishkom vse bylo iasno dlia naroda', *Istochnik*, 0 (1993), pp. 107–16.
Iuvanalii, Archbishop of Kursk and Ryl'sk, 'Slovo na II Vserossiskom monarkhicheskom soveshchanii', *Nash sovremennik*, 1 (1996), pp. 144–6.
Iuvenalii, Metropolitan of Krutitskii and Kolomna, 'O muchenicheskoi konchinoi Tsarskoi Sem'i: doklad o rabote Komissii Sviashchennogo Sinoda po kanonizatsii

sviatykh, prochintannyi na zasedanii Sviashchennogo Sinoda Russkoi Pravoslavnoi Tserkvi 10 oktiabria 1996 goda, *Tserkovno-obshchestvenniy vestnik*, 2 (Special Supplement to *Russkaia mysl'*, no. 4147), 31 October 1996, pp. 4–5.

Ivanov, Pavel, 'Zakhoronenie tsaria – do sikh por goriachaia tema', *Izvestiia-nauka*, 27 July 2001. Available online at http://www.romanov-center.ural.org/news/otvet_ivanov_to%20japan.htm (accessed 27 May 2004).

Ivanov, Pavel L. et al., 'Mitrochondrial DNA Sequence Heteroplasmy in the Grand Duke of Russia Georgij Romanov Establishes the Authenticity of the Remains of Tsar Nicholas II', *Nature Genetics*, 12 (1996), pp. 417–20.

Kasvinov, M.K., *Dvadtsat' tri stupeni vniz*, Moscow, 1978, first published *Zvezda*, 1972.

Kirill, Metropolitan, 'Kredit nashego doveriia k Vsemirnomu sovetu tserkvei ischerpan', *Tserkov' i vremia*, 2 (1998), 24–9.

Knight, A., L.A. Zhivotovsky et al., 'Molecular, Forensic and Haplotypic Inconsistencies Regarding the Identity of the Ekaterinburg Remains', *Annals of Human Biology*, 31, 2 (2004), pp. 129–38.

Kol'tsov, Mikhail, 'Poslednii reis', *Pravda*, 24 January 1924, p. 2.

Kulikovskaia-Romanova, Ol'ga, 'Eshche raz o "Ekaterinburgskom dele": Rassledovanie obstoiatel'stv ubiistva tsarskoi sem'i vedetsia tendentsiozno', *Izvestiia*, 28 October 1994, p. 4.

Kulikovskaia-Romanova, Ol'ga Nikolaevna, *Nevravnyi poedinok*, Moscow: AO ZT Rodnik, 1995.

Kulikovskaia-Romanova, Ol'ga, 'Dorogoi vladyka Ioann . . .', *Nash sovremennik*, 4 (1997), pp. 208–16.

Kulikovskaia-Romanova, Olga [interview], 'The Bones of Contention', *Road to Emmaus*, 12 (winter 2003).

Lebed, Aleksandr, *Za derzhavu obidno*, Moscow: Moskovskaia pravda, 1995.

Livadia dot org. Available online at <http://www.livadia.org/scrapbooks.html> (accessed 15 September 2005).

Maiakovskii, Vladimir, 'Imperator', *Polnoe sobranie sochinenii*, 13 vols, vol. 9, Moscow: Gos. Izd. Khudozhestvennoi literatury, 1958, pp. 27–30.

Mefodii, Metropolitan of Voronezh and Lipetsk, 'Znamenie edintsva: O proslavlenii Tsarstvennykh Muchenikov', *Rus' pravoslavnaia*, 3–4 (2000), pp. 4–5.

Mel'gunov, S., *Sud'ba Imperatora Nikolaia II posle otrecheniia: Istoriko-kriticheskie ocherki*, Paris: Editions 'La Renaissance', 1951.

Michael, Prince of Greece and Andrei Maylunas, *Nicholas and Alexandra: The family albums*, London: Tauris Parke Books, 1992.

Monastyr' v chest' sviatykh tsartsvennykh strastoterptsev, pamphlet. Ekaterinburg: Ganina Yama, 2002.

Murzin, Aleksandr, 'O chem rasskazal pered smert'iu tsareubiitsa Petr Ermakov?', *Komsomol'skaia pravda*, 25 November 1997, pp. 1, 4.

Narinskaya, Anna, 'The Real Life of Nicholas II', *Moscow News*, 16–22 July 1998, p. 12.

Osipov, Aleksei, 'Osobennosti kanonizatsii poslednego tsaria', *Nezavisimaia gazeta-religii*, 14 July 1999.

Paganutstsi, P., *Pravda ob ubiistve tsarskoi sem'i: Istoriko-kriticheskii ocherk*, Jordanville: Sv.-Troitskii Monastery, 1981/Moscow: Tovarishchestvo russkikh khudozhnikov, 1992: Belaia kniga Rossii, vypusk tretii.

Panfilov, Gleb, 'Chelovecheskaia tragikomediia', *Izvestiia*, 17 July 1998, p. 6.

Petrov, Vadim, Igor Lysenko, Georgy Egorov, with personal reminiscences by the family of Vasily Filatov, *The Escape of Alexei, Son of Tsar Nicholas II: What happened the night the Romanov family was executed*, trans. Marian Schwartz and Antonina W. Bouis, New York: Harry N. Abrams, 1998.

Platonov, O.A., *Ubiistvo tsarskoi sem'i*, Moscow: Sovetskaia Rossiia, 1991.

Platonov, O.A., *Ternovyi venets Rossii: zagovor tsareubiits*, Moscow: Rodnik, 1996.

Platonov, O.A., *Ternovyi venets Rossii: istoriia tsareubiistva*, Moscow: Entsiklopediia russkoi tsivilizatsii, 2001.

Platonov, O.A., Sviatoslav Rybas and Vladimir Soloukhin, 'Zhizn' i tragediia Imperatora Nikolaia II po arkhivnym materialam i pisatel'skim issledovaniiam', *Literaturnaia Rossiia*, 32, 9 August 1991, pp. 16–22.

Popov, Professor V.; Prosecutor V., Solov'ev, 'Bor'ba za istinu ili igra v kosti?', *Izvestiia*, 15 January 1998, p. 4.

Pospelovskii, D.V., 'Vopros o kanonizatsii Nikolaia II i Aleksandry Fedorovny', *Vestnik russkogo khristianskogo dvizheniia*, 176 (1997), pp. 243–55.

Pospelovskii, D.V., 'Ne pora li vspomnit' o khristianstve?', *Nezavisimaia gazeta*, 24 (November 1999).

Pozdniaev, Mikhail, 'Desiat' voprosov k Patriarkhii', *Ogonek*, 28 July 1998, pp. 17–20.

Radzinskii, Edvard, 'Rasstrel v Ekaterinburge', *Ogonek*, 21 May 1989, pp. 4–5, 30–2.

Ramazanov, V.V., 'Rasputin's Night-time Orgies (the Tsarist Miracle-worker): A Tale in One Act' (1917) in James von Geldern and Louise McReynolds (eds), *Entertaining Tsarist Russia: Tales, songs, plays, movies, jokes, ads and images from Russian urban life, 1779–1917*, Bloomington and Indianapolis: Indiana University Press, 1998, pp. 385–92.

Riabov, Gelli [interview], 'Zemlia vydala tainu', *Moskovskie novosti*, 16, 16 April 1989, p. 16.

Riabov, Gelli, 'Prinuzhdeny vas rasstreliat'', *Rodina*, 4 (1989), pp. 84–95, 5, 79–92.

Riabov, Gelli, *Kak eto bylo: Romanovy: sokrytie tel, poisk, posledstviia*, Moscow: Politburo, 1998.

Rodikov, V., '"Grob, torzhestvenno vnesennyi ...". Pravda i lozh' o rasprave nad tsarskoi sem'ei', *Inzhenernaia gazeta*, 7 (1990).

Romanov, Prince Nicholas. Available online at http://media.dagospia.com/public_html/articolo_2272.html (accessed 4 July 2005).

Romanov, Prince Nikolai Romanovich, 'Da khraniat nas Bog i Rossiia!', *Rossiiskie vesti*, 6 June 2001, pp. 4–5.

Ross, Nikolai (ed.), *Gibel' Tsarskoi Sem'i*, Frankfurt, 1987.

Salymskaia, Anna, 'Chudo na meste zakhoroneniia ostankov Tsarskoi Sem'i', *Zhizn'*, 27 November 2000, p. 8.

Sedova, N., *Blagodatnyi dar Gosudaria: Ikona Tsaria-Muchenika ot mirotocheniia do skhozhdeniia blagodatnogo ognia*, Moscow: Novaia kniga, Kovcheg, 2000.

Sem'ianinov, V.P. (ed.), *Poslednie dni Romanovykh*, Moscow: Kniga, 1991.

Serafim, Igumen (Kuznetsov), *Pravoslavnyi Tsar'-Muchenik*, Moscow: Khrizostom, 2000 (first published Peking, 1920).

Shargunov, Aleksandr, *Novye chudesa Tsartsvennykh muchenikov*, Moscow: Novaia kniga, 1996.

Shargunov, Aleksandr, *O znachenii kanonizatsii tsarstvennykh muchenikov*, Moscow: Novaia kniga, 1999.

Shargunov, Aleksandr, *Bogom proslavlennyi Tsar*. Available online at <http://www.tzar.orthodoxy.ru/n2/chud/4htm> (accessed 23 August 2004).
Shirokorad, A., 'Nikolai II, informatsiia k razmyshleniiu', *Izvestiia*, 11 July 1998, p. 4.
Shiropaev, A., 'Pobeda Imperatora Nikolaia II', *Tsar' kolokol*, 1 (1990), pp. 43–53.
Slavin, Oleg, *Kovcheg spaseniia*, Moscow: Russkii dom, 2001, [ch. 4, 'Kanonizatsiia Gosudaria Nikolaia II i chudesa nashikh dnei].
Sokoloff, Nicolas, *Enquête judiciare sur l'Assassinat de la Famille Impériale Russe*, Paris: Payot, 1924.
Sokolov, N.A., *Ubiistvo tsarskoi sem'i*, Moscow, St Petersburg, 1990 (first published Berlin: Slovo, 1925).
Soloukhin, Vladimir, 'U Ganinoi iamy', *Literaturnaia Rossiia*, 32, 9 August 1991, pp. 20–2.
Solov'ev, V., 'Ugolovnoe delo No. 18/123666–93', *Izvestiia*, 19 November 1994, p. 6.
Solov'ev, V. [interview] 'Razstreliat' i skharonit' tak chtoby nikto i nikagda ikh trupa ne nashol', *Rodina*, 7 (1998), pp. 11–14.
Stansgate, Margaret, *My Exit Visa*, London: Hutchinson, 1992.
Steinberg, Mark D. and Vladimir M. Khrustalëv, *The Fall of the Romanovs: Political dreams and personal struggles in a time of Revolution*, New Haven, CT: Yale University Press, 1995.
Stepanchuk, Taras and Zinaida Stepanchuka (eds), *Dom Romanovykh: k 300-letnemu iubileiu tsarstvovaniia 1613–1913; Poslednie dni poslednego tsaria (unichtozhenie dinastii Romanovykh)*, Moscow: TsEK Zhivaia voda, 1991.
Tal'berg, N.D., *Nikolai II: Ocherki istorii imperatorskoi Rossii*, Izdatel'stvo Sretenskogo monastyria, 2001.
Townend, Carol, *Royal Russia: The private albums of the Russian Imperial Family from the James Blair Lovell Archive*, London: Smith Gryphon, 1995.
Trotskii, Lev, 'Ssylka, vysylka, skitaniia, smert'', *Znamia*, 7 (1990), pp. 173–90; 8 (1990), pp. 165–98.
Trufanov, S.M., *The Mad Monk of Russia Iliodor. Life, Memoirs, and Confessions of Sergei Michailovich Trufanoff (Iliodor)*, New York: Century, 1918.
Ushkuinik, V., *Pamiatka russkomu cheloveku*, New York: Politicheskoe vospitanie, 1982.
Vasilevskii, I.M. (Ne-Bukva), *Chto oni pishut? Memuary byvshikh liudei*, Leningrad: Gos. uchebno-prakt. shkola-tip. im. tov. Alekseeva, 1925.
Vil'ton, Robert, *Poslednie dni Romanovykh*, Moscow: Pamiat', 1998.
Viner, Vadim [interviewed by Strana.Ru], 'Izuchenie "ekaterinburgskikh ostankov" budet prodolzhenko', *Pravoslavnaia gazeta*, Ekaterinburg, 22 (2001), pp. 12–13.
Voloshina, Viktoria, 'Burial Ceremony: A Great Success', *Moscow News*, 23–29 July 1998, p. 10.
von Geldern, James and Louise McReynolds (eds), *Entertaining Tsarist Russia: Tales, songs, plays, movies, jokes, ads and images from Russian urban life, 1779–1917*, Bloomington and Indianapolis: Indiana University Press, 1998.
Vorob'evskii, Iu., *Bog i Tsar'*, Moscow: Anastasiia, 2000.
Wedgwood Benn, the Right Hon. Tony and Margaret Benn, *Beckoning Horizon: The story of a journey around the world*, London: Cassell, 1935.
Wilton, Robert, *The Last Days of the Romanovs, from 15th March 1917. Part I: The narrative; Part II: The depositions of eye-witnesses*, London: Thornton Butterworth, 1920.

Yeltsin, Boris, *Against the Grain: An autobiography*, trans. Michael Glenny, London: Jonathan Cape, 1990.
Zhivotovskii, Lev [interview], 'Oshibki bluzhdaiushchikh atomov', *Literaturnaia gazeta*, 2002. Available online at http://www.romanov-center.ural.org/news/com_o%20nagai.htm (accessed 27 May 2004).
Zhivotovsky, L.A., 'Recognition of the remains of Tsar Nicholas II and his family: a case of premature identification?', *Annals of Human Biology*, 26 (1999), pp. 569–77.

Secondary sources

Acton, Edward, *Rethinking the Russian Revolution*, London: Edward Arnold, 1990.
Alexander, Robert, *The Kitchen Boy: A novel of the last Tsar*, New York: Viking, 2003.
Alfeev, Hilarion, 'Reviving the Russian Orthodox Church: A Task Both Theological and Secular' in Heyward Isham (ed.) with Natan M. Shklyar, *Russia's Fate through Russian Eyes: Voices of the new generation*, Boulder, CO: Westview Press, 2001, pp. 235–49.
Ananich, Boris Vasilievich and Rafail Sholomovich Ganelin, 'Emperor Nicholas II, 1894–1917' in *The Emperors and Empresses of Russia: Rediscovering the Romanovs*, ed. Donald J. Raleigh, comp. A.A. Iskenderov, Armonk, NY, and London: M.E. Sharpe, 1996, pp. 369–402 (first published in *Russian Studies in History*, 34, 3, 1995–1996).
Arasse, Daniel, *The Guillotine and the Terror*, trans. Christopher Miller, London: Allen Lane, 1989 (first published Paris: Flammarion, 1987).
Arens, Olavi and Andrew Ezergailis, 'The Revolution in the Baltics: Estonia and Latvia' in Edward Acton, Vladimir Iu. Cherniaev and William G. Rosenberg (eds) *Critical Companion to the Russian Revolution, 1914–1921*, Bloomington: Indiana University Press, 1997, pp. 667–78.
Ashton, Janet, 'Locked Windows, Locked Minds: The Fictional Portrayal of the Romanovs', *Atlantis*, 5, 1, pp. 166–88.
Bakhtin, Mikhail, *Problems of Dostoevskii's Poetics*, trans. R.W. Rotsel, Ann Arbor, MI: Ardis, 1973.
Barker, Adele Marie (ed.), *Consuming Russia: Popular culture, sex, and society since Gorbachev*, Durham, NC, and London: Duke University Press, 1999.
Beatie, Bruce A. and Phyllis W. Powell, 'Story and Symbol: Notes Towards a Structural Analysis of Bulgakov's *The Master and Margarita*', *Russian Literature Triquarterly*, 15 (1978), pp. 219–51.
Belyakov, Victor, 'Russia's Last Star: Nicholas II and Cinema', *Historical Journal of Film, Radio and Television*, October 1995. Available online at <http://www.findarticles.com/p/articles/mi_m2584/is_n4_v15/ai_17782468> (accessed 15 September 2005).
Bethke Elshtain, Jean, 'Introduction. Bodies and Politics' in Bethke Elshtain and J. Timothy Cloyd (eds), *Politics and the Human Body: Assault on Dignity*, Nashville, TN, and London: Vanderbilt University Press, 1995, pp. xi–xvi.
Betts, Richard (Thomas), 'From America to Russia: The Myrrh-streaming Icon of Tsar Nicholas II', *Road to Emmaus*, 1, 1 spring 2000, pp. 39–54.
Billig, Michael, *Banal Nationalism*, London, and Thousand Oaks, CA: Sage, 1995.
Bokhanov, A.N., *Sumerki monarkhii*, Moscow: Voskresen'e, 1993.

180 Bibliography

Bokhanov, A.V., *Nikolai II: Seriia biografii Zhizn' zamechatel'nykh liudei, no. 739*, Moscow: Molodaia gvardiia, 1997.
Bokhanov, A.N., *Imperator Nikolai II*, Moscow: Russkoe slovo, 1998.
Bovin, Aleksandr, 'Primirenie i pokaianie', *Izvestiia*, 11 July 1998, p. 4.
Boym, Svetlana, *Common Places: Mythologies of everyday life in Russia*, Cambridge, MA, and London: Harvard University Press, 1994.
Brovkin, Vladimir, *Russia After Lenin: Politics, culture and society, 1921–1929*, London and New York: Routledge, 1998.
Brubaker, Roger, *Nationalism Reframed: Nationhood and the national question in the New Europe*, Cambridge: Cambridge University Press, 1996.
Brudny, Yitzhak M., *Reinventing Russia: Russian Nationalism and the Soviet State, 1953–1991*, Cambridge, MA: Harvard University Press, 1998.
Cannadine, David, *History in Our Time*, New Haven, CT, and London: Yale University Press, 1998.
Carr, E.H., *The Bolshevik Revolution, 1917–1923* (3 vols), London: Macmillan, 1950.
Clarke, William, *The Lost Fortune of the Tsars* (rev. edn), London: Orion Books, 1996.
Coleman, John A. SJ, 'Conclusion: After Sainthood?' in John Stratton Hawley (ed.), *Saints and Virtues*, Berkeley: University of California Press, 1987, pp. 205–25.
Condee, Nancy (ed.), *Soviet Hieroglyphics: Visual culture in late twentieth-century Russia*, Bloomington and Indianapolis: Indiana University Press; London: BFI Publishing, 1995.
Crawford, Rosemary and Donald Crawford, *Michael and Natasha: The life and love of Michael II, the last of the Romanov tsars*, New York: Scribner, 1997.
Cunningham, James, *A Vanquished Hope: The movement for church renewal in Russia, 1905–1906*, Crestwood, NY: St Vladimir's Press, 1981.
Davies, R.W., *Soviet History in the Yeltsin Era*, London: Macmillan, 1997.
de Baecque, Antoine, *The Body Politic: Corporeal metaphor in revolutionary France 1770–1800*, trans. Charlotte Mandell, Stanford, CA: Stanford University Press, 1997 (first published as *Le Corps de l'histoire: Métaphores et politique (1770–1800)*, 1993).
Dixon, Simon, *Church, State and Society in Late Imperial Russia: The Diocese of St Petersburg 1880–1914*, Ph.D. thesis, London: SSEES, 1993.
Dumin, Stanislav, *Romanovy: Imperatorskii dom v izgnanii: semeinaia khronika*, Moscow: Zakharov. ACT, 1998.
Duncan, Peter JS and Martyn Rady (eds), *Towards a New Community: Culture and politics in post-totalitarian Europe*, London: SSEES, 1993.
Duncan, Peter JS, *Russian Messianism. Third Rome, Revolution, Communism and after*, London: Routledge, 2000.
Dunlop, John, *The New Russian Revolutionaries*, Belmont, MA: Nordland, 1976.
Edwards, Sue, *No Resting Place for a Romanov*, published by the author, 1998.
Engelstein, Laura, 'Culture, Culture Everywhere: Interpretations of Modern Russia, Across the 1991 divide', *Kritika: Explorations in Russian and Eurasian History*, 2, (2001), pp. 363–93.
Engelstein, Laura, 'New Thinking about the Old Empire: Post-Soviet reflections', *The Russian Review*, 60 (2001), pp. 487–96.
Epstein, Edward Jay, 'The Spy Wars', *New York Times Magazine*, 28 September 1980. Available online at http://www.edwardjayepstein.com/archived/spywars_print.htm (accessed 27 September 2005).

Bibliography 181

Fennel, John and Antony Stokes, *Early Russian Literature*, London: Faber and Faber, 1974.
Ferro, Marc, *Nicholas II: The Last of the Tsars*, trans. Brian Pearce, London: Viking, 1991.
Ferro, Marc, *Les tabous de l'Histoire*, Paris: NiL éditions, 2002.
Figes, Orlando, *A People's Tragedy: The Russian Revolution, 1891–1924*, London: Jonathan Cape, 1996.
Figes, Orlando, 'Burying the Bones', *Granta: Russia: The Wild East*, 64 (winter 1998), pp. 95–111.
Figes, Orlando, 'Czar Vasily? Another account of a Romanov survivor', *New York Times Book Review*, 22 November 1998, p. 46.
Figes, Orlando and Boris Kolonitskii, *Interpreting the Russian Revolution: The language and symbols of 1917*, New Haven, CT, and London: Yale University Press, 1999.
Fitzpatrick, Sheila (ed.), *Stalinism: New directions*, London and New York: Routledge, 2000.
Fitzpatrick, Sheila, 'Making a Self for the Times: Impersonation and Imposture in 20th Century Russia', *Kritika: Explorations in Russian and Eurasian History*, 2 (2001), pp. 469–87.
Fletcher, William, *A Study in Survival: The church in Russia, 1927–1943*, London: SPCK, 1965.
Freeze, G.L., 'Handmaiden of the State? The Church in Imperial Russia Reconsidered', *Journal of Ecclesiastical History*, 36 (1985), pp. 82–102.
Freeze, G.L., 'Subversive Piety: Religion and the Political Crisis in Late Imperial Russia', *Journal of Modern History*, 68, (1996), pp. 308–50.
Freud, Sigmund, 'Family Romances' in *The Standard Edition of the Complete Psychological Works of Sigmund Freud*, trans. and ed. James Strachey, London: The Hogarth Press, 1959, Vol. IX, pp. 235–41.
Galeotti, Mark, *A Glossary of Russian Police and Security Service Acronyms and Abbreviations*. Available online at PDF: <www.keele.ac.uk/depts/hi/resources/modern%20resources/PoliceGlossary-v3.pdf> (accessed 9 September 2005).
Geertz, Clifford, 'Religion as a Cultural System', in *The Interpretation of Cultures: Selected essays*, London: Hutchinson, 1975.
Gentes, Andrew, 'The Life, Death and Resurrection of the Cathedral of Christ the Saviour, Moscow', *History Workshop Journal*, 46 (1998), pp. 63–95.
Gessen, Masha, *Dead Again: The Russian intelligentsia after Communism*, London and New York: Verso, 1997.
Gill, Peter, Pavel L. Ivanov *et al.*, 'Identification of the Remains of the Romanov Family by DNA Analysis', *Nature Genetics*, 6 (February 1994), pp. 130–5.
Gregg, Pauline, *King Charles I*, London: J.M. Dent & Sons, 1981.
Hallencreutz, Carl F. and David Westerlund, 'Anti-secularist Policies of Religion' in Westerlund (ed.), *Questioning the Secular State: The worldwide resurgence of religion in politics*, London: Hurst, 1996, pp. 1–23.
Harris, Robert, *Selling Hitler*, London: Faber and Faber, 1986.
Hemenway, Elizabeth Jones, 'Nicholas in Hell: Rewriting the Tsarist Narrative in the Revolutionary *Skazki* of 1917', *Russian Review*, 60 (2001), pp. 185–204.
Hobsbawm, Eric and Terence Ranger (eds), *The Invention of Tradition*, Cambridge: Cambridge University Press, 1983.
Hunt, Lynn, *The Family Romance of the French Revolution*, London: Routledge, 1992.

Husband, William B., *'Godless Communists: Atheism and society in Soviet Russia, 1917–1932*, DeKalb, IL: Northern Illinois University Press, 2000.
Isham, Heyward (ed.) with Natan M. Shklyar, *Russia's Fate through Russian Eyes: Voices of the new generation*, Boulder, CO: Westview Press, 2001.
Izvestiia, 'Tam, gde rasstreliali tsaria', 16 July 1998, p. 5.
Jansen, Marc, 'International Class Solidarity or Foreign Intervention? Internationalists and Latvian Rifles in the Russian Revolution and the Civil War', *International Review of Social History*, 31, (1986), pp. 68–79.
Johnston, Robert H., *New Mecca, New Babylon: Paris and the Russian exiles, 1920–1945*, Montreal: McGill-Queen's University Press, 1988.
Juergensmeyer, Mark, *The New Cold War? Religious nationalism confronts the secular state*, Berkeley: University of California Press, 1993.
Kendrick, John M.L., 'Russia's Last Tsar: Why are Alexei's Bones Absent?', *The St Petersburg Times*, 2001. Available online at <http://www.sptimesrussia.com/special/tsar/why.htm> (accessed 27 January 2004).
Kendrick, John M.L., 'Russia's Imperial Blood: Was Rasputin not the Healer of Legend?', *American Journal of Hematology*, 77, 1 (2004), pp. 92–102.
Kendrick, John M.L., 'The Spala Crisis of 1912: Rasputin Explained and Alexei Found'. Available online at <http://www.npsnet.com/alexei_found/> (accessed 27 January 2004).
Kendrick, John M.L., 'Tsarevich Alexei: Lenin's Greatest Secret'. Available online at <http://www.npsnet.com/tsarevich_alexei/> (accessed 23 January 2004).
Kenez, Peter, 'The Ideology of the White Movement', *Soviet Studies*, 32, (1980), pp. 58–83.
King, Greg, *The Last Empress: The life and times of Alexandra Feodorovna, Tsarina of Russia*, London: Aurum Press, 1995.
King, Greg and Penny Wilson, *The Fate of the Romanovs*, Hoboken, NJ: John Wiley & Sons, 2003.
Kirsta, Alix, 'The Crying Game', *Guardian Weekend*, 9 December 2000, pp. 26–34.
Kizenko, Nadieszda, 'Ioann of Kronstadt and the Reception of Sanctity, 1850–1988', *Russian Review*, 57, (1998), pp. 325–44.
Kizenko, Nadieszda, *A Saint's Two Bodies: John of Kronstadt and the Russian people*, University Park, PA: Pennsylvania State University Press, 2000.
Klier, John and Helen Mingay, *The Quest for Anastasia*, London: Smith Gryphon, 1995.
Kotkin, Stephen, *Magnetic Mountain: Stalinism as a civilisation*, Berkeley: University of California Press, 1995.
Kurth, Peter, *Anastasia: The life of Anna Anderson*, Glasgow: Fontana, 1985.
Kurth, Peter, 'The Mystery of the Romanov Bones', *Vanity Fair*, January 1993. Available online at <http://www.peterkurth.com/ROMANOV%20BONES.htm> (accessed 6 November 2003).
Lawton, Anna, *Kinoglasnost: Soviet cinema in our time*, Cambridge: Cambridge University Press, 1992.
Lebzelter, Gisela C., *Political Anti-Semitism in England, 1918–1939*, London: Macmillan, 1978.
Leggett, George, *The Cheka: Lenin's political police*, Oxford: Clarendon Press, 1986.
Levitt, Marcus C., 'Pushkin in 1899', in Boris Gasparov, Robert P. Hughes and Irina Paperno (eds), *Cultural Mythologies of Russian Modernism*, Berkeley: University of California Press, 1992, pp. 183–203.

Lewin, Moshe, *Russia/USSR/Russia: The drive and drift of a superstate*, New York: The New Press, 1995.
Lieven, Dominic, *Nicholas II: Emperor of all the Russias*, London: John Murray, 1993.
Lincoln, W. Bruce, *Red Victory: A history of the Russian Civil War*, New York: Simon & Schuster, 1989.
Litvin, Alter L., 'The Cheka' in Edward Acton, Vladimir Iu. Cherniaev and William G. Rosenberg (eds) *Critical Companion to the Russian Revolution, 1914–1921*, Bloomington: Indiana University Press, 1997, pp. 314–22.
Lovell, James Blair, *Anastasia: The lost princess*, London: Robson Books, 1992.
Luukkanen, Arto, *The Party of Unbelief: The religious policy of the Bolshevik Party, 1917–1929*, Helsinki: Societas Historica Finlandiae, 1994.
McNeal, Shay, *The Plots to Rescue the Tsar: The truth behind the disappearance of the Romanovs*, London: Century, 2001.
Maksimova, Ella, 'V pravitel'stvennom tupike zastrialo sledstvie po delu o rasstrele tsarskoi sem'i', *Izvestiia*, 2 December 1997, pp. 1, 7.
Maples, William R. and Michael Browning, *Dead Men Do Tell Tales: The strange and fascinating cases of a forensic anthropologist*, London: Souvenir Press, 1995.
Massie, Robert, *The Romanovs: The final chapter*, London: Jonathan Cape, 1995.
Mawdsley, Evan, *The Russian Civil War*, Boston, MA: Allen & Unwin, 1987.
Meerson, Michael A., 'The Life and Work of Father Aleksandr Men' in Stephen K. Batalden (ed.), *Seeking God: The recovery of religious identity in Orthodox Russia, Ukraine, and Georgia*, DeKalb, IL: Northern Illinois University Press, 1993, pp. 13–26.
Meier, Andrew, 'RIP – at long last', *Time*, 151, no. 8, 1998. Available online at http://www.time.com/time/magazine/1998/int/980302/europe.r.i.p.at_long_las8.html (accessed 30 June 2005).
Merridale, Catherine, *Night of Stone: Death and memory in Russia*, London: Granta Books, 2000.
Miller, Martin A. (ed.), *The Russian Revolution: The essential readings*, Oxford: Blackwell, 2001.
Moynahan, Brian, *Rasputin: The saint who sinned*, London: Aurum Press, 1998.
Mukhin, Aleksei, *Pravoslavnye monarkhisty v Rossii 1988–1998 gody: Istoriia, ob'edineniia, biografii*, Moscow: SPIK-Tsentr, 1997.
Munslow, Alun, *Deconstructing History*, London and New York: Routledge, 1997.
Naiman, Eric, *Sex in Public: The incarnation of early Soviet ideology*, Princeton, NJ: Princeton University Press, 1997.
Nikolaev, P.A. (ed.), *Russkie pisateli 20 veka: Biograficheskii slovar'*, Moscow: Bol'shaia rossiiskaia entsiklopediia, 2000.
Occleshaw, Michael, *The Romanov Conspiracies*, London: Chapmans, 1993.
Orlov, Boris and Sophia Kotzer, 'The Russian Orthodox Church in a Changing Society' in Nurit Schleifman (ed.), *Russia at a Crossroads: History, memory and political practice*, London: Frank Cass, 1998, pp. 147–71.
Ouspensky, Leonid and Vladimir Lossky, *The Meaning of Icons*, Crestwood, NY: St Vladimir's Seminary Press, 1983.
Parland, Thomas, 'Christian Orthodoxy and Contemporary Russian Nationalism' in David Westerlund (ed.), *Questioning the Secular State: The worldwide resurgence of religion in politics*, London: Hurst, 1996, pp. 117–39.

184 Bibliography

Parland, Thomas, 'Russia in the 1990s: Manifestations of a Conservative Backlash Philosophy' in Chris J. Chulos and Timo Piirainen (eds) *The Fall of an Empire, the Birth of a Nation: National identities in Russia (Nationalism and Fascism in Russia)*, Aldershot: Ashgate, 2000, pp. 116–40.

Perry, John Curtis and Constantine Pleshakov, *The Flight of the Romanovs: A family saga*, New York: Basic Books, 1999.

Phenix, Patricia, *Olga Romanov: Russia's last Grand Duchess*, Toronto: Viking, 1999.

Pickering, Robert B. and David C. Bachman, *The Uses of Forensic Anthropology*, Boca Raton, FL: CRC Press, 1997.

Pipes, Richard, *The Russian Revolution, 1899–1919*, London: Vintage, 1991.

Pitcher, Harvey, *Witnesses of the Russian Revolution*, London: John Murray, 1994.

Pospielovsky, Dmitry, 'The Russian Orthodox Church in the Postcommunist CIS' in Michael Bourdeaux (ed.), *The Politics of Religion in Russia and the New States of Eurasia*, Armonk, NY, and London: M.E. Sharpe, 1995, pp. 41–74.

Punter, David, *The Literature of Terror: A history of Gothic fictions from 1765 to the present day* (2 vols), London and New York: Routledge, 1996.

Radzinskii, Edvard, *'Gospodi...spasi i usmiri Rossiiu': Nikolai II: zhizn' i smert'*, Moscow: Vagrius, 1993.

Radzinsky, Edvard, *The Last Tsar: The life and death of Nicholas II*, New York: Anchor Books, 1993.

Radzinskii, Edvard, *Nikolai II: zhizn' i smert'*, Moscow: Vagrius, 1998.

Raeff, Marc, *Russia Abroad: A cultural history of the Russian emigration, 1919–1939*, New York and Oxford: Oxford University Press, 1990.

Read, Christopher, *From Tsar to Soviets: The Russian people and their revolution, 1917–21*, London: UCL Press, 1996.

Remnick, David, 'Letter from St Petersburg: The Next Tsar', *The New Yorker*, 6 July 1998, pp. 40–53.

Richards, Guy, *Imperial Agent: The Goleniewski–Romanov Case*, New York: The Devin-Adair, 1966.

Richards, Guy, *The Hunt for the Czar*, London: Peter Davies, 1970.

Richards, Guy, *The Rescue of the Romanovs: Newly discovered documents reveal how Czar Nicholas II and the Russian Imperial Family escaped*, Old Greenwich, CT: Devin-Adair, 1975.

Richards, Jeffrey, 'Review of Barrell – *Imagining the King's Death*', *Reviews in History*, 2 October 2000.

Richards, Thomas, *The Commodity Culture of Victorian England: Advertising and spectacle, 1851–1914*, Stanford, CA: Stanford University Press, 1990.

Ries, Nancy, *Russian Talk: Culture and conversation during Perestroika*, Ithaca, NY, and London: Cornell University Press, 1997.

Rogger, Hans, 'The Beilis Case: Anti-Semitism and Politics in the Reign of Nicholas II', *Slavic Review*, 25 (1966), pp. 615–29.

Roslof, Edward E., *Red Priests: Renovationism, Russian Orthodoxy, and Revolution, 1905–1946* (Indiana-Michigan Series in Russian and East European Studies), Bloomington: Indiana University Press, 2002.

Schama, Simon, *Citizens: A chronicle of the French Revolution*, London: Viking, 1989.

Schama, Simon, *Dead Certainties (Unwarranted Speculations)*, London: Granta and Penguin, 1991.

Shalin, Dmitri N. (ed.), *Russian Culture at the Crossroads: Paradoxes of postcommunist consciousness*, Oxford: Westview Press, 1996.
Shenfield, Stephen D., *Russian Fascism: Traditions, tendencies, movements*, Armonk, NY, and London, 2001.
Shirokorad, Aleksandr, 'Nikolai II, informatsiia k razmyshleniiu', *Izvestiia*, 11 July 1998, p. 4.
Simon, Gerhard, 'Church, State and Society' in George Katkov *et al.*, *Russia Enters the Twentieth Century, 1894–1917*, London: Temple Smith, 1971, pp. 199–235.
Simpson, Mark S., *The Russian Gothic Novel and its British Antecedents*, Columbus, OH: Slavica, 1986.
Slater, Wendy, 'Boris and Gleb in Hagiography and Iconography, 11th to 14th Centuries', unpublished MA dissertation, Cambridge: University of Cambridge, 1991.
Slater, Wendy, 'A Modern-day Saint? Metropolitan Ioann and the Postsoviet Russian Orthodox Church', *Religion, State* and *Society*, 28 (2000), pp. 313–25.
Slater, Wendy, 'Relics, Remains, and Revisionism: Narratives of Nicholas II in Contemporary Russia', *Rethinking History*, 9 (2005), pp. 53–70.
Smith, Kathleen E., 'An Old Cathedral for a New Russia: The Symbolic Politics of the Reconstituted Church of Christ the Saviour', *Religion, State and Society*, 25 (1997), pp. 163–75.
Smith, S.A., *The Russian Revolution: A very short introduction*, Oxford: Oxford University Press, 2002.
Sobolev, G.L., 'Dinastiia Romanovykh i Vremennoe Pravitel'stvo' in *Dom Romanovykh v istorii Rossii*, St Petersburg: Izd. Sankt-Peterburgskogo universiteta, 1995, pp. 277–95.
Sontag, Susan, *Regarding the Pain of Others*, New York: Farrar, Straus & Giroux, 2002.
Steele, Valerie, *The Corset: A cultural history*, New Haven, CT, and London: Yale University Press, 2001.
Steinberg, Victoria S. and John W. Steinberg, 'Romanov Redux', review article, *Russian Review*, 60 July 2001, pp. 420–29.
Stephan, John J., *The Russian Fascists: Tragedy and farce in exile, 1925–1945*, London: Hamish Hamilton, 1978.
Stites, Richard, *Russian Popular Culture: Entertainment and society since 1900*, Cambridge: Cambridge University Press, 1992.
Stites, Richard, 'Crowded on the Edge of Vastness: Observations on Russian Space and Place' in Jeremy Smith (ed.), *Beyond the Limits: The concept of space in Russian history and culture*, Helsinki: SHS, 1999, pp. 259–69.
Stone, Richard, 'Buried, Recovered, Lost Again? The Romanovs May Never Rest', *Science*, 303 (2004), p. 753.
Summers, Anthony and Tom Mangold, *The File on the Tsar*, London: Orion Books, 2002 (first published London: Victor Gollancz, 1976).
Tebbut, John, 'Video Vulture', *FFWD Weekly*, 12 March 1997. Available online at http://www.ffwdweekly.com/Issues/1998/0312/vid1.html (accessed 16 September 2005).
Timasheff, Nicholas, *The Great Retreat:The growth and decline of Communism in Russia*, New York: E.P. Dutton, 1946.
Tkachev, Il'ia, *Dinastiia Romanovykh*, Moscow: Izdatel'skii Dom GELEOS, 1998.

186 Bibliography

Tökés, Rudolf L., *Béla Kun and the Hungarian Soviet Republic: The origins and role of the Communist Party of Hungary in the Revolutions of 1918–1919*, New York and Washington, DC: Frederick A. Praeger, 1967.
Tumarkin, Nina, *Lenin Lives! The Lenin cult in Soviet Russia*, Cambridge, MA, and London: Harvard University Press, 1983.
Tumarkin, Nina, *The Living and the Dead: The rise and fall of the cult of World War II in Russia*, New York: Basic Books, 1994.
Verdery, Katherine, *The Political Lives of Dead Bodies; Reburial and postsocialist change*, New York: Columbia University Press, 1999.
Verkhovsky, Aleksandr, 'The Role of the Russian Orthodox Church in Nationalist, Xenophobic and Antiwestern Tendencies in Russia Today: Not Nationalism, but Fundamentalism', *Religion, State and Society*, 30 (2002), pp. 333–45.
Vitale, Serena, *Pushkin's Button*, New York: Farrar, Straus & Giroux, 1999.
Ware, Timothy, *The Orthodox Church* (new edn), London: Penguin, 1993.
Warth, Robert D., *Nicholas II: The life and reign of Russia's last monarch*, Westport, CT: Praeger, 1997.
Wedgwood, C.V., *The Trial of Charles I*, London: Collins, 1964.
Wettering, Frederick L., 'Counterintelligence: The Broken Triad', *International Journal of Intelligence and CounterIntelligence*, 13, 3 (2000), pp. 265–300.
White, Hayden, *The Content of the Form: Narrative discourse and historical representation*, Baltimore, MD: Johns Hopkins University Press, 1987.
Williams, Robert C., *Russia Imagined: Art, culture, and national identity, 1840–1995*, New York: Peter Lang, 1997.
Wortman, Richard S., *Scenarios of Power: Myth and ceremony in Russian monarchy. Volume Two: From Alexander II to the Abdication of Nicholas II*, Princeton, NJ: Princeton University Press, 2000.
Youngblood, Denise J., *Movies for the Masses: Popular cinema and Soviet society in the 1920s*, Cambridge: Cambridge University Press, 1992.
Zeepvat, Charlotte, *Romanov Autumn: Stories from the last century of Imperial Russia*, Stroud: Sutton Publishing, 2000.

Filmography

Gosudar' Imperator Nikolai II: vozvrashchenie, author Elena Kozenkova, dir. Andrei Plakhov, 1999.
Padenie dynastii Romanovykh, dir. Esfir Shub, 1927.
Poslednii russkii Tsar, dir. Aleksandr Aleksandrov, 2000.
Romanovy: Ventsenosnaia sem'ia, dir. Gleb Panfilov, 2000.
Russkaia Golgofa, dir. Viktor Ryzhko, 2000.
Wondrous is God in His Saints, dir. Yury Balovlenkov, 2000.

Photographic collections

Bokhanov, Alexander *et al.*, *The Romanovs: Love, power and tragedy*, UK: Leppi Publications, 1993.
Kurth, Peter, *Tsar: The lost world of Nicholas and Alexandra*, New York: Little, Brown, 1995.
Yermilova, Larissa, *The Last Tsar*, trans. Vladimir Pavlov, Bournemouth: Parkstone Press/Planeta, 1996.

Zeepvat, Charlotte, *The Camera and the Tsars: A Romanov family album*, Stroud: Sutton Publishing, 2004.

Author's interviews

Borovoi, Father Vitalii, Daniilevskii Monastery, Moscow, 25 April 1996.
Chaplin, Father Vsevolod, Director of Public Relations, Department for External Church Relations, Daniilevskii Monastery, Moscow, 27 October 1998.
Chirikin, Artem, secretary to Fr Hilarion Alfeev, Secretary for Inter-Christian Affairs, Daniilevskii Monastery, Moscow, 27 October 1998.
Dushenov, Konstantin, Editor, *Rus' Pravoslavnaia*, St Petersburg, 19 April 1996.
Novik, Hegumen Veniamin, lecturer at St Petersburg Orthodox Academy, Keston Institute, Oxford, 26 January 1996.

Index

23 Steps Down 55
Abramov, Sergei 40–1
Aldermaston (UK Home Office
   Forensic Science Service) 29–30,
   33–5, 37
Aleksii II, Patriarch 115, 117–8
Alexander II, Tsar 93, 117
Alexander Palace 48, 95, 145, 149
Alexander, Robert, *The Kitchen Boy*
   104–5
Alexandra Feodorovna, Tsarina:
   decapitation story 60–3, 72–3;
   execution of and burial of 2–15;
   family life of 59, 111, 129–30,
   134–7, 145–9, 156; identification
   of body 27–9, 36–40, 45, 98;
   and Rasputin 67, 130, 138,
   141–3; as saint 57, 107, 120, 127
Alexandra, Queen 34
Alexei Mikhailovich, Tsar 62, 118
Alexei, Tsarevich: body of missing
   19, 27, 31, 42–3, 45, 58, 156;
   execution of and burning of body
   2–15; family life of 137, 148–9;
   as heir 48, 87, 148; illness of 50,
   88, 131, 148; and impostors 58,
   81–105, 156; in Romanov
   propaganda 131–2, 137–9, 141;
   as saint 118
Alexis Romanov, Prince 91
Alice, Princess 33–4
Anastasia (impostors) 29, 81, 83–4,
   86–7, 99–100
Anastasia, Grand Duchess 19, 27–9, 31,
   41–2, 83–4, 86–7, 137–8
Anderson, Anna 29, 86

András 1–2, 5–6, 8, 11
anniversaries of Romanov deaths
   32, 44, 52–3, 55, 117, 122
anti-Semitism 46, 58, 63–4, 72–8
archives 22, 31, 47, 53, 55, 64, 71,
   138, 146–7, 155
Arseniev, Sergei 125
Atlantis Magazine 144
Avdeyev, Aleksandr 53
Avdonina, Aleksandr 16–25, 33,
   36–7, 39
Avdonina, Galya 16, 20

Baker, James A. 28
Balabanov, Angelica 66
Balovlenkov, Yury 112, 122
banal Orthodoxy 124–5
Baring's Bank 98
Barnaul 81–3
Barnes, Julian 44, 47
Beilis, Mendel 78
Belchenko, Dr Oleg 119, 122
Beloborodov, Aleksandr (chairman
   of Urals Regional Soviet) 65, 88
Benckendorff, Count Paul 102
Black Hundreds 53, 108
Blake, George 99
bodies of Romanovs and servants,
   disposal of 8–15
Bokhanov, Aleksandr 113
Bolshevik Revolution 2–4, 14,
   46–9, 51–3, 67, 71, 73, 78–9,
   153–5
Bolsheviks, 30–1, 45–54, 59–61, 63–6,
   68–71, 73–80, 83–5, 93–5, 98,
   101–2, 109, 151, 153–6

bones of Imperial Family and their servants 17–20, 24–8, 30–40, 42–3, 45, 98, 114–7, 155–6
Boris and Gleb, saints 111–2
Borisov, N.S. 70
Botkin, Dr Evgeny (Eugene) 5–8, 11, 14–5, 27, 38, 40, 42, 45, 71, 80, 106, 114
Breshko-Breshkovsky, Nikolai Nikolayevich 60, 63–4, 73, 76, 79
Brest Litovsk, Treaty of 101
Brown, Dorothy 103
Brown, Gill 103
Brown, Sandra 103
Bruce Lockhart, R.H. 143
Bukharin, Nikolai 65–6
Bulgakov, Mikhail 80, 85
Buxhoeveden, Baroness 149
Bykov, Pavel, *Last Days of the Romanovs* 22–3, 52–3

Canada 91, 102
Cannadine, David, 145–6
Captain Lepa 1–2, 5
Carr, E.H. 48
Cathedral of Christ the Saviour, Moscow 114–5
Cathedral of Sts Peter and Paul, St Petersburg 32, 94, 115
Central Executive Committee of the Soviets (VTsIK or CEC) 52, 153
Chaplin, Father Vsevolod 108
Charles I 49–50, 78
Charles II 102
Chebotarev, Grigory 94–8
Chebotarev, Nikolai (alias for Alexei), 95–8
Chebotareva, Valentina 95
Cheka 2–3, 5, 11, 51, 73
Cheremeteff Sfiri, Countess Xenia 34–5
Cheremeteff, Irina 34
Chernomyrdin, Viktor 115
Chicherin, Georgy, Commissar for Foreign Affairs 52
Christ, imitation of 111–12
Christianization of Rus' 106, 117
Church of the Saviour on the Blood, Ekaterinburg, 117

Church of the Saviour on the Blood, St Petersburg, 117
CIA 99
cinema, and Nicholas II 134–5
Civil War 50–2, 116
Clemens, Hans 99
Commandant *see* Yurovsky, Yakov
Commission on the Identification and Reburial of the Remains of Russian Emperor Nicholas II and Members of His Family (Russian government commission) 30–2, 36, 41–2, 114–6
Constituent Assembly 48
Cooke, Natalie, 96
corsets 1, 9–10, 91
Couriss, Nikolai, 95–7
craniofacial superimposition, 40–1
Cromwell, Oliver 78
Czech Legion 3, 11, 50–1, 71, 152–3

Dalsky, Nikolai 91
daughters of Nicholas II: Bolsheviks lie about death of 49, 52; bones of 18–19, 42, 115; controversy over identity of missing body 28–9, 33–4, 41–3, 45; and escape 95, 97, 99, 101; execution and burial of 1–15; family life of 40, 50, 148, 150; and imposters 82–3, 86–7, 90; in Romanov propaganda 59, 92, 128–9, 131–2, 137–8, 148; as saints 126–7
dead bodies, symbolism of 55–6, 116–17
Demidova, Anna (Imperial Family's maid) 6–7, 21, 27, 40, 42, 114, 150
Derevenko, Doctor 92
Derevenko, sailor nanny to Alexei 92
Diana, Princess of Wales 127
diaries of Nicholas and Alexandra 111
Disney, Walt 86
Diterikhs, General Mikhail 71–4, 76
Diuzheva, Elena 125
DNA 29–30, 33, 37–9, 45, 55, 86, 91, 98–9, 103, 155
DNA, mitochondrial 33–6
dog 8, 12
domestic life of Romanov family 46–7, 56, 58, 111–2, 132–3, 137–8, 143, 147–50

Dushenov, Konstantin 109
Dzerzhinsky 65–6

ecumenism 108, 110
Edward VII 34
Edward VIII 103
Eiduk 66
Ekaterinburg 3–4, 11–13, 15, 45, 49–51, 117–8, 153–4; renaming of 27–8, 53; and rivalry with Moscow, 27–8
Ekaterinburg remains, controversy over authenticity of 27–32, 35–40, 42, 45, 114, 118
Ekaterinburg Soviet 23, 52
Elchaninov, Maj. Gen. Andrei, *The Tsar and His People* 131, 137–8, 148–50
Elisabeth (Ella), sister of Alexandra Feodorovna 37–8
Elizabeth II, Queen 103
émigrés 22, 29–31, 46, 57, 60–4, 68–71. 76–80, 95–6, 113, 155
Enel (Mikhail Skariatin) 74–5
English Revolution 78, 153
Ermakov, Petr 5, 7–12, 15, 41, 53
escape of Imperial Family 3–5, 46, 53, 69, 83, 91–5, 98–102, 153
espionage 99
Essad-Bey, Mohammed 67–8
Estonia 91, 102
Evtushenko, Evgeny 80
execution of Imperial Family 1–8, 15, 41–2, 44, 48–9, 51–5, 71, 76, 104–5, 128, 152–6

Felfe, Hans 99
Feodosy of the Caves, 125–6
Fife, the Duke of 34–5
Figes, Orlando 49, 104–5
Filatov, Ksenofont 92
Filatov, Oleg 93–4
Filatov, Vasily 91–4
Filatova, Anzhelika 93
film *see* cinema
forensic science 19–20, 24, 27–42, 45, 58
Four Brothers Mine 10–11, 14–15, 17, 22–3, 67–8, 72, 117–18

Frankenstein, 77
French Revolution 76–8, 153
Freud, Sigmund 89, 104

Gendelevich, Professor 88
George (Georgy), 'Grand Duke of Russia' 56, 115
George V 34, 96
Georgii, Father 100
Georgy Alexandrovich, Grand Duke (NII's brother) 30, 34–7
Gerasimov Institute 19
Gilliard, Pierre 40, 87–9, 131
Gladkikh, Mikhail 92
Glazunov, Ilya 54
Glebov, Archpriest Boris 115
Gogol, Nikolai, *The Government Inspector* 85
Goleniewska, Janina 100
Goleniewski, Michal (sr) 100
Goleniewski, Michal 98–101, 103
Goloshchekin, Philip (Isaac) 12, 71–5, 78
Gorbachev, Mikhail 25, 57, 108
Gothic fiction 63–4, 66–7, 70, 74, 76–80, 127, 155
Grabbe, Bishop Anthony 38
Grand Duchesses *see* daughters of Nicholas II
Grand Duke Vladimir (impostor) 81, 83–4
grave of Imperial Family and servants, discovery of 16–28, 33–38, 43–6, 54–5, 70, 87–8, 98, 156
Gray, Michael (William Lloyd Lavery), *Blood Relative* 81, 97–98, 105
Guillotin, Dr 77–8
Gus(s)eva, Khionia 68

haemophilia 43, 59, 91–4, 131, 143, 148
hagiography 111–2, 125–6
Harris, Robert 86
heads of Nicholas and Alexandra 31, 46, 61, 63–74, 76–7, 79–80
Heath, Edward 103
Heine, Heinrich 74
heteroplasmy 35–6
Hill, Capt. George 95

historiography of Nicholas II's death 48–55
history and narrative 47–8, 63, 89, 91, 104–5, 152–6
Hitler, Adolf 31, 49, 86
Houghton, Harry 99
House of Special Purpose *see* Ipatiev House
Hulbert, John and Iya 97

icon 'Heavenly Glory' 118–20
icon 'Holy Tsarist Martyrs' 122–3
icon 'Tsar Martyr' 118
iconography of Nicholas II 118–9, 126
icons 107, 118–23, 125
Ilf and Petrov 85
Iliodor (Sergei Trufanov), *The Mad Monk of Russia* 67–9
inscriptions on cellar wall 74–6
internet 46, 90–1, 144–5
Ioann, Metropolitan of St Petersburg 108–9
Ioannites, 81, 83
Ipatiev House demolition of 25, 44, 55; and Imperial Family's arrest and execution 2–4, 7–9, 11–12, 27, 44–6, 49, 53–4, 89, 91–3, 98, 114, 129, 138, 150, 152; as Museum of the Revolution 53–4; as site of cathedral 117; as site of pilgrimage 55; as site of ritual murder 74–6; visit by Geli Ryabov 21
Ipatiev, Nikolai 50
Ivanov, Pavel 29–30, 35–7
Izvestiya 36–7

Japan 36–7, 68, 99
jewellery and valuables of Nicholas II and family 1–12, 71, 91, 96, 147, 151
Jewish plot *see* anti-Semitism
John (Ioann) of Kronstadt, Father 81, 83

Kabanov brothers, 2
Kagirin, Father Aleksei 106–7, 123
Kalinin, Mikhail 65, 68
Kamenev, Lev 65–6
Karlenko, Mikhail 83

Karlovtsy Synod *see* Russian Orthodox Church Outside Russia (ROCOR)
Kartashova, Nina 126–7
Kendrick, John 103–5
Kent, Duke of 95
Kerensky, Alexander 50, 62
KGB 20, 57, 99
Kharitonov (Imperial Family's cook) 27, 114, 150
Khodynka Field 134
Khrushchev, Nikita 71, 80
Kimsey, Herman E. 99
King, Mary Claire 35
Kiril Vladimirovich Romanov 56
Kirill, Metropolitan of Smolensk and Kaliningrad 110
Klimenkova, Lidiya 93
Klimov, Elem, *Agoniya* 55
Kochurov, Mikhail 17
Kolchak, Adml Aleksandr 71
Kollontai, Alexandra 66
Komsomol 19, 23, 82, 84–5
Koptiaki 17, 23–4, 102, 104, 117
Korlykhanov, Col Ivan 21–2
Koryakova, Liudmila 24–6
Kremlin, Moscow 31 61, 64–71, 76–77, 80
Krylenko, Nikolai 65–6
Kseshinskaya, Matilda, 146
Kudrin *see* Medvedev-Kudrin
Kuibyshev, Valerian 70
Kulikovskaya-Romanova, Olga 30, 36
Kulikovsky-Romanov, Tikhon 30, 34, 36
Kusova, Natalia 82

Latsis 66
Latvian Rifles Battalion (*Strelki*) 3, 41
Lawlor, Sandra 90–91
Lebed, Aleksandr 116
Lee, Christopher 146
Lenin Library 22, 71
Lenin Museum 71, 80, 116–7
Lenin, Vladimir 2, 50, 61, 65, 99, 101, 152–3, 156; body of 116–17
Leningrad 23–4
Leonid (kitchen boy) 4, 105
Likhachev, Dmitry 56, 115
Lisin, Gennady 23

Literaturnaia Rossiia 64
Lloyd Lavery, William *see* Gray, Michael
Loraine, Sir Percy 95–6
Louis XVI 49–50, 76, 78, 141, 154
Louise of Hesse Cassel 34
Lyle, Noel 98
Lyukhanov (Ipatiev House chauffeur) 8–9, 13–14

Maples, William 28–9, 35, 41
Maria Feodorovna, Dowager Empress 34–5, 95
Maria Nikolaevna (imposter) 81–4
Maria Vladimirovna 56
Marie (Maria), Grand Duchess 27, 29, 41–2, 50, 98–99, 126–7, 137
Marie Antoinette 141
Marie, Queen of Romania 94
Marina, Princess of Greece 96–8
martyr princes 46, 111, 156
Mayakovsky, Vladimir, 1, 15, 22–3, 54
Medvedev, Pavel 7–8
Medvedev-Kudrin, Mikhail 5, 7, 10, 41, 54
Mefody, Metropolitan of Voronezh and Lipets, 109
Meinertzhagen, Richard 95
Melgunov, Sergei 68–71
Men', Father Aleksandr 108
Merchant's House *see* Ipatiev House
MI6 99
Mikhail Alexandrovich, Grand Duke (NII's brother) 38, 48, 60, 63
Mikhail Feodorovich, Tsar 129
Mikhalkov, Nikita 116
Milyutin, Vladimir 152
miracles 46, 58, 106–7, 118–27
monarchists 3, 51, 56–7, 60, 67, 69, 84, 113, 143, 154
Moscow News 115
Moscow Patriarchate 30–2, 57, 107–11, 117, 123
MVD (Soviet interior ministry) 21–3

Nagai, Tatsuo 36–7
Nagorny, sailor nanny to Alexei 148
Natalia Feodorovna 83

national patriots 31–2, 37, 49, 57–8, 64, 74–6, 80, 119, 123, 155
Nemtsov, Boris 32
NEP (New Economic Policy) 78–80
Netrebin 3
Nicholas II, Tsar, and decapitation story 60–80; execution and burial of 2–15, 152–6; family life of 128–51; historiography of death 44–59; identification of body 16–43; last words of 6–7; in Romanov propaganda 128–51; as saint 106–27; teeth of 39; trial of 1, 4, 49–51, 152–6
Nikulin, Grigory 5–6, 8, 53–4
Northern Ireland 95–8

OGPU 82–4
Old Bolsheviks 53–4
Olga Alexandrovna (NII's sister) 30, 87
Olga, Grand Duchess 27, 137–8
Omsk 3, 52, 71, 88
OTMA(A) 137, 145

Pamiat' (Memory) organisation 54
Panfilov, Gleb 145–6
passion-bearers 111, 118, 125
Patriarchate's 'ten questions' 30–31
Pchelin, V.N. 54
Pesotsky, Vladislav 18
Peter I (Peter the Great) 62, 108, 130, 138
Peters 65–6
Philip, Duke of Edinburgh 33–4
photographs of Romanovs 40, 46, 128–32, 138–41, 146–7
Pichugin Lt Col 27
Pipes, Richard 48–9, 51
Plaksin, Vladislav 28–9, 40
Platonov, Oleg 49, 64–6, 74–6
Pokrovsky, Mikhail 24, 53
Poland 98–9
Politburo 55, 70
Popov, Professor Vyacheslav 31, 36–7
Populism 117, 126
Pospielovsky, Dmitry 113–4
postage stamps 132, 134, 141
Pravda 52, 152–3
pre-Petrine Russia 118–9, 130

Protopopov, Aleksandr 143
Provisional Government 48, 50, 62, 93
Pushkin, centenary of 133–4

Radzinsky, Edvard *The Last Tsar* 43, 46, 86, 88, 128–9, 145, 147
Rasputin 1, 9, 55, 67–8, 92, 130, 138, 141–3, 146
Rasputin, Valentin 54
reburial of Romanov remains (St Petersburg) 28, 32, 55, 114–7
remains *see* skulls, bones, grave, Ekaterinburg remains
Remnick, David 86, 94
rescue of Imperial Family 3–5, 46, 53, 69, 83, 91–5, 98–102, 153
restoration of monarchy in Russia 51, 56, 87, 102
Richards, Guy *Imperial Agent* 99–101, 105
Richardson, Hilda Wakefield 96–7
ritual murder 31, 58, 72–5, 77–8, 80, 127
ROC *see* Russian Orthadox Church
Rodikov, V 70
Rodina 24
Rodzinsky, Isai 3
Rogaev, Evgeny 36
Romanov fortune 31, 86–7, 89, 98, 104
Romanov, Prince Nicholas 56, 87
Romanovs, books about 44, 46–7, 55, 128, 138, 146–7; romanticisation of 46, 5–9, 127, 143–51
Rossel, Eduard 25, 27–8
Rus' pravoslavnaia 109–10
Russian Expert Commission Abroad 31, 37
Russian Orthodox Church Outside Russia (ROCOR) 32, 57, 100, 103, 110, 123, 155
Russian Orthodox Church, and canonization of Imperial Family 46, 57–8, 107–17, 123, 127, 145–6; Holy Synod of 30, 32, 46, 107–8, 113–5; in Imperial Russia 108–9; Jubilee Bishops' Council of (2000) 110, 114; in post-Soviet Russia 108; reform of 85, 107–12; and Soviet state 107–8
Rutskoi, Aleksandr 109

Ryabov, Geli 17–25, 33, 39–40, 71
Ryabova, Margarita 16–18
Ryazan 119

scenario of power 129–32, 137, 141, 144
Schama, Simon *Dead Certainties* 47–8
Semashko, People's Commissar for Public Health 152
Semyonov ('Tsarevich Alexei') 88–9
Sergei Alexandrovich, Grand Duke (NII's uncle) 37–8
Sergi, Metropolitan 110
servants of Imperial Family 4–7, 14, 21, 24, 27, 38–9, 42–5, 49–50, 114–5, 117
Shargunov, Archpriest Aleksandr 123, 126
Shchelokov, Interior Minister 22
Shitov, Aleksei (Alexei) 81–7, 89
Shukshin, Vasily 54
skulls of Imperial Family and servants 18–21, 25–6, 33, 39–42
Slavophilism 67
Smirnov 66
Smith, Eugenia (Anastasia) 100
Smolensk 83
Smythe, James P. *Rescuing the Tsar* 100
sobornost' 112
Sokolov, Nikolai 17, 19, 45, 69, 71, 73
Soloviev, Vladimir 30–1, 36, 41
Somow, Father Andrei 103
Sontag, Susan 128–9
Soviet Union, demise of 25, 30, 46, 54–7, 80, 110, 138
Sovnarkom (Council of People's Commissars) 49, 51, 72, 152–3
Speller, Robert 100
St Petersburg 31–2, 36, 93–5, 109, 117, 119, 129, 134
St Petersburg Times 104
Stalin 44, 59, 70–2, 80, 99, 114, 150
strastoterptsy see passion-bearers
Strekotin, Aleksandr 92
Strekotin, Andrei 92
sulphuric acid 14, 16, 18, 24, 27, 72, 117

194 Index

Sverdlov, Yakov 27, 49, 61–3, 72–4, 78–9, 152–3
Sverdlovsk 16–17, 19–23, 27–9, 53–5, 83
Sverdlovsk region 24–5, 27–30
Synodal Commission for the Canonization of Saints 110–11, 114

Tallinn 102
Tammet, Heino 104
Tarkovsky, Andrei 145
Tatyana, Grand Duchess 19, 27, 137
teeth 18–21, 25, 28–31, 39–40, 73
tercentenary of Romanov dynasty 129–31
Tikhomirov, Pavel 119
Tikhon, Patriarch 108, 110
Tobolsk 50, 146
Toporkov, Father Fyodor 83–4
Trotsky, Lev 3–4, 49–51, 61–6, 78–9, 99, 155
Trupp (NII's valet) 5–6, 14, 27, 42, 114
Tsar kolokol 75
Tsarevich *see* Alexei
tsarist affair 30, 32, 55, 58
tsarskoe delo see tsarist affair
Tsarskoe selo 92, 95, 135, 138, 144, 149–50
Tyumen 92

Upper Isetsk 3, 9, 27
Urals Bolsheviks 38, 49–50, 153–4
Urals Regional Soviet 50–2, 88, 150, 153
Urals Republic (1993) 27
Uralskii rabochii 23, 52
USA 36, 67, 90, 97, 99, 119

Vancouver 102–3
Vasilev, Gennady 46, 18–20, 25
Vasilevsky, I.M. 79
Veerman, Ernst 102
Veerman, Johann 102–3
Victoria of Hesse, 33
Victoria, Queen 33, 136–7
village prose 54
Viner, Vadim 30, 37
Vladimir (Kotliarov), Metropolitan of St Petersburg 109

Vladivostok 51–2, 71, 86
Voikov, Petr (Urals Commissar of Supplies) 3, 14, 74
Von-Benkendorff-Känna, Paula 102
Vyrubova, Anna 143

Warsaw 98–9
weapons 5, 8, 41, 53
websites 44, 59, 90, 94, 143–6
White investigation of Romanovs' death 17, 22–3, 40–1, 45–6, 54, 69, 71, 74, 117
Whites 2–4, 11–12, 17, 50–52
Whiteside Boyle, Lt-Col Joseph 94–5
Wilhelm, Kaiser 101
Wilton, Robert 73–4
Windsor, House of 96–7
World Council of Churches 110
World War I 3, 41, 51, 73, 101, 141, 143
World War II 32, 54
Wortman, Richard, *Scenarios of Power* 119, 130

Xenia Alexandrovna (NII's sister) 34

Yakovlev, Special Commissar Vasily 50
Yeltsin, Boris 25, 27, 55, 115–6
Young Pioneers 53
Yurovskaya, Rimma Yakovlevna 23–4
Yurovsky, Aleksandr Yakovlevich 24
Yurovsky, Yakov, and burial of Imperial Family 8–15, 20, 42–3; and execution of Imperial Family 1–8; in fictionalised accounts 60–64, 74–5, 92, 98–9, 101–2, 128–9; and house arrest of Imperial Family 3–4, 150; testimony of 16–17, 24, 33, 41–3, 53
Yusupov, Felix 34
Yusupova, Irina 34
Yuvenaly, Metropolitan of Krutitsky and Kolomna 32, 109–10

Zeepvat, Charlotte, 147, 149
Zhivotovsky, Lev 37–9
Zinoviev, Grigory 64–5
Zyuganov, Gennady 109

eBooks – at www.eBookstore.tandf.co.uk

A library at your fingertips!

eBooks are electronic versions of printed books. You can store them on your PC/laptop or browse them online.

They have advantages for anyone needing rapid access to a wide variety of published, copyright information.

eBooks can help your research by enabling you to bookmark chapters, annotate text and use instant searches to find specific words or phrases. Several eBook files would fit on even a small laptop or PDA.

NEW: Save money by eSubscribing: cheap, online access to any eBook for as long as you need it.

Annual subscription packages

We now offer special low-cost bulk subscriptions to packages of eBooks in certain subject areas. These are available to libraries or to individuals.

For more information please contact webmaster.ebooks@tandf.co.uk

We're continually developing the eBook concept, so keep up to date by visiting the website.

www.eBookstore.tandf.co.uk